# Change
## Your Encodements,
# YOUR DNA
## Your Life!

# AMMA THROUGH
# CATHY CHAPMAN

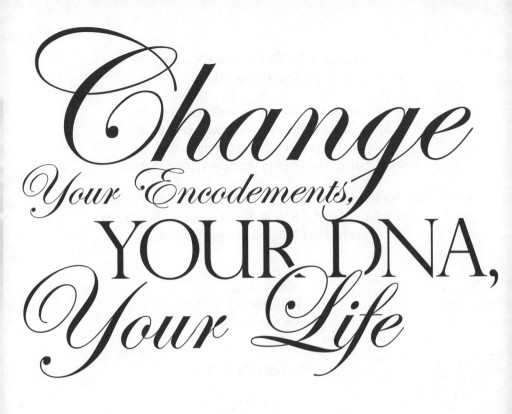

# Change Your Encodements, YOUR DNA, Your Life

## AMMA THROUGH CATHY CHAPMAN

Light Technology Publishing

This book has been compiled from articles previously printed
in the *Sedona Journal of EMERGENCE!*, a monthly magazine
published by Light Technology Publishing.

Cover art by
Frank Hettick
www.skyhighgallery.com

ISBN 1-891824-52-X

Published by

800-450-0985
www.lighttechnology.com

Printed by

PO Box 3540
Flagstaff, AZ 86003

# Contents

# Introduction

Dear one! Yes, you who are reading this page! You are very much a dear one. You have been dear since you sprang from the oneness of Source. This does not mean that you are separate from Source; you have never been separate, even though you might believe that you are. Separateness is a fallacy of your life here on this planet of duality.

You have in your hands one of the many books that will help you see past the myth of separateness. This is the first book channeled through this one [Cathy Chapman]; however, there are many others. You have been called to read this one—if you had not been, you would not be reading these words.

What does this book offer that is different from other such books? Know, first of all, that it is simply another way to explain what is happening in your reality. The more of these books you read, the greater your perspective will be about what is happening. Enjoy learning, remembering and stretching!

This particular book has three basic parts. The first part discusses various aspects of what you call love. Please be aware that "love" as I use it has nothing to do with your romantic songs, movies or novels. Love is the most powerful energy. It is an energy of great vibration. You are made of this energy. You can learn to do many creative actions with this energy. When you learn to harness the energy called love, you can do whatever you wish to do in your life. The only caveat is that your intent and your actions must be in accordance with the vibration of love energy.

Understand, dear one, that I am this love energy without any change in vibration. You sprang from this same love energy without any initial change in vibration. The difficulties you have in your life come from changes in that vibration. When you act in any way contrary to the vibration from which you came, discordance occurs. That is what you are experiencing on this planet—discordance. The first part of this book reminds you of what love is.

The second part of this book contains an introduction to powerful techniques for working with your DNA encodements. Over the course of time, you will receive much information on encodements. Read the material here to discover what encodements are and how you can use them to make great changes in your life.

I will tell now that encodements are energy structures particular to you that assist you in learning what you came here to learn. They can be damaged. They can be changed. Artificial ones can be inserted. You have, within the second part of the pages in your hand, specific information on encodements that will help you do what some would call miracles. Use and enjoy this information!

Dear one, the time for living a life of difficulty is over, unless you wish it not to be. All you need in order to have joy and ease in your life is to align your thoughts, beliefs, feelings, words and actions in the highest way possible with the energy from which you sprang—love. The information you have before you will assist you in learning how to do so. Take the information available to you in this book and in others, and make your life what you wish it to be.

Does that mean you can eliminate all suffering? Yes, it does mean that! Does it mean that what you might call "bad" things or "painful" things will no longer occur? No, dear one, it does not mean that at all. What it does mean is that you will discover who you truly are and how to release that which is not you. You will receive instruction on how to accept the lesson and release the "packaging" of the lesson. Peace and joy result when you take the lesson and release the package in which the lesson comes. You might have received a most valuable gift in an utterly plain or even ugly package. The package does not determine the value of the gift inside. The lesson available to you is the gift. The lesson is priceless. The event—or the people—that brings the lesson is the packaging. Once you have the lesson, you will no longer need the packaging. Release it. You will discover joy and peace.

The third part of this book contains what some call predictions. Predictions are nothing more than a reading or interpretation of the energy at the time when the energy was read. Very few predictions cannot be changed. When you find things that did not occur as predicted, there are one of two reasons: Humanity changed the energy, or this one [Cathy] misinterpreted the energy. Channels can only be as clear as they are. There are times when a channel's own belief system interferes with the interpretation of the energy. Predictions can be changed to have a more positive outcome—the point of my making predictions is so that you can change them.

Dear one, each time you begin reading, I suggest that you do the following: Breathe in and out of your heart center. Set your intention to tap into the energy of the message you are reading. Ask that all necessary information come to you. Ask that you be given the secrets contained within the message and ask to be shown how to implement these secrets. You have powerful information in your hands. It is dormant unless you use it. Have fun exploring!

One further comment. If, while you are reading, you have the thought, "I wonder if I could . . . ," know that the answer is almost always, "Yes, yes, yes!" As you read, I will have one hand upon your heart and one hand touching your mind. You are love, and you are beloved. I am Amma, the divine mother of the divine mothers.

# 1
# Using the Pillar of Light

*September 2002*
*Melchizedek and Quan Yin*

*M*y dear ones, I welcome you tonight. I am your Brother Melchizedek. We are of the light, all of us. We are light of the light. We are related in the deepest possible way that anyone could be related. We are from the same source.

I come to you for a few minutes this evening to lead you through a meditation. This meditation has to do with an energy and a pillar of light. Some of you have already experienced such a thing, but anchoring it in, of course, is always a positive experience. Behind you are gathering your own angels, guides and master teachers. I give you a moment at this time to feel them gathering.

## THE PILLAR OF LIGHT MEDITATION

*Become aware now of your own pillar of light that goes through the center of the crown of your head, down through your spine, anchoring into the center of the Earth. For one of you, this pillar is three inches in diameter, for another, it is six inches and for others, it is twelve inches in diameter. There is no difference other than that the larger ones allow in more light. The diameters of your pillars will be adjusted as you are able to hold more light. At this time, the diameters will expand until the pillar of light encompasses your entire body. Feel that light passing through you at this time.*

*Your angels, guides and teachers are standing behind you, focusing energy from what you would call the heart center (since they have no physical bodies, they do not have a heart center). They are sending love energy straight into the pillar of light that goes through your body. Feel it.*

Those of you who are used to receiving light in this manner will be receiving more light whether you are consciously aware of it or not; those of you who are not quite used to this will not be receiving as much. This is regulated by the diameter of the pillar. It will help the light come into your body more easily if you set your intention to be fully open to this energy coming in, coursing through your body. As it comes in, it is clearing your spine.

And now, dear ones, comes the pillar of light that most of you are not aware of. Directly in front of you is another pillar of light. It is approximately two feet in front of you. Feel it . . . feel its energy. This pillar also comes from Source, God, All That Is, and it goes down into the center of the Earth. This pillar will always be in front of you, whether you are aware of it or not.

To access the power of this pillar in front of you and to increase the power of this pillar and your use of it, you have to do only one thing: Send a beam of energy from your heart to this pillar of light in front of you. Do it now, if you wish. There is, of course, no obligation. A completed circuit of energy is now flowing through you.

This pillar of light that we are bringing onto the planet, the one in front of you, is a tool that you can use to stay in the Now, to stay in the present moment. By staying in the Now you will be able to raise your consciousness, your awareness of who you are. You now have a completed circuit. Can you feel the power that is here, the energy that is coming in?

## ONE PILLAR OF LIGHT FOR ALL

I wish to tell you something else about this pillar of light in front of you. You know that each one of you has his or her own separate pillar of light going through the crown of the head down the spine. That is your personal pillar of light and has to do with this incarnation, in this body, in this lifetime. Now you might think that the pillar of light in front of you is a separate pillar just for you, but that is not correct. It is actually all one pillar; it is a multidimensional pillar that is in front of you. The pillar in front of each of you is the same one in front of all of you. It is one pillar. Those of you who have participated in the Melchizedek method have experienced connecting from their hearts to a pillar of light in the center of the room, thus connecting to everyone in the room, to Source and to Mother Earth. Dear ones, this is the same pillar.

It is a pillar of light being given to everyone. It has always been there in small, fragmented form. Now it is being made manifest because of the energies all of you need to be on your path as human beings and to be aware of who you are as spiritual beings. This is a tremendous gift being given to those on your planet; it has not been given before.

Dear ones, there is no way to express to you how excited we are and how pleased we are about what those of you on this planet have been doing. I know that many of you have heard this from many other beings coming through channels, but I wish to express our deep love and gratitude to you for your commitment to following this path. It does not matter which way you follow the path. Whatever your spiritual path, whichever way it takes you, whatever tradition, whatever ritual, whatever prayer or meditation, it is connected to the same Source—All That Is.

As you remember to send a beam of energy from your heart to the pillar of light in front of you—and that is your conscious choice to do—you are in the present and connected to every other person who is connected to that pillar. This is one way of fulfilling what is called "praying always" in the Christian scriptures. Know that I am also connected to this pillar. I'm going to give you a few moments to experience the energy that comes from your connection to this pillar of light in front of you.

## HONOR ONE ANOTHER'S SACREDNESS

Now, my dear ones, I wish to talk to about something that has been very much in the news lately, and that is the issue of sexual abuse in the Roman Catholic Church. My channel did not want me to talk about this, but I think it is important that you know exactly what is happening. Yes, we are coming to the end times, and in the end times—about which you can read in what you know as the Christian scriptures—what is in the dark will be made light. Your news media is focusing on the issue having to do with the Roman Catholic Church. You do know, don't you, that this event in the Roman Catholic Church is simply bringing to light what is happening in your country—the abasement of a very precious gift, the expression of your love, one to another. The purpose of it happening, with all its pain and turmoil, is for each one of you to begin to examine how it is that you relate, one to another. How do you treat those you come in contact with? Do you honor their sacredness? Or do you use them for your own desires? This is the simplicity of the message within what is happening.

Know that many more scandals will come to light, in many other religious traditions. There are still many to come to light in your government. The unfortunate thing is how your country has such a fixation on what you call sex. Because of your fixation, you miss the higher message in all of this: the right relationship to another.

Dear ones, as you know, the right relationship, one to another, is more than a sexual relationship. It is how you speak to another. It is how you treat one another when one of you has what you consider "failed." In the grander scheme of things, there is no difference between the ways you abuse another: sexual abuse, physical abuse, emotional abuse, capital punishment, denying someone the right to work or food or housing. In the right relationship with another, it is the sacredness of every individual that is important.

I do not want you to get the idea that what I am talking about in these things has to do with what is known in some traditions as sin. There is no sin involved, not in the way that you think of it or have been taught. All I want you to realize is that everything that is being brought to light now, whether it is in a religious or governmental institution, is being brought to light so that you will know to look at yourself and within yourself and see what it is that you need to release. And, dear ones, know that if you have any judgments on the men and women involved in these acts, it says something about you.

## BE NOT ANGRY

I realize that I am speaking strongly. It is because each one of you has made a commitment to the spiritual path, and time is running short. I am giving you examples of what you can do on the "fast track": Stay connected to the pillar of light; every time you see or hear news about any type of violence of any kind, look into yourself and see how it is symbolic for you.

The Master Jesus said, "Be not angry." He said that because anger is violence. There is a difference in the emotion of anger that you have momentarily let pass out of you. Although it is still violence—to yourself and to your energy and to the energy of another—by allowing that anger to pass through you, you also allow that energy to pass through you. The violence comes when you nurse those feelings. You know where that anger takes you. You have seen it on your planet. You have seen it in what you call the 9/11. You see it in your Middle East. You see it everywhere.

The best thing you can do to stop that violence, as all of you have been praying for, is to stop the violence within yourself. Yes, in the human condition, you will become angry. It is what you do with it that makes the difference. Notice what it is that you are angry about and what that says about you. Use that as a growth point. Hold no judgment of those who performed the act about which you are angry. This is all energy and only energy. You will be able to let those lower vibrations pass through you by staying connected to the pillar of light in front of you. When you do have lower-vibration energies come through you—be they anger, jealousy or fear—send them out into the pillar in front of you. Direct that energy straight into the pillar, and it will dissolve.

## YOU ARE LOVE AND BELOVED

I realize that I am not telling you anything you do not know yourself. I now wish to tell you something else that you might have heard and that some in here do not believe: Dear ones, you are only love. You were created from love and you are love. You will always be love. It does not matter how you choose to experience this lifetime, what you choose to do. You are love. You have no way to see the brightness of your very being. I can't begin to tell you how bright you are right now. I can't begin to tell you what joy you bring to us as we watch you on your journey. Each one of you is more precious than you could ever know. There is nothing that can separate you from the love that you are. You might deny that you are the love you are, but that does not change it. Each one of you is in a different stage of accessing his or her personal power. You all have tremendous power. You are all just beginning to learn how to use that power. Continue learning. We are here to help you.

Be aware that what is going on on your planet, whether it happens in the room you are in or across the seas, is just something that is happening. The way you can change it is to change yourself and your response. The more you work on that, the more at peace you will be and the more you will be able to be in this world but not of the world—the more you will be in your physicality but remain in your spiritual essence.

Dear ones, you are so beloved. You are dearly beloved. The great masters have come to tell you that. We send you angels all the time to tell you that. Some of you have a block to believing that this is so. Do you realize that the block has only to do with the past? If it has to do with the past, it's over. In the present, at this very moment in the present, you are beloved. At this very moment there are only beings here telling you that you are beloved. Simply release those things that you remember, that told you that you were not beloved. Why hold on to them? Do you continue to grasp a hot poker? Do you continue to keep your hand on a hot burner? Of course not. So no longer hold on to those other things that have seared your soul. I give you this truth, and I ask you to plant it deep within you and let it flower. The truth is you are only love. That is what you are. In your daily life, you might experience those parts of yourself that are "not love" or have an experience of "not love." This only shows you what love you are, because those parts you experienced as "not love" were so uncomfortable. You are love. That is my message for you this evening. We are sending tremendous light and love to each one of you to awaken within yourselves the knowledge that you are love.

I wish you to simply remember several things:

- The pillar of light in front of you—be connected to it through your heart.
- Anything that happens on this planet is a symbol of something that is happening within you or something you can change within you.
- You are love, love incarnate.

Now, dear ones, I am willing to answer some questions. Of course, remember that I will not tell you anything that would interfere with your path in any way. There are some things you just cannot know. I hope you understand that.

## ABOUT LOSSES

*Dear Melchizedek, thank you for being with us. I would like to know—if it is my right to know—the meaning of the losses in my life this past year. I feel an urgency, especially with the last loss, and I'm afraid that I am not getting the message. Would you be so kind as to help me understand this? I'd be very grateful.*

Oh, precious one, do you not remember the prayer that you said at one time, to be in total union with God, to be able to do what God asks you to do, to strip away all that needed to be stripped away so that you could be of service? Do you remember those prayers? You have said them at different times in your life, in different ways.

Your loss is the experience of removing all that which was familiar to you and which you based your identity upon, so that you can be the purity of who you are without interference from this third dimension. Your last loss had to do with your sense of efficiency, your sense of attending to detail. Even that needs to be stripped away at times so that you can rest in the fullness of who you are—which is love—and be in communion with the rest of us. Does that make sense to you? Are there any other questions?

## ABOUT A CURRENT LESSON
*Yes. I would like to know what I need to learn about my husband's cancer. What is the lesson for me?*

The lesson for you is twofold. One is to allow him to be on his own path. He must struggle in his own way with the cancer. That is his path. Your part is to allow him to do that. The primary lesson for you is to learn to be there with an open heart and to not fix it. It is a very difficult lesson put in simple terms. Did you wish to ask something else about that?

You can give support to him. You actually can do whatever you wish, but know that you can't fix him, you can't change him. He must do that for himself. Of course, you can do the things that people do, like drive to doctors and things like that. But there is no need for you to expend your energy in trying to convince him to do things to make him well. That part is his path. You might wish to try to detach yourself from him as much as possible. That does not mean that you do not care, but it does mean that you let him be on his way. If he says that he doesn't want to do something, don't try to convince him otherwise. Let him be.

## ABOUT FUTURE LESSONS
*I'd like to ask if you could tell me my next test and my next lesson on my path.*

No, but I can tell you this: We will be with you. You have been given all that you need to navigate it. I can tell you this also, and this applies to everyone: You can ask that you learn your lessons with joy and ease. Some of you have the idea that every lesson has to be difficult. You are the only ones who make it difficult. If you believe that a lesson has to have much pain, we will be glad to give you exactly what it is that you want to believe. I cannot tell you what your next lesson will be. It's like cheating on the test. Know that we will be with you and that you will be able to be even more conscious and see the possibilities of response and action within yourself by staying connected to the pillar of light before you. But fear not. Be in the present. If you fear your next lesson, you're in the future. Who knows, you might leave the planet before the next lesson comes. Ah, but that leaves a lesson for your family, does it not?

## ABOUT HOLDING THE GRID IN PLACE
*Melchizedek, I would like to ask a question about the light grid of the Earth, if I may. A short while ago, masters informed us that the grid was depending on the lightworkers. Has the work*

*of the lightworkers grown enough to create a critical mass of this Christ-consciousness grid around our beloved planet?*

It is almost there; it will happen soon. We are so excited about it. It is almost there. Can you not feel it? When you are not involved in what is going on in the drama of the planet, can you not feel the lightness that is coming? Yes, it will happen soon. But know that when it does happen, it does not mean that there is suddenly going to be total peace on your planet. Do you realize that? In fact, it might even feel worse, because all the lower-vibration energies will be released as this grid becomes firmer . . . being released to be released. It is almost there. That is one of the reasons you have been given the pillar of light in front of you. It connects you to that grid, to the Christ-consciousness grid.

Now I want to tell you something else. Those who have incarnated on your planet as the Christ, the Master Yeshua, the Buddha, Krishna and others are there in different places, holding the grid in place. It is like holding pieces of material down for the final fastening so they do not slip. It is an exciting time.

## THE DIVINE FEMININE AND REPTILIAN ENERGY

*I have a question, Melchizedek, a really far-out question. Is there some clarity that you could shed for us on the ancient energies of the divine feminine that apparently were here on the planet in the beginning, embodied in the symbol of the snake? Now there is much literature out about reptilian energy. This is not a need to know, but rather a curiosity thing. Are these one and the same? Have they been perverted? Is there any comment that you would make for me on that? And stop laughing. No . . . it's okay to laugh.*

We do enjoy you! One of the things to realize is that this is a multipart question that you've asked, with multipart answers. Yes, the divine feminine energies were here at the beginning of your planet. What you do not realize is that your feminine energies now on this planet—such as all of you gathered here—have become so excited about the feminine being recognized again that you now believe that the divine feminine energies at the beginning of your planet were extremely strong. I want to tell you that they were not. That is not to say that they were less than they are now; that's not true. They were there at the birthing of your planet. Look at this as an example of "as above, so below," the microcosm and the macrocosm. There are some of you who have given birth. You all went through pain when you gave birth and were presented with a precious, wiggly, wrinkled being. It was precious and glorious just looking at it.

When this Earth was manifested, the feminine energies were what was born and what gave birth to it. They were growing and developing and were much, much stronger than they are now. When the divine feminine energy comes in now, it is going to be stronger than the masculine energy ever was, because the feminine energy is the energy of the heart. As I am talking about this, it happened over thousands and thousands of years of your time. The feminine energy has always been about the heart, about breath, about life and about connection. You women, even those of you who have not given birth, can in some way imagine what it must be like to be connected to another human being within your body—and not just to other human beings, but to nature, to all that abounds. Women have always done that. That is how you were made.

Now then, what happened on the planet is that you as a race began to experience the other energies within yourself. You began to experience the separation of mind and heart. Although it was known that this would happen, it was not the preference to have it happen, because it was known that once you began to separate the mind and heart, you would begin to lose your androgyny. The thing about the divine feminine at the beginning of this planet is that there was androgyny, a perfect melding of what you now call the masculine and feminine energies. What is happening now is that as the divine feminine becomes more prevalent, there is a rejoining of the energies of the heart with the energies of the mind.

I want you to know that the female energies—the female—are correct: The heart is more powerful. Your science is showing this in many different ways. You go into your heart, and it will relax your mind. If you go into your mind, it does not relax your heart. So which is the more powerful, the one with control? It is the heart that has the control. What is actually happening as the divine feminine energies come in? This is the beginning of the process of coming into androgyny again. Know that anything that is said to come from the heart—a meditation, an activity—is a manifestation of the feminine energies, whether it is stated to be feminine or not. At the separation of the masculine and the feminine, the feminine took the heart and the masculine took the mind. The heart cannot make war, only the mind can do that. The heart cannot remain disconnected—it would die. You all know people who are disconnected from their hearts, and you know of times in your own life when you have been disconnected from your heart and felt as if you had died.

About the reptilian energies and the symbolism of the snake, they are two different things and two different symbols. The reptile that you know as the snake is a symbol for this planet. The reptilian energies you speak of from another planet have their own sets of symbols, which are separate from the symbology of this planet. You will be better able to understand them if you just consider them as another symbol structure, another set of beings from another planet, which, for the most part, the masculine has taken over. They also go through their process of getting in touch with the feminine. They have to do that when they come to this planet. That is not to say that all reptilian energies are of the masculine, any more than all human energies are of the masculine or the feminine. Many of you know masculine beings on your planet who have strong feminine energy and vice versa. It is the melding that is coming—

the merging, the coming into androgyny. The reptilian energies, the ones from the other planet, are separate from what is happening here. That is where the confusion comes from. Does this help?

*Yes, that was very fine. Thank you very much.*

Are there any other questions for me? No? All right then. My sister wants to speak to you. Would that be permissible? *Melchizedek*

## QUAN YIN IS SPEAKING

My dear ones, I am Quan Yin, and I am here to bless you. I do not want you to be left with a heavy heart. My brother, Melchizedek, has been heavy today. We have agreed that I would finish this discussion with you. He has told you the truth about yourself, that you are love. Not only are you love, but you are beloved. Dear ones, each one of you has been so strong upon his or her path. Some of you might feel you are in a place of confusion and wonder what it is you are supposed to do. Just put your next foot forward. It is that simple.

I wish to give you a gift. Actually, it is not just I who wishes to give it to you. Gathering in this place at this moment are many representatives of the divine feminine. They are gathering behind you right now, and we are going to do two things. First, we are going to give you a flower to place in your heart. You will not all receive the same flowers. The second thing we are going to do—you will have to listen with your heart for this—is that we are going to sing to you. We are going to sing you a lullaby. This lullaby is not meant to put you to sleep. Lullabies are meant to calm and to express love in another form. They are really love-abies. Now, dear ones, be connected to the pillar of light in front of you and be aware of us behind you as we give you this gift.

Thank you, my sisters and brothers. Blessed be. Namasté. Adonai.

# 2

# Let It Go

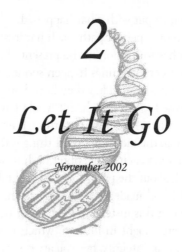

*November 2002*

O h, my children, I am so excited to be here with you today. I can't even begin to tell you the excitement I feel sharing this with each one of you. I have been waiting and waiting to come in. You needed to be ready for me and ready for the energies I have to share with you. We have been guiding you and telling you exactly what you needed to do to prepare for these energies. You were led to begin a discussion about the Now. I am going to tell you why you were to learn about the Now.

The Now, dear ones, is about creation. It is about the creative energy that each one of you has. I want to tell you how I create. Are you ready? My dear ones, I can only create by being who I am and what I am in the time—which is no-time—that I am in. By being in that space, in that place, I can manifest exactly what is needed. That is how I manifested you. I manifested your coming together in this group by being in the place—my place, who I am, what I am, in the Now of me—in my time, which is no-time.

You know about creation and being in the Now. You have to be fully present, because when you are focused on the past, you are not who you are now, you are who you were then. You are no longer who you were. It does not matter what happened in the past, whether it was in this lifetime, in another lifetime, on another planet, in another galaxy, in another form or even when you were totally with the I Am. That is not who you are now, so it is imperative for you to let this go. You need to release the shackles of your belief in who you were and the guilt, shame, embarrassment, frustration or disappointment—

whatever word you want to put with what happened.

Each of you has been on a perfect path; each has frustration about his or her path. Each one of you has frustration in the present about what has happened in the past. Why didn't certain things happen sooner, and why couldn't they have happened faster, and why couldn't they have happened differently? Dear ones, they weren't supposed to! If they had it would have happened differently. Let it go! You have had many teachings on this. I am telling you that if you want to work on anything, the most important thing is to let it go. Don't regurgitate the past, don't go over each thing, don't hash it out—let it go.

Sometimes you think about the past, "Gee, if I had taken this job, if I hadn't married this person, if I had made this other decision, well, possibly in three months, I could have been this instead." That is not true! Know that you are lying to yourself. You are caught in illusion, which is a lie. Each one of you believes fully and strongly in integrity, but you are not in integrity when you are in the past. In the past, when you were not who you are now, you all had times when you failed—if you want to call it failure, though it is actually learning. Now you are where you are. Of course, each of you struggles at times when you slip or deviate from the path a bit. It does not matter. That is why you are here, to support one another. You would not be together if you did not have your past experiences. You planned this—not the minute details, but you did make a general plan of what you wanted.

# 3

# Accepting Michael's Sword

*December 2002*

*This piece was channeled on September 11, 2002.*

Good evening, dear ones. Silver love is vibrating in this room tonight. You know me, but you might not all know of me. I am Amma. I am the divine mother of the divine mothers. It is in my womb of love that you grew and from which you were birthed. That means, of course, that you are love because you were created from love. That is all you were created from. You are the very essence of love.

Now you might wonder why there is so much talk of war. Let me speak of it in this way: Think of how you would feel if someone invaded your home. Would you not wish, is it not the natural inclination to bring together every force you can to protect yourself and your family? Being invaded is an action against you, against love, contrary to love. Is it not in human nature to respond to something that is not love in the same "not-love" manner? In other words, you respond with fear. Because you are set in the past, you believe that the invasion could happen to you again. The reality is that your house could be broken into again.

You respond by getting an alarm system. In your home you bring together defenses. Some people go out and buy guns or other weapons; some people put baseball bats by their beds. You become nervous at every little strange sound you hear. Think about how you would respond. Would you not want to hurt someone before he or she hurts you? Offense becomes your defensive mode. This is acting out of fear.

This is what your leaders are doing: acting out of fear. They have their alarm systems and alert systems. They broadcast every little wrinkle or wave they hear about that is different. This hypervigilance is occurring, dear ones, because they are living in fear. Fear is not love. It is not what you were called to, because it is not what you were made of.

## ABOUT DISCIPLINE ON THE SPIRITUAL PATH

All of you here are very special, deeply spiritual people; you are connected to the love energy. Some of you are more aware of that than others. You are love. Your job right now, those of you who are wondering about your purpose in life, is to hold that love energy. On this planet, in this city, right now, there are desperate needs for anchors of love. Why were you put here on this planet? To hold love. Why were you put here on this planet? To give love. Why did you volunteer to be here? (And you did volunteer.) To hold love. It does not matter how you do it. By that I mean that it does not matter what your profession is, what your job is. For many of you, it does not matter where you do it. For some of you, location does matter. Some of you have a direct contract to be in a certain place. This is the challenge for each one of you: how to anchor love.

Have you noticed how you have had a difficult time managing your thoughts and emotions of late? Fears, anxieties and maybe angers have been coming up; old memories have been coming up. These are things for you to release.

You have heard about discipline on the spiritual path. Dear ones, discipline is not really about meditation and prayer. Those practices teach you how to discipline your mind. The discipline you need right now is not only discipline over your mind but also over your emotions. To do what you came here to do, to be beacons of love, you must, and I do mean must, discipline your mind and your emotions. Be aware of any negative, fearful, anxious thoughts that come to you and let them go. Do not beat yourself over the head if they come, because then you go into negativity. Just let them go. Very simply, let them go. And, not so simply, bless them. Bless them in every way you can. So if you have a negative thought about someone from another country, such as the leader of Iraq, surround him with love.

## TAKE MICHAEL'S SWORD

All of you know that hate begets hate. You are in a sense warriors, but remember that war means conflict, so is there such a term as "loviors"? Your job is to do the work with love, fight the battle with love.

You have seen pictures of Michael the Archangel with his sword. It is a sword of love, and he uses it with great love. We will now give you the gift of his sword. *Extend your right hand right now, and Michael will place his sword in your hand. Feel it . . . grasp it . . . feel the energy that is there. Feel the weight of it in your hand. Feel the energy come up into your arm. Hold the sword in front of you. Focus on your heart and move the energy from your heart into the sword. Use the sword, dear ones, to wield love and truth. The sword will also help you to sever from you all that is not love.* SWORD RT. HAND
ENERGY UP HAND
ENERGY INTO SWORD

*If you have an attachment to a particular thought, such as your own unworthiness, hold the sword before you. Now wield the sword by severing that thought from yourself. Release the energy of that thought. Learn how to wield that sword. When you are fearful that someone in some way is coming to attack you, hold the sword in front of you. Focus on your heart, and feel the energy of the sword blaze and surround you. This is a protection.*

*Be consciously aware that from this point always you now have the sword of Michael, the sword of truth and love, in your hand. Hold it now before you and watch its blue-white light blaze in front of you and around you to protect you. Carry it wherever you go. Be aware that you are carrying it. Do not put it down or forget that you have it. By the way, if you do forget you have it, pick it up again. It is that simple. Use the sword to release those thoughts and feelings that have been plaguing you. Use the sword to protect you from the fear that is permeating your planet right now. Use it when you hear any report of fear, even if that report might be true. It might be true that someone really is getting ready to attack or break into your home. Surround the whole situation with love. Use the sword, send energy from your heart, hold it in front of you and send it in love. This is your biggest weapon.*

## HELP YOUR LEADERS IN THEIR FEAR

Many people will speak out against you, as you have already experienced. They will say you are being unpatriotic if you do not wish to go to war. In fact, it is perfectly right to say that you agree to go to war, but you prefer to do it with love. You will do battle in a different way. The battle is not one of conflict, but one of openness and compassion.

Realize that most of your leaders are in a place of fear. Look at it that way; they are in a place of fear. What do you who are parents do when your children are in a place of fear? Does it work better when you yourself are fearful with them or when you do everything you can to keep yourself as calm as possible? Do you not show them that perhaps there is nothing to fear, that there is a way to handle it? What would happen if you became hysterical and fearful along with your child? Would that not increase the fear? Look at your leaders, the ones who are so fearful, as your children. That seems kind of strange, doesn't it? But on the spiritual path they are children. They are children in the fact that they need help in addressing the issues in a loving and compassionate way. There are ways to handle things without guns, without bombs and without angry words. All of you know that.

I wish you to carry this message to everyone around you. You do not have to do it verbally. You do it by your life and by the way you are leading your life. You do it by the words you use, by the way you respond when someone responds to you in an angry manner and by the way you respond to fear.

I wish I could tell you how much love there is. In your lives as humans, as they has been constructed, so often—in fact most of the time—you do not feel and are not aware of love. But everything you touch is love, the chairs you are sitting on, the pillows, the floor, the air around you, the water. It is all love. If you can look at it that way and bring it into yourself, you will find you can live on the air around you. The breath of God is around you. That is the love that is there.

Now I would be willing to answer some questions. But before we go to questions, I am showering love down upon you now, directly into your crown and into your heart. I am also showering this love on those reading this message. Feel that love come into you, and as it comes into you feel the brightness. Perhaps you can see the brightness of Michael's sword. And I will continue pouring this love into you for the rest of the evening. And now for your questions.

## BE WHERE YOU END UP

*How are we supposed to discern where we are supposed to be?*

You are supposed to be where you end up. You are asking about your particular situation?

*Yes.*

You weigh the possibilities in your heart. You have a decision to make very soon, and you weigh the possibilities in your heart. You take it into your heart because either place is a good place. So you get to choose what would give you the greatest sense of life and freedom and joy. But take each situation into your heart and evaluate it from that standpoint. The one that gives you the most joy and the most peace, take that one. Is that more helpful?

*A lot more helpful.*

But know that where you end up is where you are supposed to be. Other questions?

## WHAT ABOUT WAR?

*Will there be war?*

It depends upon what your leaders choose and upon how people respond. The forces are actually gathering to prevent such a thing. It is rather surprising to many of your leaders that the forces are gathering to not go to war. Very few people in the world wish war. The fear is greatest against the intruder. So it has not been decided yet, but the balance is more toward "no." Hold peace in your heart and surround the whole situation with love. You might feel powerless about how to prevent it. If you do not want war, let your leaders know that. Do not be angry with your leaders who want war. Know that they are responding to fear and yes, some are responding out of the desire for power, but it is mostly fear. Yes?

## REVEALING SECRETS

*Are there many secrets of different societies of the past that are going to be coming out to help us?*

There are many, many secrets that are coming out. You are going to discover many more secrets, not only from within the corporations and the churches, but from many more places. The secrets are going to seem awful to many people. But I'd like you to know that spiritual secrets will also be coming out. These spiritual secrets from Atlantis and Egypt are life-giving and ancient. Those are what to focus on. The secrets soon to be revealed were hidden not to keep things from you, but to wait for the proper time. Those will be coming out very likely within the next decade and maybe sooner rather than later.

But those spiritual truths and spiritual secrets will also bring about a division. Their revelation will be fearful to some people. Remember that Jesus, the master who walked upon this Earth some two thousand years ago, said his own words would divide families. Well, there is one family you know—the family of all of you on this planet. So, many of those things will also divide people. It is out of fear that people have difficulty in changing. Hold all of that in love. Hold all the fears in love. Some of you have already had problems due to those kinds of fears, but just hold it in love.

They will be coming soon; know that the most wondrous secrets that seem impossible are true. You do not remember the depth and the power of this other world you came from. Remember, the good that you can envision can happen. You might think of something and wonder, "Can this occur in healing?" If you wondered it, yes, it would. "Is it possible to do this good thing?" If you thought it, yes, it would. There is not a thought that can come to you that is not possible, be it of good or ill. And, of course, your thoughts are of good. Anything else?

## WORKING THROUGH EGO

*How do we work through this ego?*

Do you mean the ego of who you are?

*I mean pride, individualizing yourself.*

Know that the way this world was constructed for you to grow and develop might seem perverse. Because you were born from your mother, as you developed the first thing you learned was how to be separate. You thought you were one with her for so long.

You grow and you develop and you learn about separateness. The next task is to learn about unity. So you come in unity, you grow away from unity into separateness and then you are to grow back into unity again. But you go at a much deeper level. The best way is to learn how to avoid what I call the little ego, the small "e." Remember that ego means I am. There is the I Am presence, the capital "E" Ego. All of you have the I Am presence and are part of that. And then there is the little I am, the little part of you that believes you are separate. That is the ego you are referring to.

The task is to stay in your heart and to remember that you are good and that all is good around you. You are being directed if you ask, but only if you ask. We do not tell you what to do if you do not ask. You did come here with a contract, and I am speaking directly to you. You came here with a contract to show great wonders to many different people. Your heart is being opened, and you are learning a lot about how to live a life of love. You came into a family so that you could learn about love, but in a very different way. As you learn and struggle with what you did not receive, you will learn what love truly is.

Open your heart. When you open your heart, you let go of your pain. The little ego will release. Soon you will find that you don't need the pride that you feel you must have in small accomplishments to be able to feel good about yourself. You will then need only the pride that comes from being in a place of love, understanding and compassion with your brothers and sisters. Does that make sense?

*Yes.*

Thank you. Anybody else?

*As far as these secrets and wonders that are going to be revealed, are any of them going to have to do with the Dead Sea Scrolls?*

Actually, some of the secrets of the Dead Sea Scrolls are already out; you just have to find the right books. The reason that they are not out publicly is because. . . well, can you imagine why?

*Yes, I know exactly why. That is why I am wondering if that will ever change.*

Yes, and they will come out more and more. There is a group trying to keep that down, because it will completely blow the lid off and change the whole view. Know that when the Dead Sea Scrolls do become public and if people choose to believe some of the things that are being said in them, you will see one very important truth about the Master Yeshua who came to this planet. He came here to talk about and display love and to stay single-minded. His death was not a sacrifice; Yeshua did not die because you had to be saved. Yeshua died because he continued to state the truth, which was contrary to what was accepted in that day. Know also that Yeshua died because of a few people, not because of many people. You are actually seeing something similar to that which you call the 9/11. Thousands of people died because of a few people, not because of the many. Know that the many are good; the many have hearts of clarity and of love.

## HELP WITH GRIEF

*What can I do to help myself with the grief in my heart? I am working on releasing it.*

As you have been sitting there, I have been talking to the spirit that is in your heart. Realize that you have energies living within you that are not of you.

Release those. There is something you might not be aware of about yourself, and I would be glad to tell you now, or if you would like to know it privately, I would be glad to tell you privately. Which is your choice?

*You can tell me now.*

You wonder about being here on this planet, and I want you to know you were very pushy about coming. You came earlier than was recommended. You had not healed completely from two previous lifetimes. Those wounds became activated when you were here, and that is part of the despair you have been feeling. You are a spirit of tremendous love and compassion, and that is why you rushed to get here. It might not feel like that as I say it because you have struggled so hard. It is rather difficult to convince you of things, even when you are not in the body, because you have a single-minded plan to bring healing to the planet, and you do that each time you come. You have experienced deep wounds and betrayals in the past few lifetimes. You have not been totally healed of those before you came. I guess, in a sense you could say you recycled very quickly. That is part of where your wounds come from and part of the deep sadness. It is not just from this lifetime. Does that resonate within you?

What you could do at night before you go to bed is to open your heart as much as you possibly can. Your heart is pretty closed. Not that you do not have great compassion—you have tremendous compassion. Your heart is closed in fear of being wounded again, and some of that is on a very subconscious level. Ask each night that it be opened a little bit more, that the healing be a little bit more. You have very deep wounds. You will need to work on those yourself. There really isn't anyone outside of yourself who can help you. That might be discouraging, but I want you to know that you have the power within you to heal. It will be a little bit at a time, one struggle at a time. I also want you to know that as you do this, you are like a metaphor for the world. The little bit of healing that occurs bit by bit is a metaphor for the little bit of healing that can happen in the world. It is a very tough job that you have.

Surround yourself with caring people who love you and will support you. Does that help at all? Do you have any more questions?

*Does that mean that the rest of my life will be painful?*

Is it going to be as painful as you are experiencing? Hopefully not, as you open your heart to more love and allow that to occur. It is not as if you have been resisting it on a conscious level. I want you to know that I know that. And I want you to know that it is true. There is great pain in what has happened to you. You have the possibilities of achieving great joy and peace. That will occur when you are able to truly love yourself. Does that mean love yourself a hundred percent? No, it does not. But at least love yourself twice as much as you love yourself right now.

I do not want you to become discouraged. It is difficult at times to know how our struggles help anyone. One of the things you want to do in life is to help people. Know that your struggles do help others. It is very difficult to see that. If you will call upon me every night, I will be there with you. I will help you heal your heart. And ask specifically to be taken—we can do this only if you ask—ask specifically to be taken to places that can heal your heart from the other lifetimes and to be shown those things that occurred. If you wish, you can be directed to books, movies, articles and pictures that might remind you and resonate with you about something very painful. That will be a reminder of something that happened in another lifetime that needs to be healed. Ask for healing in that.

Do not be discouraged. Know that there is a chance of great joy and, yes, there is a chance of great love. You will not be alone the rest of this lifetime.

*I feel kind of lost. Can you tell me what I need to know at this time?*

Yes. I would like you to know, dear one, that your life is now opening in a way that you did not know it could open. In a way, your life is beginning over again. The feeling of being lost is because of all the changes that have occurred. Soon you will stabilize, and you will find exactly what it is you need to do. Just know you are in rough waters right now and give yourself some time. You need a few months. It is too soon. Just relax and release the guilt you feel. Use the sword of Michael and sever the guilt. Know that your life as it was led had a purpose. You learned the things from it you needed, and the journey is now over with him. There is nothing else to know. You did, meaning you and he did, the things you needed to do together. It was difficult but you did it well. And he is fine.

## INDIVIDUAL MESSAGES FROM AMMA

I have a message for each one of you individually. I have already given the message to some of you. I can do this in one of two ways, whichever you prefer. I can give it to you in the deepness of your heart, or I can give it to you here. It is whatever you prefer.

*Better here or I might not hear it!*

Yes, then I will give you your message: Know that the restlessness in your heart is only due to your not believing who you really are. It is difficult to believe that you are love when you do not believe that you are love. Ask for healing in that. Ask that you be shown. Call upon your angels or your guides and, of course, you can call upon me to lead you and direct you to those areas that need to be healed and released. You will be guided to some people, one in particular, in about three months. You will come to some books, some reading.

If something jumps off the shelf, read it. It is not necessary to read the whole thing; you will be directed to what to read. You are doing exactly what you need to do. Is there anybody else who wanted to know now?

*I want to know now.*

This is also a time of change for you. You know that. It is time for you to move on with what it is that you have been considering in your heart. Have no fear. Have no fear. You need to know you are right where you belong. What I wish to tell you right now more than anything is that your main job is going to be with your family and that is the place to focus on.

*That's a tough one!*

Know that you will have choices facing you regarding your job situation and that it doesn't really matter on the deepest level what you choose as long as you stay in integrity. You will have chances to love more and to open yourself to love. You will also learn more about love as you love more in your family. You are in a good place, so know that there are not any direct changes facing you, but soon you might have some opportunity if you wish. Anyone else?

*Sure.*

More changes will come in a few years. Know that you are now given the opportunity to prepare for your future, which is what you are doing in your work. All that you have done is actually to give you the material basis you need in order to do what is going to happen later. Follow your heart in what you are being led to in regard to the healing area. You, of course, will not be the same type of healer as your partner, but you will complement each other greatly in what you do. Know that your mental capacity and your ability to think critically are important in what you are going to be doing. Your healing will take more of a mental form. That is not to say you won't be in your heart, of course, but it will be more the weighing and analyzing of things. Does that make sense to you?

*Yes.*

Then that will open up greatly for you. Continue the learning you are doing. Be patient as you are waiting for that time of change. Know that much will open before you, and you will be a great blessing to many people and to many animals.

*I would like to hear a message.*

You, like many people in here, are facing a time of change. You will have a decision facing you also. Know to follow your heart. Know also, and it is totally up to you, that if the decision is to move out of your town, that is fine. Allow your grief to be released. Do you know to what I am referring? Just allow that to be released and know that, when the time comes to move, it will be because of the job, and it could take you out of the state if you choose that. But know that it isn't mandatory. Is that cryptic enough? Do you wish to ask a question about it?

*In my same field?*

Yes, if you wish, but it will be an expansion of your field. You do not trust yourself in your field. You do not believe you are as good as you actually are. You are a master in what you do. You do not believe that, do you?

*Ummm, sometimes.*

Believe it all the time. If you wish and if you desire, we will help you with the book. You have great things you could share. There is a children's book you could write that will open up the child within you and bring great healing to the child within you. You are very precious, and you are right where you belong. There is really nothing more to say to you.

*What about me?*

Continue as you are doing. You are doing well. Do not forget the interpersonal as you work on job and school. That will be one of the things you will have to work on throughout your life. You will become very focused on a job or an activity and will forget to relate to the one you are with. Remember that. That does not just include your living situation. It includes coworkers and other people. You might make a choice to change what you are studying and it is okay. You have much of the healer within you, and you are not aware of that.

Anybody else?

*(A woman points to herself.)*

You know you will soon be leaving, don't you? Not from your body but from this state? When you finish your work and your training in the spiritual direction, you will be opened to other possibilities for where this will take you. But you have known that. Follow what is there in your heart and do not limit yourself. All in your family are on good footing now. It is time for you to spread your wings and fly. Know that what you have been learning about love has been one of the major lessons you came here to learn. And you have been doing a good job in learning about that. One of the things that you have been discovering is patience. Continue to learn about that. There are no major changes for you in the next year that I see. That doesn't mean something can't change, of course. But know that you are in a good place and there will be some possibilities of different things that you can do, but not major job changes or things like that. But there are some broadening things that possibly could occur.

You are doing well in learning about love. That is what you came down to learn so much about. That is why you chose the lifestyle you have—yes, to learn a different aspect about love from what you have learned before. You had a lifetime, two lifetimes, in which you did not handle love very well. And now you are relearning the other side of it. You are right where you need to be. Learn to use your creativity, and you will open and blossom even more with that. I will speak more to you tonight in your heart, so listen.

Anybody else?

*My heart is burning.*

Yes, your heart is burning. I will be speaking to you much over the next few months. You will have possibilities open in your new position, and you will grow and broaden there and do many other things that are going to be exciting for you. You have been prepared for that in your work that you did within your church, and you will take some of that—the organization that you learned, the working with groups. It will bring you to other places. Remember that in the end, all is going to be fine with your families, know that. Let your family go, every one of your family members.

Your brother asked me to tell you how much he loves you and that he is with you and that you have a very special soul connection. He wanted me to assure you that he no longer has the tattoo.

*I would like a message.*

I want you to know how important you are to your son. The thoughts you were having of the special needs and care he needs for school are true. He needs a good, safe environment. He is a very special and tender spirit, and that is one of the reasons he was given to you. He chose you and your husband, because he knew that the two of you could help him grow and develop. Know that he is your main purpose in life in the next few years. But you knew that, didn't you? You might also want to open up possibilities for yourself in using your creativity and talents and doing what you are able to do in this information field. So know that whatever choices you make in where it is you are going to be moving, you will be able to open your own business and do well and provide your son with exactly what he needs.

Be sure you stay openhearted with your husband and love him. He struggles with depression and he hides that. Let him be there but also love him. Know that things that might happen do not have a lot to do with you, but have a lot to do with what is going on with him. Do you have any questions to ask about that?

*It is kind of unexpected.*

Which is unexpected? About your son or your husband? Your husband is a very beautiful spirit and very tender. He is actually more tender than you know or he knows. He hides things very well. He and your son are very much alike in their tenderness. You will provide much strength for them. Continue to allow yourself to heal. Any other questions?

To close, I wish to take you through a method to use Michael's sword to heal the planet.

*Close your eyes and go into your heart. Feel Michael's sword in your hand. Allow yourself to become comfortable with it in your hand. Now bring the sword in front of you, point upward. Activate your heart by bringing light into your crown. Simply ask and then imagine, see or feel the light coming into your crown. The light goes into your heart and amplifies the energy of your heart. Have that wonderful heart energy travel down your arms into Michael's sword. Feel the sword grow brighter. The energy of the sword is now surrounding you. Now see the planet in front of you. Ask, "Where do I most need to go to hold the light and dispel darkness?" Go there. You might feel yourself transported there. Whether you feel it or not, you are going there. Now look for a place of darkness. The darkness is due to the energy of anger, fear, hatred, jealousy. Thrust your sword into the darkness and watch and feel what happens.*

Thank you for your service of love this night. Blessings to you. I am Amma, the divine mother of the divine mothers.

# 4

# *What Do You Really Need?*

*January 2003*

*A*ll my precious ones, how good it is to be here with you again! I am Amma. I am your mother. I am the divine mother of the divine mothers. I can't tell you how much I have enjoyed coming in to speak to you and how excited I am to be able to share with an even wider audience.

We are going to continue our discussion about love. That is why I am coming in, to talk to you about love. That is what your life is about; that is what all our lives are about. Life is about love. Always remember that you were created in love and that you are love. You have heard it said that you are in the image and likeness of God. God is love. That is all God is—love. That is all there is—love. Today we are going to talk about compassion, a very important part of love. There is often a misunderstanding about compassion. Compassion is the opening of your heart to all that is around you.

## FEEL WITH DETACHMENT

It is sometimes believed that if you don't feel anything for someone else who is in pain, then you are not compassionate. That is not true. Sometimes, when people feel the pain of another, it is not compassion. It is more, shall we say, an egocentric way of looking at things in that the experience of the other resonates with their own pain within. With true compassion, what you are doing is being aware of the other person's pain, but you are still detached from that person. You do not get caught within his or her drama. The other's experience might resonate within you and you might feel pain due to the compassion you feel. However, the pain you feel is not due to the compassion. That sounds contradictory, doesn't

it? The pain is actually due to the fact that what you are sensing in another person, what you are feeling from another person, resonates with your own memories, within the cellular memory. So compassion really has nothing to do with
feeling, but it has to do with being open—to resonating, to being present, to not
judging. It has to do with being who you are, which is love.

You will demonstrate great compassion at this time in your country's history if you are able to watch what is happening and not get caught up in the
fear—if you are able to hold in love all those who are caught up in their fear.
You can be aware of what is happening within them, that their fears are surfacing. If your fears surface, know that it is an opportunity for you to let go of
them. Compassion is to be there in openness, being nonjudgmental and
standing with others, anchoring love. When people are in a state of fear, they
have no anchor. They are drifting about in the sea, drifting about in the
ocean with nothing to hold on to. That is a terrifying experience.

So what you, as people of the light, can do, is show other people of the
light—who don't know they are people of the light—what it is they can hold
on to. That is love. You stay there focused within your heart; you stay there
with Michael's sword.

## TAKE UP MICHAEL'S SWORD

Remember, we have used Michael's sword before. It is good for all of us to
review how to use it.

*Hold out your hand, palm up. And those of you who have already been given
Michael's sword, feel it, grasp it. If you have not already received Michael's sword,
we are now placing its hilt in your palm. Close your hand upon it. Feel it, grasp
it. Feel the weight of it; feel the energy of it. Now hold it in front of you, in front
of your heart, point up. Focus on your heart. Ask for the light from All That Is
to come into your crown and go into your heart. Claim the love that you are, and
open your heart even more. Allow that energy to go through your hands into
Michael's sword and feel it; see it blaze in front of you. Feel the energy, the power
of it surrounding you. Now see yourself doing it without physically holding your
hand in front of you. (You would look kind of strange doing that in the mall, would
you not?) Holding on to Michael's sword will remind you of your anchor since it
can be a very tangible experience.*

So in your compassion, when you have someone who is caught in fear—and
you do realize that anything that is not love is fear—you can use Michael's
sword to surround and protect him or her. You can etherically place yourself in
front of the one in fear. Remember that there is no time or space. See yourself
moving in front of the person, standing before him or her and holding Michael's
sword in front of you, point up. Amplify the energy so that it surrounds you and
the person behind you, providing protection. Think of what you would do if
you were with a little child and something dangerous like a ferocious dog came

into the room or the child became afraid. Wouldn't you place yourself in front of the child to protect him or her? Those of you who have had little ones, if some thief or brigand came in, wouldn't you place yourself in front of your child and do all that you could to protect? Well, that is what you are going to do with the compassion you have when you are using Michael's sword. You will not get into fear, but if you do, use Michael's sword to dissolve the fear around you. Simply stand there with that high-vibration energy of Michael's sword. This will dissolve the energy of the fear and help anchor that person so that she or he does not feel unstable.

## COMPASSION IS NOT RESCUING

Now, dear ones, compassion has nothing to do with rescuing. I repeat, compassion has nothing to do with rescuing. In the human conception of love, it has been said that you need to serve one another. That is true. However, what service is has been misunderstood. If you see a car barreling toward someone who is unaware of it, most of you would have the instinct to yell and warn that person. And some of you might, if there was a chance, push him or her out of the way. That is honorable and could very well be what you were called to do and what you were put on this Earth to do. But take something such as drinking and drug use. Let's say some people you know are destroying their lives with such things, and you keep rescuing them in many different ways. It could be that they go to jail time and time again, and you bail them out time after time. It is not compassion, dear ones, to continue bailing them out, not allowing them to learn their lesson. Doing it once, yes, maybe even twice—but you know when it comes to the third time, it is time they learn their lesson.

Think of your children; we'll take something very simple. They refuse to do their homework. You do not want them to fail; therefore, you do their homework for them. And so where are you going to be when they are thirty-five? You can't keep doing their homework for them, or they cannot learn. That is not compassion. Look at your own motives for doing something.

## YOU ARE ALL HEALERS

Many of you are healers. There is a time in the healing when continuing to give your service to someone is not compassion. Rather, you are enabling that person to stay in place without moving forward in life. You will know—and we will tell you if you ask—when it is that you need to be aware of this. So, very succinctly, compassion is not doing something for others that they can do for themselves. Of course, there are going to be things that you do of service for one another. I don't want you to think that I am speaking in a very black-and-white manner, because I am not. As a courtesy, you would get coffee, tea or a drink for someone. That is a courtesy. But you do not walk for someone when he or she could walk yet refuses to do so, choosing to stay immobile. Am I being clear about what it is we are saying?

It is time to open your heart. It is a time to stand in solidarity with people, but do it in love. There is no way for any one person to rescue everyone else from what is happening. There is no way you can rescue everyone from fear, no way you are called to do so. No one in this room (or reading this) is called to stand in front of every member of humanity with Michael's sword right now. There are some who are called to do similar work, but it is not anybody in this room. (There are two people reading these words who are called to do extraordinary work with Michael's sword. If you believe you are called to do that, let me give you your characteristics: you have overcome great adversity; you have released much anger and have little of that left in your heart—you do not erupt in anger at any time; you have great gentleness and tremendous strength.)

I said that some of you are healers—actually, all of you are, although some of you are called more specifically to work one on one with healing. But you are all healers when you open your heart to another, when you stand anchored in love. You are all healers when you respond to anger with love. You are all healers when you respond to insecurity with love. You are all healers when you have what you call good boundaries and you don't let people run over you. You set those boundaries with love. That is also compassion. Do you have any questions about this message?

## DO WHAT YOU ARE

*I would like to know what I am here to do. Maybe I should figure it out on my own? Is there something you can tell me?*

Let me answer this generally. Your society has a tremendous emphasis on being what is called productive. Now, how does your society define production? Is it not how much money you make? How many books you write? It is very difficult to realize who you truly are when you grow up with that kind of notion of what production is. I am sure you have heard the phrase, "You are a human being, not a human doing." That is a little simplistic, because the complexity of it is that you do what you are. Now many of you are aware that numerous people who have jobs in this country are not happy with what they do. Most of you in this room are fortunate enough to do what you enjoy doing, because you are doing what you are being. In other words, what you are doing is in line with the vibration of who it is you are. It does not have anything to do with production, as in money or papers, that type of thing. It has to do with the "production" of the vibration that is expanding to others from you. Am I making sense here?

Now, as much as you rebel against it and as much as you yearn to be where you want to be in ten years, you are still here. You are vibrating in the mode of learning. In other words, your vibration right now is calling into you the things you need to learn to do, what it is that you are to be doing in, actually, fifteen years. All of this now is preparation. Does that mean that you are not going to be feeling comfortable or anything? No, that is not what it means. But what I would like you to take within your heart is that you are doing exactly what you need to do, because you are being what you need to be.

## ABOUT INTERPERSONAL CHALLENGES

Let's look at the interpersonal challenge. All interpersonal challenges are learning experiences. You can have this interpersonal challenge now or you can have it in about ten years. I want to give anybody who has interpersonal challenges some strategies. You have been given Michael's sword. You know to stay anchored in the heart. All interpersonal challenges come to us because of what other person surfaces within us.

Now we are looking at things from a global perspective. When I say global, I am talking about your global perspective, not the planet. When you drop the pebble into the water, you know how it ripples out? If you take your interpersonal challenge now, it will cause some tension. You can work through it. Anytime someone is going through an interpersonal challenge, it causes challenges in other relationships because of the stress. Continue to stay in your heart. Remind yourself of what you are going through so you can work through it. Go through this interpersonal challenge now and work through the problems.

## DISSOLVE FEAR WITH MICHAEL'S SWORD

Here is one of the things you can do with Michael's sword when you feel the energy of the fear. You are going to have fear and tremendous anger coming up in you. Remember that this is okay. Do not berate yourself or beat yourself over the head. You can use Michael's sword to dissolve some of that and to stand there in a place of love. It will be a tremendous learning experience, more productive than anything else you could do. It is your choice. You are in this school here on the planet. Look at it as if you have decided to skip grades and are going into something that might make you feel like you are in over your head for a while. You can do this. There are others who will be there to help you.

## EVERYONE IS IN A PLACE OF OPPORTUNITY

Let's talk about opportunity. Every moment of every day is an opportunity to learn, to grow and to develop. What we were just talking about in interpersonal relationships is opportunity, and this does correspond with compassion, which is what we began with. Part of compassion is having compassion for yourself, being open to yourself. One of the ways to do this is to look at everything as opportunity. If you have a conflict with yourself, if you have a conflict with another person, if you are struggling in your job or if you are struggling with housework, look at it as an opportunity to be in a place of love and compassion for yourself and another. Right now everyone on your planet is in a place of opportunity. It is imperative for you to accept this opportunity, no matter what happens. It is an opportunity to learn how to remain in a place of peace, the peace within your heart when the world is in turmoil. There has never been a time in the recent history of your planet—and when I say recent history, I am speaking of the past five thousand years—when there has not been war. You must realize that on other planets where there is no more war, your planet is considered to be in a state of perpetual world war.

Most of the people on your planet seem to have the misconception that world war is when there is continual fighting among countries. You have these artificial divisions between one another. War is conflict. Have you heard of any place on your planet where there is not conflict? So many people have the misconception that war means fighting with guns or bombs. You even have the term "cold war." Do you not see how almost everyone on this planet walks in a place of cold war? And how cold—deep-freeze cold—burns?

## LET GO OF THE NEED FOR RECOGNITION

*If everyone walks around in fear of everyone else, how is it possible for us to have love without fear?*

There is no way to have love with fear. There is no way for you to have fear if you are in a place of love. But how do you do this? This is where opportunity comes in. Once we spoke about ego. Where fear comes in is when you become afraid that something is going to be taken away from you, that you are not going to be enough, that you are not going to have enough. You are not going to have enough notoriety, recognition or power. That is what your leaders look at. How many of your leaders are concerned about not having enough food on the table? How many of your leaders are concerned about not having enough clothing? Do you not think that something would be done about your health care crisis if your leaders did not have health insurance? So what is it that you think your leaders are most concerned about? Power, money, fame—and that is because they are in the public arena.

Now let's look at the small arena of yourself. How many of you become upset and feel offended when you are not recognized for what you do? Now, your psychology teaches how it is important that you recognize each person for what it is he or she does. You have laws that are based upon recognition, upon recognizing people—copyright laws, trademark laws. I am not saying that these things are wrong. What I am doing is putting them on a different, spiritual level. If you are fully in a place of love, you accept information that comes to you as something to be given to the world. When it goes out to the world and then someone else proclaims it as his or her own, it does not change that what you brought into the world went out into the world. So if your intention is to bring out something for the good of humanity, then even if others steal it (if you would like to say it that way) and claim it as their own, did you not still do your job?

## LET GO OF THE ATTACHMENT

Do you fear that you will not be taken care of? How much money do you need to have in your bank account? What do you need most at the end of the month, a dollar more or a dollar less in your bank account than what you need to pay your bills? A dollar more or a dollar less? Would it make any difference in paying your bills if you had a million dollars more or ten dollars more? Do you really need more than ten dollars more than you have to take care of your bills? Think about it. The extra ten dollars might give you security, but the bills are paid. What I am saying is, trust that it will come to you. This is the opportunity to learn. Some of you have very deep lessons to learn about the energy of what you call money. The fear of not having enough is there. We will not take those lessons away from you.

Let me tell you that there is nothing wrong with wanting a million dollars more at the end of the month when you pay your bills. There is nothing wrong with the desire to have security. Where you come into the fear is when you are attached to having to have the security. Do you see the distinction?

Would you like to have a pen or a pencil to write with at times? Does it matter which kind—a 19-cent pen, a 150-dollar pen or a gold-plated pen? You would just like to have a pen to write with when you need one, and of course, you would prefer that it works. If you can only write with the gold-plated pen, then it is the attachment causing the problem, not the writing instrument.

There is nothing intrinsically wrong with having a gold-plated pen, money, power and prestige. The challenge is to use it wisely. You see, the more power and prestige you have, the more opportunity you have to learn. It is more difficult to handle great power and prestige than it is to not have great power and prestige. You do more damage with great power and prestige. Who has the opportunity to do the greatest damage in your world right now?

*The president of the United States.*

That's right. And who has the most power and prestige in your world right now? Corporations, world leaders and the president of the United States together. What you have are opportunities. As you progress into positions in which you have more power and prestige, each one of you has power over people. You have the opportunity to do great damage or great good. It is your attachment to the power and prestige that causes difficulties.

Back to the financial issues now. If you are not happy unless you have a million dollars in your bank account, even though all your bills are paid, there is a problem within you. There can be great joy when you are writing out checks for all your bills at the end of the month. You come to the end of the month, and you are wondering if you can pay all your bills. You deduct the last bill and have one dollar left. Think of how much better you feel with that one dollar left than if you were fifty cents short. Can you feel the difference in how that would be? Yes, there is greater security, but do not be attached to the security. It is fine to have prestige, but do not be attached to the prestige. You are all going to be given ideas to give to people, but do not be attached to them. Some of you are going to go through great trials of feeling betrayed, because people are going to steal ideas from you. But you brought the idea out, so allow it to be that way. You might not remember these words when it happens to you. They are very difficult words, but you are here to learn spiritually what to do.

Look at the spiritual giants who have walked the Earth. Think about it. Have they had any attachment to fame or power? But have they not had great fame or power? Do not think there is anything wrong with money, fame or power. It is just the attachment that inhibits spiritual growth. This is where the opportunity to learn comes in—compassion, opportunity, openness, being in your heart.

## WORK ON YOURSELF AND HELP EARTH

Now, dear ones, get a sense of how big you really are. Practice with Michael's sword. Know that Michael's sword can change sizes. I will always refer to it as a sword, but it can actually become dagger-sized. Know that anything the sword touches—and we are speaking of energy here, any discordant energy—will be dissolved. You can use it to slice and sever attachments. First, I would like you to find the place within you that holds the greatest pain. For some of you, it is in the heart. Place the sword in the fear, the sense of betrayal, the anger, the abuse, and use it to dissolve that discordant energy. Feel the energy course through you as though there is an opening.

You can use the sword at any time. Let me show you another way to use it, just as an example. Think about financial insecurity, what it feels like. Where is it in your body? Touch that energy mass of insecurity with the sword and allow it to burn away. You would be amazed at how much abundance you have when you don't care whether you have it or not.

Do not think that doing this work on yourself is selfish. As you do it on yourself, you also do it for the planet. Now we will do it specifically for Earth. Notice how big you are. Do you think this room can contain you? It cannot. See yourself surrounding this planet of yours and look down upon it for those places that look dark. With the sword that is in your hand, now much larger than a dagger, reach down and place it where you are called to place it. Feel and watch what happens. You did not know you had such power, did you?

Thank you, dear ones. I send you my blessings. Know that my love is always surrounding you.

# 5

# *Turn Jealousy into Acceptance!*

*February 2003*

$G$ ood evening, dear ones. Thank you for coming. We are going to continue our discussion on aspects of love. What I am going to talk about today is actually an aspect of "not love." I do this so I can then enter into an aspect of love.

## JEALOUSY, ENVY AND COVETOUSNESS

I would like to talk about the aspect of "not love" known as jealousy. Jealousy is an emotion in your human condition that stems from the basic lack of satisfaction within yourself. Jealousy is the emotion that has to do with the inability to accept people as they are. Many people have the inability to accept that people have desires, joys, sorrows, needs and wants that may not include them. In a way, I am talking about the aspect of love that concerns acceptance and nonjudgment.

The reason I am discussing jealousy is that it is rampant in this world. Offshoots of it are covetousness and envy. Jealousy stems from the fact that people do not accept that they are aspects of love. They mistakenly believe that they can become more of who they are if they have someone else. Jealousy usually revolves around someone, whereas covetousness and envy revolve around something. Jealousy seems to believe that a person can become whole if there is someone else just like him or her, with the same beliefs, to make the person whole.

Let's expand on the above. Jealousy and its companions, envy and covetousness, are what you see so much in the world today, are what is bringing about the great strife that is here. There is a lack of acceptance of people and their dreams and beliefs. In some way, people become jealous of those beliefs and want them to be theirs, but theirs in the way that they want to interpret them. For instance, look at religion.

## JEALOUSY AND RELIGION

Take any of the religions you know. You can take a small sect or a large population. They want others to believe in their own beliefs. They have to feel within themselves that their acceptance of the belief needs the validation of someone else accepting that belief.

There is no need for anyone to have to believe what you believe in order to make what you believe valid. Each of the religions or schools of thought—be it a philosophy or a religion—has to do with what makes the individuals in that particular group feel comfortable about their particular beliefs. Some of the religions, thoughts and philosophies are such that there is much control within a hierarchical structure. This control is for people who do not have the necessary strength and confidence to make their own decisions. What causes difficulty is that they believe that other people also do not have this strength. They then become afraid that people will make a decision contrary to their own beliefs, which to them would be a wrong decision. So they believe they have to get the other person to believe as they do. In a sense, they are jealous of their own belief in such a way that they have to force it upon someone else.

That is not the way of love. Know that jealousy stems from a lack within yourself of your own knowingness of who and what you are. Know that your desire, if you have the desire that someone must believe the way you do, stems from your insecurity that perhaps your belief is wrong. It is a shadow aspect of belief, of holding to basic precepts. This leads to the question, "Are there any basic truths?" The answer is, "Yes, there is one basic truth. That is love, because all is created of love." Each of you is created of love. You have to decide, "How do I become love? How do I experience love? How do I be that of which I am made?"

It is an interesting question, because the only way to be that of which you were made is to be that of which you are made. Unfortunately, what has happened in the human condition is that your society has determined that there are certain ways in which this thing called love should be defined. Some societies have many different words for love. In English, as you know, there is only one. Many concepts are lumped into this one word "love." Love is the highest aspect of who you are. Love is the best way that you care for and nurture yourself. Love is the best way in which you care for and nurture others, calling them to grow, to know that of which they are created.

## JEALOUSY OF CHILDREN

Those of you who have children know the awesome responsibility of calling to growth these young personalities who are forming and struggling to discover who they are and how they are to be and live in this society. Young ones are often unruly. The unruliness comes from their freedom and joy of life. They are unruly only according to your definition of what is proper deportment. Many times adults are jealous of children's freedom and therefore limit that freedom. The adults believe they cannot have that same joy and freedom of life and, in many ways, attempt to snuff it out in the young ones.

There are things young ones need to learn. They need to learn that there are ways you care for yourself and that there are times when you care for others as well. As you grow and develop, the task is discovering how you care for yourself and how you care for others. Unfortunately, what happens as you struggle in the woundedness of this society is that the lessons of your own wounds get lost, and that is what happens on this planet. That is why you are here: to learn and to grow through the wounds you have and learn to heal those wounds. You learn about aspects of yourself that are not love, since there are aspects that are not love in this society and in this world. You are facing those wounds on your planet this very day. There are those who wish to start war. There are those who wish peace. There are those in fear. There are those who are in want. And yes, there are those who jealously guard their land, their security, their weapons. Ironically, they jealously guard their peace. You cannot jealously guard peace because it dissolves.

## LEARNING TO ACCEPT YOURSELF

Let's go to the other aspect of jealousy, the part that is love. The part that is love is acceptance of who you are and acceptance of the other. Dear ones, if you could only know how precious you are. If the persons in your governments across this planet knew how precious they were, how priceless they were, there would be no war. Unfortunately, there are energies that feed upon negative energies and keep the conflict going between countries, between individuals. Your job as people of the light is to remain in your heart, to shine that light among all, to come to know the love that you are and to come to know and understand the love that each person is. If all persons realized that they and everyone else are love, they would not dare strike out with any sword other than Michael's sword—the sword of love, the sword of peace and the sword of truth. Then they would use Michael's sword to eliminate the thought forms of fear, anger, hatred and insecurity—the thought forms within each person that are not love.

This is what you must do: Learn to accept yourself and learn to love. You see, God really is not a jealous God. God is a loving God and an accepting God. God knows that when you focus on something other than God—and we are defining God as love, pure love, the source of love, the essence of love—then you lose who you are. In a certain sense, God is a jealous God, in that God wants you to be one always with God, with love.

you focus on that is not love becomes an idol, becomes that which is
it which is not love and that which is not you. To find the source of
love, focus within your heart. You have heard it said that the eyes are the windows
of the soul. I challenge you, however, to learn, see, feel and know the heart
energy within each person. The heart is the entryway into yourself. By feeling the
heart energies within other persons, you will come to know who they truly are.
People have learned how to hide what comes from their eyes. Very few know how
to hide what comes from their heart energy, from their heart center.

I ask you, dear ones, to let go of any desire to have someone think like you,
believe like you, feel like you or be you. Let go of your desire or the need you
have for people to be within your life if they do not want to be. If they do not
want to be within your life, then they do not need to be. You do not become
more complete by having someone fulfill you. Your completeness comes only
from going within your heart and finding the love that I have for you and that
the Father has for you. Let go of all that is not love. Let go of jealousy, envy,
covetousness. Learn the joys, the preciousness, the delight that you are. Not
only will you be well satisfied with yourself, but all that you desire will come to
you. Abundance will be yours.

Are you ready to do some healing tonight? First, let us work on your planet.

## A HEALING MEDITATION FOR THE PLANET

*Connect with the pillar of light in front of you. You do that simply by being aware
of the pillar of light that goes from the source of God through your crown, through your
spine and into the center of the Earth. Now, in front of you, about two feet away, is
the pillar of light that goes from the source of God to the center of the universe. Send
a beam of energy from your heart into that pillar of light before you.*

*Now accept Michael's sword in your dominant hand, the hand you would use to
wield a sword. Focus on your heart, bringing in energy and light from above and below.
Have them merge together in your heart, go through your arm and, like an electric current, go into Michael's sword. Feel, sense, see the sword blaze in front of you.*

*Now ask to be taken by Spirit to the place you are to go to thrust the sword into
thought forms of war, hatred, jealousy, covetousness and the desire for control and
power. You might be surprised at where you are taken. Once you are there, use the
sword to penetrate the darkness. Watch the darkness be transmuted into light.*

*Being fully aware of your own self, your own spirit within you, connect with your
higher self. Ask to be shown within yourself the energies that prevent you from recognizing who you truly are. Whether it be unforgiveness of yourself, fear or a disbelief in who
you truly are, ask to be taken to that place, that system within you where these energies
are held. Place Michael's sword within that place and watch those energies dissolve.*

*Feel the energy of my love coming into your heart. Allow it to course through you
and strengthen you. Accept my love for you. Accept my knowledge of how precious
you are. Now believe it yourself.*

# 6

# *Time to Use What You've Learned— School Is Over*

*April 2003*

$G$ood evening. It's so good to be here with you again and to see some new faces. It is just wonderful to have you here. So what is on your minds tonight? Are you listening to what your news people and government are putting out? It's going full force, isn't it—the attempt to have you in as much fear as you can possibly be.

The trick of all this is that what they are talking about may indeed happen. You do not need to be in fear about it. This is very important to realize. It does not matter what happens on this planet, what your government says or what other people say; there is no reason to be in fear about what happens. Remember that fear changes nothing about an event. If something is going to happen, it will happen whether you are in fear or not. But when you are in fear, it makes that event worse for you, no matter what it is. As you know, it is impossible to stay in a place in your heart and be in a state of fear at the same time.

## DO YOU WANT TO CHANGE WHAT'S HAPPENING?

Do you wish to change what is happening on your planet now? I know the answer is yes. Dear ones, the way to change what is happening with the planet is to change what is happening within you.

Think of those you are not reconciled with at this time in your life. If there cannot be peace between you and another person or two, how do you expect countries with millions of people to have peace among them? To have true peace—not just the absence of war—which is not peace? Peace is when you have in your heart the calmness, the evenness and the joy of life. Peace happens when there is nothing that you allow to interfere with it. Peace within yourself can occur in the midst of other people warring. Peace can occur within yourself even if you are living or working in a situation where there is great turmoil.

I have a suggestion for you at this critical time in your world—not just in your country. Do not listen to the news on the radio or television or read your newspapers. Be aware that what you do hear has some factual truth, but there is also a lot of obfuscation in it. You are not being given the total truth about what is happening on your planet at this time. You can choose peace. Each person on your planet can choose peace. Your governments can choose peace. It all depends upon what it is that you focus on.

There is nothing to be afraid of. What is the worst thing that could happen? That you leave your body? Well, you don't seem to get upset when you take off your clothes at night, and leaving your body is no different from taking off your clothes. Are you afraid that others you know and love will leave their bodies? Yes, that is possible. But, dear ones, you will see them again soon. This is the time to be in a place of total detachment, total detachment from fear—and total attachment to the love energy that comes from your heart. Do not be afraid and do not be dismayed if there is violence over the next few weeks. Do not be dismayed if there is none. There are choices that can occur. If you stay in a place of fear, you perpetuate fear. One of this country's leaders said about fifty years ago, "We have nothing to fear but fear itself." He did not know how true these words were.

## BE AWARE OF MANIPULATION

You can do anything when not in fear. But you cannot move mountains if you are in fear; you cannot move your heart and you cannot open yourself to the good things of life if you are in fear. It does not matter what is happening or what is going to happen. Fear does not change anything that will happen, except to make it worse for you and bring about a vibration in other people that increases their fear. Every one of you has answered the call on a deep soul level to break up the vibration of fear. That is a strong calling. It is powerful, powerful work to do. Whatever it is that you do in your daily lives, know that your most important job, a most crucial job, is to stay in your heart.

With all the fear coming out of your country today, all the buildup and talk of alerts, being prepared and so on, the fear is rising to extreme heights. That is the intent of those who are doing it. The people will want to break the heightened tension of fear in some way, and therefore they will agree to war. Think of the concept of waiting for the other shoe to drop. Tension builds and builds until you scream out, "Would you throw the other shoe?" This is what they are trying to do.

Be aware of what is happening regarding the psychological manipulation that is occurring. Be very aware of this. Be aware, but do not be in anger. Be aware, but do not be in fear. Be aware, but do not be jealous, do not be envious, do not be resentful, do not be suspicious. Just know that it is happening. Know that it is there. And know that you were not made in fear. You were made in love.

You were made in the image and likeness of the God Source. The God Source is only love. It is not the love you hear in your songs or on your radio. It is the love that is the total consciousness and essence of is-ness, the being-ness. It is energy. It is life. And you call it love.

## CONNECT WITH YOUR COMMUNITY

Unfortunately, most people are not aware of exactly what this creative force is that you and we are made of. Therefore, they—and you—do not realize how creative you yourself are. I have spoken before: You are a creator. You can be a creator in your own right. You do not need someone else to cocreate with you, although it can be helpful. You are beings of community, because you come from the Oneness. You are One and you know you are One. That is why you are community. You reach out, one to another, which is reaching out to the other parts of yourself that are there. So it is helpful in the physical to gather as community to create. Know that you do not need one another to create. Know also that it is easier, on this planet of duality, to stay out of fear when you are together in community. You can be together in community even when you are not together physically.

Remember the pillar of light in front of you. There are some who do not know of this pillar of light. Simply be aware that there is the pranic tube, also known as the pillar of light, that goes through your crown, down your spine and into the Earth. This pillar of light is a part of every person. It is actually a part of every living substance. By the way, "living" has nothing to do with replication of cells. The pillar of light I wish to speak of is the one before you. It goes from the Source of God to the center of the universe, whereas the one within you goes from the Source of God to the center of the Earth. Be connected to the pillar of light in front of you by sending a beam of energy from your heart to the pillar. As you are connected to this pillar, you are also connected in a real way to all persons in the universe who are connected to the pillar of light in front of them. Learn to live within this pillar, not just to be connected with it. Connect now. Feel the community that is here as you do that now.

Know that to change the movement of this planet, the cleansing can occur with pain and travail—or with greater ease. You have a large group of people who want it to occur with pain and travail for their own ulterior purposes. If you wish to help move the planet to a place of cleansing through ease, consciously and continually be connected to the pillar of light in front of you and know that as you are connected in such a way—connected from your heart— your vibration of calmness and love energy radiates out to others and helps them to raise their frequencies so they are not in such pain, anxiety and fear. Some of you will find this exercise more difficult than others, because some of you came to this planet to learn about fear and how to release it.

## CLAIM WHO YOU ARE

Do not be concerned about knowing what the news is. Someone will tell you. When you hear about what is going on, whatever alert, whatever precautions, be in your heart. You might want to practice a reflexive action of just placing your hand over your heart so that you can stay there. You are strong people. You have strong wills and strong spirits. Even if you do not believe this is true, I tell you that it is so. Claim that truth for yourself. At this very moment, claim who it is you choose to be. It does not matter what has happened in the past, in this life-time or any other. You are a creator, and you can even create yourself anew at this very moment. Do you wish to be one who is continually connected from the heart to the pillar of light in front of you? Choose that this instant and live it. Make that your consciousness. Make that your job.

If there is violence over the next few weeks or months, you may get caught up in the anger that may occur. Remember to stay in your heart and to stay connected to the pillar of light in front of you. It is time. It is time. The teaching about love is now to be put into action. All you have heard about love in every lifetime, all the experiences that you have of learning about love through each lifetime, this is the time, in this moment, of putting it into action. The action is being. Isn't that interesting? You think of being as a place of inaction, yet the action of being love is what you are called to do.

One of the things you can do before going to sleep is to connect to the pil-lar of light if you are not already connected, and ask the beautiful angels and guides surrounding you (who happen to be part of you) to bring all the energies and knowledge of love from every lifetime that you've had or will have to your spirit while you sleep. It can happen. Ask that it all be collected and placed right in your heart so that you can live who you are and be who you are. The greatest action that you can do now is to be who you are.

A somber message but an important one. Although I will teach you a few things in the future, I need to tell you that school is over. You have already graduated. So use that degree for which you have worked so hard over these hundreds of lifetimes. Be aware and be in love. Are there any questions?

## BE CONSCIOUS OF ENERGY

*I remember that before you had said that you didn't think there would be a war, and now I feel a shift in your perspective. Am I right?*

Yes, there has been a shift. However, know that although this could occur, there is a greater chance right now of what your country calls terrorist activity. Remember that you are working with very wounded people on this planet.

What would you do if your next-door neighbor kept threatening to come in and take over your home and had tremendous weapons to be able to do that, but would not allow you to have weapons to defend yourself? Do you not think, being human, that you might reach a breaking point? These are possibilities only. Know that. It can change.

Just think, if you had a leader of a country who's leading the way to war, it would only be that leader who needed to change, would it not? It is the same with those within what you call terrorist activities. I want you to know, the chance of terrorist activities is not as strong as your government is saying it is. So my message seems contradictory, does it not? Just be aware. Be aware of your own anger when you flare out at someone you love and care for. Be aware that that action contributes to what is going on in the world. Be very conscious of your actions. You know energy. Be conscious of it.

*When releasing fear, is it the same thing as being in fear?*

That's a very good question. Releasing fear is recognizing that you have the fear and then letting it go. Being in fear is often not even recognizing you are in fear and holding on to it. It is the difference between taking out the garbage and putting it into the garbage can or letting it build up in your house. So when you are releasing fear, you are taking the garbage out of yourself. Release the fear into the pillar of light and have it transmuted into love. Do not just release the fear into the atmosphere. You want the energy of fear to be transmuted into love, and by releasing it into the pillar of light, it will be transmuted into love.

*How many more years of this chaotic consciousness do you see occurring here?*

I cannot give you an answer to that, because on this planet you have not yet decided. Know that everything is being created anew. I will tell you that at this moment in time, it will be at least ten more years. You have had the idea that all of this would change completely in 2012. There will be a big change, but there will still be chaos that is occurring. Do you wish to be part of the chaos? People around you can be in chaos, but you do not need to be a part of it. The more you are in a place of being connected to the pillar of light, that place of love that is a place of freedom, the sooner the chaos will end. Know that there are some people who have a belief system that the only way to give up the battle is to die, their physical lives dying. You do not have to be part of that. Anything is possible.

## GET OUT OF BED AND CREATE WITH ADAMANTINE PARTICLES

*When you say it hasn't been decided yet, does that mean that humans as individual creators are the ones who make the choice? And is it possible, if enough people awaken to that fact, to shorten the time period of the chaos?*

You are right. It is humans as individual creators who will make the choice. You have enough people on this planet who have awakened. But, to use an analogy, they also have to get out of bed! What I mean by that is they have awakened to the possibilities, but they have not yet claimed their possibilities and power. All of you have been awake for a while, and look how you still struggle to claim who you truly are. If you knew to the deepest part of yourself who you truly are, do you realize that none of you would have any aches or pains? If you knew to the depths who you are, do you realize that the financial worries you have would be gone? And then there are those who are just awakening—opening their eyes in bed, so to speak, looking around and wondering, "Was that a dream or is this the dream?" That's where many people are right now.

It is you, who have already awakened, gotten out of bed, selected clothes to wear and put them on, who must help people. So yes, it can definitely change. Remember, there are those who have made a choice not to awaken. You can't change that choice, but what you can do is send out the vibration of love. As you are sending out this vibration of love, have your intention be that it nullifies the fear. Those of you who are energy workers know how much stronger the energy is when you form an intention consciously.

You can have your intention to send out love and also have the intention that it nullifies the fear. This will increase the vibration of love, because what you are sending out are particles that some call adamantine particles. They are ruled by love and only by love and are what you create from. These are the most powerful particles found in the universe. They cannot be ruled by anything but love, as they will be ineffective. I would like you to become aware of the adamantine particles right now. If you have unconsciously dropped your connection to the pillar of light in front of you, go ahead and reconnect now. Open your hands. Go into your heart and ask that you be able to feel one adamantine particle in each hand. Feel the pure potential in each one. Now, dear creators, what do you wish to create with these two adamantine particles, one in each hand?

You can ask for as many adamantine particles as you want. Perhaps going through your head are the many, many things you could create. There are an infinite number of these adamantine particles and they can only be commanded by love. It is a responsibility having these adamantine particles, isn't it?

## WHAT IS REALLY BEHIND THESE CONFLICTS?

*I'm not quite certain how to phrase this, because my own feelings on it are somewhat confused. It seems to me that this conflict or the potential for various conflicts that exists is much more than just battles for territory, oil or whatever. I would like some information from you, Amma, as to what are the real motivation and the real purpose behind the experiences that we're all going through on the planet at the moment.*

What I am going to tell you is nothing you have not heard before. The true thing that is occurring is a cleansing of the old energies and a moving into the new energies. People are very entrenched in the old energies, and they live in fear because they are afraid of change.

On one level, what is occurring is the cleansing that needs to happen. There are those who are very much aware of these new energies. They know that they will lose their power when the new energies are accepted and people come to know who they themselves truly are. So in one way it is a power struggle.

If the new energies and the new Earth do not come in, these people of the old energy who are into power in a negative way will remain so. But I wish to tell you that there is no way that can happen. It is just a question of whether the new energies will come in with ease or with conflict. It is a desperate fight to remain in control and in power. You do not need someone in power, control or authority, since your authority is in the heart. Each one of you who has broken out of the structure—be it out of a church, be it out of a governmental force (that is what civil disobedience is) or be it out of making your own decisions about what you should do—has broken out of the old energy and flowed into the new energy.

## MICHAEL'S SWORD HELPS YOU TRANSMUTE FEAR

*How can we use Michael's sword with this?*

Some of you are not aware of Michael's sword. There is the one you call Archangel Michael (or Mich-a-el), and your pictures often show him with a sword that is always unsheathed. This is a sword that is a tool for truth and for raising vibration. This sword is also used for protection. Simply open your dominant hand and ask that Michael's sword be placed in it. Feel the hilt of it, the heft of it. It is now yours to use. Consciously activate your heart and bring energy from your heart down your arm and into the sword. See, feel and sense the sword blaze before you. Hold it in front of you. Any time the fear vibration comes toward you, use the sword to deflect it and transmute it into love. You could, if you so chose, go about your day not only consciously connected to the pillar of light in front of you, but also carrying Michael's sword. Of course, you do not need to always have your hand up. You can carry it in the etheric. That can be your work tomorrow and these next few days. You can use Michael's sword to transmute the energies of fear, and you can ask to be taken anywhere you are needed. Place the sword within the energies of that place. You can also use the sword as a protection for yourself. You can hold it in front of you, open your heart even more and allow the energy of the sword to surround you. It will act as a protection. The crisis will be over when the planets exchange places. When this astrological time is over, then you will be more at ease

*Can you tell us what is happening astrologically?*

You have certain planets coming into alignment that are presenting the same kind of energy that occurred on what you call your 9/11. These planets are bringing a force of change, producing that which will bring forth the energy of change. Whenever you have planets/stars going into alignments, you can flow with that energy or you can battle against it. If you flow with the energy, you know this is a time of change, and you look within yourself and ask, "What is it that I can do to change and move into the new at this time?" And you flow with that. If, however, you want to resist that change, you will feel yourself being pulled apart. Very simply, that is what's happening.

## Avoiding Unwanted Influence

*Regarding fear, as a lightworker opening myself up to do more energy work, I find myself having quite a bit of fear of presenting myself. What should I be concerned about or aware of to get past this?*

What you are saying is that you have a fear that what you are presenting yourself as is not true. You have those limiting beliefs that were placed within you at a very young age when you were told that you could not be such and such. Simply release these fears and claim that which you are.

*I think it goes a little deeper. I was concerned about our government having a negative influence on people trying to do this kind of love work.*

If you believe who you are, they cannot have an influence. You have already seen this not only with your government, but also with others who want you to go into this place of war. You are termed unpatriotic or clueless. If you believe who you truly are, it does not matter what it is they think you are, because they cannot influence those who are truly into who they are. If you have doubts about who you truly are, then yes, you can be influenced.

## How Can We Still Have Fun?

*So, Amma, you have been very serious, and I understand in the past you have said that we are here to have fun. Would you comment on how we can have fun with all this seriousness?*

First of all, be aware that you are beings of love. As a being of love, do things that love would do. Is love not joyful? Where can you go to experience joy? Be with your friends, your loved ones and your families and experience love. Avoid the things of fear. I am not telling you not to be prepared, but when you work from your heart and look for the light and the love in each person, you will experience joy. As you go out tomorrow, notice the flowers and trees and clouds and communicate with them. Being aware of the consciousness of everything is another way of having fun, because you discover just how connected you are to everything and everyone.

Every day pick something you would like to do that is fun for you. This will be different for each of you. Some find it great fun to listen to country and western music; others find that to be drudgery. Choose what it is that is fun for you. Some of you like bawdy jokes; some of you think they are uncouth and are offended by them. So don't read or listen to them. Your sense of humor is different.

The fun comes from staying in the heart. Extreme seriousness is a result of fear; it is not a result of love. Know that however difficult this may be in a four-dimensional world, it is simply transitory. When you leave your body, you will look back as you gather together and you will laugh in much the same way you may have laughed at home movies when you were learning to walk: "Look when we were learning about who we were." And you will laugh with joy at your struggles. No more questions? Shall we do some work; shall we do some fun?

Check to be sure you are connected to the pillar of light in front of you. Choose a memory of one of the most joyful or most peaceful times in your life, something that has great meaning for you. Ask those precious ones who surround you, your guides and angels, to bring to you the energies of love and joy and fun from every lifetime you have already experienced and are yet to experience. Allow your heart to open. Now form the picture in your mind of pouring all the joy and love and fun that's in your heart into a big bowl, where all of it is coming together. Pour it upon the planet. If you do not yet feel the joy, open your heart and ask that joy be poured upon you. Now take that joy being poured upon you and pour it upon others.

My blessings to you, dear ones, as I place my hand upon your heart and awaken within you the love that you are.

# 7

# *It's All About the Adventure and Self-Discovery*

*July 2003*

ood evening, dear ones. Yes, I did decide that we'll have a little variety
tonight. It's always fun to have a little variety. But first, do you realize
what bright lights you are? You don't, do you? Your light is so bright! And
that's just wonderful. You are coping well with all the fear, are you not? You are
doing a good job. It's difficult to stay out of the mass consciousness, very difficult. And you are doing a good job. So just for a little variety, why don't you
ask some questions first and then I'll sum up tonight. How's that sound? Who
wants to start?

## IS SADDAM HUSSEIN STILL ON THIS PLANE?

*Is Saddam Hussein still around? Is his spirit still on this plane? Is he physically on this plane?*

Yes. Yes, he is. He is physically on this plane. His energy will be around for
quite a while.

*Is there another leader who is available in Iraq? Is there someone there who can take over and bring
in a different kind of government?*

There is not someone there at this time whom the United States government
wants there. So there is a difference. There are some things going on. Do not
believe that this is over. This is the beginning of changing times. It's all happened. It could have happened differently if there had been choices to do that,
but there were many pressures.

Realize that the energy of a terrorist is the energy of a terrorist, no matter
whose body it is in. Each person here and each person in this world has some

of that energy within. You terrorize people when you speak ugly about some-one, when you gossip about someone—it's all a terrorizing type of energy. Flaming emails or hacking or responding in very negative ways are all terrorist acts. Saddam really isn't a terrorist. He actually . . . how shall I put it . . . He does not have the stomach for doing it himself, so he gets other people to do it, which is what happens with leaders of nations. Think of how short wars would be if just the leaders of the nations battled it out themselves.

There is a coming change. You can feel it. I hope you can feel the change. There is an energy that is here. People knew before the war began that there was another way to solve the issue. It was not so much an aspect or a question of right and wrong. When you listen to those wonderful forums of discussion, the radio talk shows (which are really quite fun), you hear from people who are caught very much in this dimension you're in, and things are black—or they are white. Are they not? Of course, it is not black or white, but when you listen to those shows, it seems to be.

## ANTI-WAR IS NOT PRO-PEACE

The last time we were together, I spoke of Saddam as being one of the great lights. Everyone involved is one of the great lights. You are one of the great lights because we are all One. You come from the same light. Some are more aware of their "great-lightedness," if you would like to put it that way. So this was a war that began and people knew there was another way before it happened.

Now you can tell the difference even in the consciousness of those who were protesting the war beforehand and those who were making a plea for peace. People who do violence—and that means in words or in actions—to protest violence are still doing violence. An anti-war protest can still be a terrorist act. A pro-peace prayer fest is not a terrorist act. It changes the energy. Do you understand the difference?

You can see how your planet is shifting consciousness. There were pro-peace rallies and many pro-peace prayer fests, and those are examples of how the consciousness is changing. Unfortunately, the violence has not ended. There is great jubilation among many people now that this war is over. It is not over yet. Know that. It will continue in physical violence, and it will continue long after in the hearts of people because there are others who are angry now.

There are other ways to find and make peace. For each one of you here, your job is to be peace itself. Know that anytime you do not have peace between you and another—whether it is in your own home, at work, on the freeway or listen-ing to the radio or watching television—if you are not at peace, then you are at war. No longer can you sit on the sidelines. Your vocalization does not actually have to be from the vocal cords. It needs to be from the heart.

## HOW CAN I BE CONNECTED AND YET DETACHED?

*I would like a suggestion. I find that the more I feel connected to the One, the more I hurt when I hear any piece of news, which I don't listen to very much. What can I do to be connected and yet be detached?*

What is happening, dear one, is that you are connected to the One while still carrying with you the energy of separateness. Does that resonate with you? It is a process, a birthing process. Be connected with the One, and at the same time honor in your heart and in your being those beautiful beings who are leaving the physical and moving into another dimension.

What you can do is to note within yourself their movement and celebrate that they are leaving and moving to a different way of being. Some of them are going to be returning very quickly, because it is so exciting here right now and they want to take a different viewpoint than the one they had in their present incarnation. It is a time of celebration. You see, you have your old belief system that you're bringing with you into the oneness. Your old belief system is triggering energies of horror, and how sad it must be for those to whom this is happening. It is not that we would wish for this to happen; it just is. This is not something that most people can understand, is it? Did that help?

## HOW LONG WILL ANTI-AMERICAN SENTIMENT LAST?

*Right now the world's opinion of our nation is very split. There is an awful lot of anti-American sentiment in Europe, China and all over the world. How long is this sentiment going to last? Is it going to grow or subside? There's a lot of emotionalism about it right now.*

Something has already begun to occur that will seem very puzzling to you. That is where the nations have seen that the U.S. was right in the sense that they could go in and oust this person; they are going to consider that right. They are going to believe then that the U.S. is the one who can go in and oust other governments. They will actually be calling for the U.S. to do that.

Each time the U.S. attempts that, if that's the choice of your president and his . . . I was going to say followers, but you know that's not the right word, because the president is the follower. Do you realize that? Your president is the follower. He's the figurehead, but he's the follower. As long as that occurs, you're going to have people wanting the U.S. to go and do these other things, whether it's in North Korea or China or another country. Every time he does it, they are going to be angrier and it will isolate this country.

Now, know there are different sides. What do you call it? The silver lining of the cloud. The more your country is isolated and the angrier people are with your country, the more those in your general population are coming to be aware of the anger toward them, and they become more confused and puzzled. Your general population believes that you are the greatest country on the planet at this time, and how could anyone not love you? How could anyone not see your joyful life and the prosperity of your country?

It is going to cause a crisis within the general population, which will, dear ones, lead to a spiritual awakening—a true spirituality and not that bound by religion. You do have your truly spiritual people at the forefronts of your religious movements. Yet more and more people are moving from your traditional religions and going into their own spirituality and their own awakening.

There will be those who will try to figure out why they are not liked by other countries. Think about yourself and your own journeys, when you have tried to figure out why you weren't liked, when you went into a period of self-reflection and inward quest and then experienced a metamorphosis. This resonates with some of you, does it not? It will happen on a national level. So it is not all as it seems. Remember that.

An image . . . Think about the worm. Before that worm's metamorphosis, it isolates itself by making a cocoon. It isolates itself totally from anything surrounding it. Is that not what is happening to this country? It is getting isolated and it too will go through a tremendous metamorphosis. There are those in this room, in this country and in other parts of the planet who have been holding the whole situation in prayer, in love, in light—whatever word it is that is used. That is the energy that feeds the metamorphosis of the worm. It will take some years, but it will happen.

## Do Not Be Afraid to Be Beings of Great Light

Again, your job is to be firm in your heart and in the light. Know that you are being the great light. Do not be afraid of being beings of great light. Have no fear of that. Yes, there is responsibility to that. The responsibility is to fear not. The responsibility is to hold firm with each person you meet, to act and not react, to notice that shadow side within yourself that wants to react with negativity and not love.

It is all right when you respond with not-love. Just notice it. And do something about it. Some of you are going through a struggle to stay out of certain aspects of fear. Perhaps not the war, perhaps not illness, but perhaps finances or other things. You recognize that there is fear. Some of you are struggling with where you are to live. Are you to stay here? What is your path? Whatever it is, stay out of fear. It's much more difficult to stay out of fear. It's much easier to stay in love. So instead of staying out of fear, stay in love. Stay within the pillar of light. Stay in love.

Just a comment. The stakes go up, the tensions escalate and the old and new forces seem to be more at odds as the stakes go up. So you have a cocoon and hopefully, at some point, the cocoon opens up and the butterfly flies. Before that, the tensions get high. I can see tensions get higher on the world stage. As individuals and as lightworkers, it gets harder because it seems as though you're getting pushed more and more.

## SARS CAN FACILITATE CHANGES IN THE DNA
*What information do you have about the appearance of SARS on the planet at this time?*

Isn't it fascinating that an illness that hasn't really affected that many people has caused pandemic hysteria? How much hysteria do you have over breast cancer? Over colon cancer? Interesting, isn't it? Very interesting. Some of you might recall that some years ago it was channeled by different people that some viruses would come in that are not treatable and that would facilitate some changes in the DNA and the immune system. That is part of what SARS is.

You would think that SARS is as bad as AIDS, would you not, the way that it has taken over in the fear? The fear has to do with not understanding it. There is no cure for it, I understand. Is that correct? There really is, but they do not know the cure, is that correct? Yet it has taken on a tremendous hysteria and they do not yet know of the cure for AIDS. There is, you understand, but they do not know of it.

*As far as cures go . . . well, I'll try to be concise. As you know, I work at a hospital and I transport patients all day. I see a lot of people in pain. I try to help them with the limited knowledge I have, which doesn't seem like much. Are these cures something that is more energetic, or are they going to make some kind of drug that will cure these things? Is it going to be a drug or is it some kind of energy and learning to use it and be more open to it?*

There will be drugs that will cure these things, but that is the slow way. The fast way is energetic.

## THE CURE IS CORRECTING THE IMBALANCE
*I've been learning a lot about energy—at least I think I am learning a lot about it. Isn't it very powerful? Can't you heal a lot of things that we normally use pills for? Can you not heal those things with energy if there's something energetically wrong with the person?*

All diseases are imbalances in the energy system, so what you do is correct the imbalance. Your traditional medical field does not correct the imbalance; it treats the symptoms. That's why medicine is so slow. It's not a sure-fire method of curing the disease, because the imbalance comes from thoughts, feelings, emotions and spiritual contracts. So if the disease is caused by shame, you could treat the disease with medication, but it will continue to manifest itself in different ways; the disease is the symptom of the shame. If it is caused by guilt, the disease is the symptom of the guilt.

So you must change the thoughts and emotions, and that is energetic; that produces the energy that sets the balance off. If each person in here, and all of you have some physical difficulties, were able to shed the energies of all of the woundedness, all of the resentments, to forgive everyone—and even to realize that no one needs forgiving as there really has been nothing done to them except a chance to learn something; they just turned to a new chapter in a book to learn—then you would be perfectly healthy.

## YOU CAN'T BE TOLD WHAT YOU WILL DO

Now my final message to you tonight, since we are reversing the order. As I have been coming and speaking to you these months, I have been talking about aspects of love. On your planet and in your lives right now, what you are experiencing and are learning is about love from the aspect of "not-love"—from that which is not love. Know that whatever your question about your path—where you are to live, what you are to do, who you are to be with—all these are questions about how best for you to express the love that you are.

I know that you would like someone to come and write on this board exactly what it is that you are to do. I want to tell you why we won't do that. It's because you wouldn't do it; you wouldn't do it if we told you. You wouldn't believe us. You'd say, "Oh yes, I would believe it." So if I pointed to you and said, "You're here to become a great healer," would you go out and do it? What it is that each one of you is to do is so magnificent that you won't believe it.

Why were some of you cold? Do you think you were sitting there by yourself? No! Each one of you, as you have been here, has had others working on you and working with your energy with love. And you've had different reactions on the physical or energetic levels. Some of you were aware of something happening on a conscious level and others were not. You didn't realize that your feeling of great cold had to do with the dismantling around you. Fear is cold. Have you ever thought about that? Fear can be frigid. If you suddenly find yourself extremely cold, ask yourself what you are afraid of right now.

I know you're not going to believe me when I tell you this, but I want you to know that each of you is exactly on the path you are to be. There is nothing to change about where you are in the nowness of where you are. You are moving exactly as you are to be. Now that I've said that, you might want to believe it for an instant and then you go, "But . . . but . . . does that mean I stay here?" Did I not say, "as you are moving along the path"?

There are certain things that are more suited for your personality as you chose to be here in this lifetime. There are some here who are extremely good at mechanical conceptualization and others who would run away from it screaming. You each have your gifts and your talents, and you can choose which one you're going to develop. The difficulty that you all have is that you are so gifted and so talented that you don't know how to focus on one talent in particular. So maybe choose your favorite three and see how they come together. Create something new out of them. There is not one of you who is not multigifted and multitalented, and you want us to tell you the one thing for you to do!

But if I did tell you one thing to do, I don't think you would do it, because again you wouldn't believe it because it did not come from within you. That is why we say that you have to discover from yourself. This is how human beings are made. You are grandly designed, with a little tinkering from others here and there, for adventure and self-discovery. That is what is happening on this planet. It is the tinkering and the adventure and self-discovery.

## EVERY SINGLE PERSON IS A GREAT LIGHT

There is not one person on this planet who is not a great light, whether it be your president or the president of any other country or the one who considers himself or herself the lowest of the low. The difference is becoming aware of the light and love that you are. That is my challenge to you, my dear, precious ones. Discover the light and the love that you are and do not run from yourself. We are very pleased with each one of you here. And you might say, "But how, in my struggle, can you be pleased with my doubts about this and about that?" Dear ones, those are your doubts. They are not ours. We are pleased with you. We enjoy you. We love you. And we are with you continually. In your struggles, we are there. And in your struggles, you are there. Know that. With every struggle that you have and that you work through, you are bringing peace and love to the planet.

Do not get caught up in what all these others are doing. Don't worry about whether or not you are going to get this dreaded disease, which very few people out of the six billion people on this planet have contracted. There is no need to worry if Saddam is, in this lifetime or another, getting ready to recycle. He is much more like a cat with nine lives, you know. Don't worry where Osama is. Have you ever wondered why, if there were all these weapons of mass destruction, they weren't used right away? Not everything is as it seems.

Your government has stopped a tremendous amount of terrorism that was to occur, so they have not lied to you in everything. Know that. The difficulty is how to tell what is truth and what is not. I would suggest that you go by your own truth that is in your heart and stay out of the mess of everything else. Just let the cocoon rupture. Work with your own cocoon and those who are around you.

Now, dear ones, a blessing. I place my hand on the front of your forehead, your sixth chakra, and on the back, and I breathe into your crown. Some of you will feel that energy going straight down you. It is the breath of love to clear you and to remind you that you are claimed as part of the One. My love is always with you. Live in joy.

# 8

# Discover the Altar within Your Heart Center

## August 2003

*G*ood evening, dear ones. How wonderful it is to be here with you. Know that I am with you always. There is never a moment in your life when I am not with you. I am always here, enjoying being with you, enjoying watching you become who you truly are and learn to discover who you truly are. That is such a delight for me and for all of those who are with you.

I am Amma. I am the divine mother of the divine mothers, and what does that mean? Who is Amma? I appear in different ways on different planets in different constellations in different galaxies in different universes. Here, in this planet of duality, I take a feminine aspect, because you have something you call genders—the masculine energy and the feminine energy. You seem to have a strange perception that all masculine energy is in males and all feminine energy is in females.

You know that's not true, don't you? Each one of you has within the masculine energy, and each one also has the feminine energy. That is because all is one; there is no separation. The only separation that occurs is because your planet does the dualities. You find a need to say masculine and feminine and assign certain characteristics to masculine or feminine. That is where you get the strange concept that all the feminine energy is in the woman and all the masculine energy is in the male.

Those of you here do not believe that, because on your own journeys and education you have learned that there are certain characteristics that feel masculine or feminine according to what society may say, but that it is all one.

You know that is the truth. We are all one. There is no separation. In the physical, you feel the separation, because you feel like you have separated from the Source. I am the feminine nature of the Source, and Abba is the masculine nature of the Source.

## TRUE SEXUAL UNION CONNECTS BODY, MIND, SPIRIT AND HEART

Let's talk about the concept of oneness. I am not going to tell you anything you have not heard before, that you do not know within the depths of your very heart. You know that you are all one. Each one of you has spent your life searching to find oneness. That is what relationship is all about. That is what the glorious sexual act you have is all about. It is the unity that is exemplified.

In your society, especially in your country, many people are not finding fulfill-ment in the sexual union you have on this planet. Not every planet has sexual union as you do. Why is it that some people do not find fulfillment in this union? It is because they are not aware of what "union" truly means. They believe that it is only a physical act and get caught up in the physical sensations of what happens.

When sexual union does not occur within the connection of the heart, then there is not its true fullness. True union occurs when the soul, the heart, the spirit are connected. That is what is exemplified in your sexual union. When you bring all those together, then you have the most spiritual experi-ence of the highest vibration that you can experience with two people. Glorious, is it not? There are those of you here who have experienced that type of sexual union where it is not just the body that is joined, but also the mind, the spirit and the heart.

Let's take that sexual union and the joining—or the not joining—of the mind, spirit and heart as a metaphor for what is happening on your planet today. You are struggling on the planet with the concept called war. It is a concept about conflict. It is a concept about the greatest form of disunion that you can have. Dear ones, if your leaders were truly working from their hearts and knew how to join mind and heart and spirit, there would be no conflict. So why are they not able to do that? First of all, nobody has taught them. Your countries and those who revel so much in the Western traditions of science have separated the heart from what is scientific, because it is very difficult to study the concept called love.

## HARNESS THE HEART ENERGY

I know some of you here become very amused when people say there is no such thing as energy. "How can you study energy when there is no such thing as this energy you energy workers do?"

Of course, you could say, "Ah, is there such a thing as love?"

And they will say, "Of course, there is such a thing as love!"

"But you can't see love."

"Well, people have certain actions."

"That's true. But some people have the same action in love as others have in manipulation. How do you know the difference?"

"You just know the difference."

Ah, but that is energy. You know the difference through the energy. That is because it is the energy that connects from heart to heart. That is what has happened. How do people allow themselves to become manipulated? Because they do not pay attention to their hearts. They bypass their hearts.

Your society has a tendency to believe that the brain is the most important organ and directs all within your body. Those of you who have studied this know that it is not true. And there are those scientists who are discovering the tremendous energy field within the human heart—its purpose as well as its potential. Dear ones, if you could harness the energy in your heart, you could move mountains. If enough of you (and it would not take many) could harness the heart energy, you would witness tremendous changes in the people of your planet.

Some of you call this energy "love." Let's not use that term right now. Many people use the word "love" for many things not related to what we mean by love. That is one of the deficiencies in your human language. Instead, let's view the heart energy as the powerful energy of creative potential. That is the energy of your heart.

When you learn to tap into the energy of your heart and direct it from your heart, you will learn how to make manifest the potential that is present. Heart energy can only be used for good. It cannot be used for ill, since it comes from the deepest source of who you are. That is pure love. If you would learn to use and direct the heart energy, the planet would change drastically. Your country would change drastically; your world and the people in it would change drastically.

It does not take that many people to focus, be aware of and learn how to use the energy in the heart. There are people who have learned how to direct this energy. Some are yogis and monks in Tibet and India and there are a few in the Western world. There are some in Russia who have learned how to do wondrous things by harnessing the energy of the heart. Aboriginal people in Australia and on some other islands have learned how to harness the energy of the heart. Why is it that people are so easily manipulated in your societies? Because they have not learned to listen to the heart.

## ENTER THE MOST SACRED SPACE WITHIN YOU

I have spoken at various times of different aspects of love. All these aspects of love are accessed by entering the heart. There is a pathway in what is called your heart chakra—your heart center—that will take you deeply into your spiritual awareness. Deeply does not refer to direction, but to your spiritual awareness. Most of you enter your heart through the front. You live out in the front, because this is what you see. Dear ones, the front is simply the physical.

Right now, I would like you to enter your heart center through the back. Do that now. Feel yourself go into your heart center through the back. Ah—now, do you see a fire or a light there, perhaps even an altar? That is because you have entered the most sacred space within you. This is where the energy of the heart is. Come here often to visit and invite me or any of those others you work with to join you. Make the altar a table—a table where you pull up chairs and sit around and drink fine wine or fine juice, whichever your choice may be. Bless the water. Break bread. And speak from heart to heart, one heart to another. Ask the question, "What is the power that I have within my heart? Tell me about this energy that is there."

You could read the scientific research and learn about the energy, but it doesn't tell you how to use or harness it. Scientists themselves are just learning. You will find out how if you go into your heart through the back. It is sacred space, the sacredness that is you. As you go deeply within, you will discover your oneness. You can connect—spirit to spirit, soul to soul—with someone.

Just think of somebody, each of you. Who would you like to talk to at your altar? Invite someone to your altar and ask the question that you would most like the answer to. (By the way, he or she doesn't even have to still be on the Earth plane.) Ah, the conversations you could have, could you not? If you are having a problem in a relationship with a loved one, call him or her to your altar and talk about it at that level. Even if he or she knows nothing about your altar in the physical, that's not true on the soul level.

## HEAL YOUR BODY FROM YOUR HEART

Now I want to show you something else. Go to your altar in your heart center and stay there. There is the pillar of light in front of you. Most of you know about the pillar of light. Just feel it and step into it. Watch the light illuminate your altar. While you are here at your altar in the pillar of light, go to an area of your body that is hurting or not working as well as you would like. Stay there in your heart and talk to that part of your body. Talk to the stem cells that are within your body and tell them what it is you want them to do.

Do you need some repair in the sinus area? Tell your stem cells that you need them to become cells within the sinuses—whole, powerful, clean cells functioning in the right way, the way ordained by a healthy DNA and RNA. Are you concerned about bone loss? There at your altar, within the pillar of light, talk to your stem cells and tell them you need them to become bone. Is it in your hip? Direct them to your hip and see and feel it happen. In your knee? Direct them to your knee. Do you need some repair in your brain or perhaps your back? Or your right big toenail?

This is the power that is within your heart. Access that power. Stay there within your heart. If you begin to doubt, then you have left your heart. You want the fullness of yourself that is within your body to be within your heart.

## YOUR HEART IS IN COMMAND

Instruct your brain that it is no longer in command. It is your heart that is in command. The heart has much more energy than the brain. People will say that if the brain doesn't work, then you are dead. And I would say to you, if your heart does not work, then you are dead. Of course, your physical heart can continue to beat, but if your heart does not work, then you are dead in spirit. The wonderful thing is that it can rejuvenate and an opening can occur.

Focus on this heart energy. Feel it. You can send your heart energy any-where. You can send it to surround anything, even the entire planet. There are those who have worked very diligently with this, but they are not in this country. They know how to send their heart energy around the planet. You can send your heart energy around someone you love and around someone you don't feel very comfortable with.

## WHOM DO I MOST NEED TO FORGIVE?

How can you change things on this planet? Send your heart energy to those you hold resentments or grudges against. Are your leaders the most important people for you to change? No, dear ones, the most important one to change is yourself. Changing yourself can and will change the world.

Go to that altar within your heart center and ask one of your favorite spiri-tual guides to sit with you. I'm going to have you ask a very risky question. Are you ready?

Ask, "Whom do I most need to forgive?" Whose name or face popped up before you? Did you groan and say, "Oh no, not that one"? Did your heart not resonate and say, "It is time. It is time for me to be free of that"?

Every person you hold in resentment and nonforgiveness reduces the energy that can come from your heart, limiting your power to create from heart energy. The energy to create is reduced, because you do not have the fullness of your-self involved in the creation. If you wish to bring peace to this planet, sit there at the altar with pen and paper and ask those wonderful spiritual guides who have agreed to be with you at this time to show you every person in this lifetime you need to forgive. Just begin making your list. You'll be surprised at the names that will pop up.

You might say, "I thought I'd already done that." That means there is another layer, another level. Ask to be directed to that layer, to that level. You might not even know the name, but you remember the sensation, the feeling, the experience. Each person you forgive will bring peace to your planet and you. Each person you are able to forgive from the depth of yourself will increase the energy that is con-tained in your heart, enabling you to send it further than you ever could before. You will know you have forgiven when you can send your most powerful energy from your heart—that energy you call love—to the one who has wounded you the most. That is how you will bring peace—by changing the energy of this planet.

Unfortunately, most people are not aware that they do not work out of their hearts. They work out of their heads, their brains. If you will allow your heart to rule—and that means be in charge of the brain—the brain will be much more powerful, and you'll see many more wonders occur. You do not need technology in a mechanical sense. All the technology you need and that is the most powerful is in your heart.

Well, dear ones, are there any questions you might have after my message this evening?

## How Do I Forgive?

*How do you forgive?*

That is a good question. There are those who are able to forgive very easily, and there are those who are not. You know which group you are in. I'm going to give you a process that might help you. It will not help everyone, but it will be something that you can use.

Go into your heart through your back and sit there with your pen and paper. Be there with your spiritual guides. Take that incident that has wounded you so much. Write the name of the person, but don't go into detail about the incident. Then write under it "What I Have Learned," and list everything that you have learned. For example, if you are angry at a parent because he or she decided to give your coat away to someone else who was cold and you didn't have a coat anymore, perhaps what you learned is that you would be sure your children had coats.

Make that list of the big things and the little things. It doesn't matter. Make that list, and then connect heart to heart with that person who has wounded you. It does not need to be done in the physical, and sometimes you have to do it with people who have left the physical. Thank the person for being the teacher in this lesson and offer a blessing. Do this for each thing you have learned.

So if this one who has wounded you grievously taught you 153 things through this wound, then you give thanks and bless each one of these things. The wounding might have sent you on a journey of self-discovery of how to be a better parent, friend or partner. This learning might not have happened if the wounding had not occurred. When you have come to realize the learning, you will find it will be easier to let go. Forgiveness is letting it go. Keep the lesson, release the package.

## There Is Someone for You

*At the beginning, you talked about oneness and relationships and the opportunity we have here. What's the best thing we can do to allow ourselves to be open to that type of relationship?*

I actually have already talked about that. It is forgiveness. You do not realize that holding on to the wounds of your life is what inhibits you from finding the friendship, the relationship, the partnership you dearly want. What happens when you hold on to these wounds is that they form a force field between you and the energy of attracting what you desire. Unforgiveness forms a force field between you and the one—and there is more than one—which repels the energy you wish to attract. What you have is the energy of the wounds. What comes to you are other people who are similarly wounded.

The best thing you can do for yourself is to do the exercise I mentioned earlier. There is someone for you—there are several someones who are potentials for you. Know that. Listen to your heart. Go in through the back and sit there at your altar when you meet someone and ask, "Does this person have the energies and healing to allow the love energy I am looking for to come to me? Is it available?" You have a tendency to find people who don't have it available. Allow it to come. Work on the healing for yourself. Do not work on the lack you have of relationship, because that simply brings more lack. Instead, focus on the healing of yourself and that one or ones will come. Then you can have your choice.

## EVERYTHING HAS CONSCIOUSNESS

*Amma, I've been thinking about consciousness, and you talked a little bit about consciousness in the form of energy and the heart and the mind. I think a lot about the balancing. Over the past twenty years, we've been trying to reproduce mind consciousness in machines, for example, chess-playing machines that can now defeat the most able human player.*

*The question that arises for scientists is what is the nature of the cognition and the consciousness that we have imparted to machines and that we will be able to impart, and what does this mean in terms of artificial versus real intelligence (whatever that is)? How do we strike a balance between heart and mind? In my experience, it has definitely been through the mind that I've gone back to the heart. Striking that balance seems to me to be an important characteristic here.*

First the machines and then the heart . . . Even though scientists are beginning to realize it, very few people understand that everything has consciousness. The chairs you are sitting on have consciousness, the walls, the lights—everything has consciousness. Some scientists are beginning to realize that as deeply within themselves as they want for something to happen, they are activating the consciousness in "inanimate" beings. That is what is helping machines to begin to work with you in developing the chess programs and others. You can work to focus your consciousness from the energy within your heart and communicate with the consciousness in the pillow, for example. When you communicate with that consciousness in the pillow or the chairs, you will find that you become more energized, because they are loving you as you are loving them. Work with that concept.

When you are doing experiments or research, begin to communicate with what you are talking about, even if it's just a concept. Talk to the concept. Feel the energy of it. It will then reveal more to you. Just as physicists have noted, they seem to be creating different physical particles and they wonder if that particle is true. They ask, "Is there such a thing?" Then they eventually discover that there is, because they have created it. That is the creative power in each person.

## BALANCE IS IN HOW YOU ENTER YOUR HEART

Now the heart . . . You have been able to go to your heart through your head because you are such a head-oriented, intellectual person. Balance is if you start to go in through your heart and then to your head; then you will learn even greater power. It is the entryway that will help bring you balance. The energy of the heart is pure, creative potentiality. Go in through the back, access the heart, go to the head or invite it to come to the altar with you, and watch the power that comes. Through the energy in your brain, the heart will unlock tremendous secrets.

Practice it. Try doing it when you are in your car, at the mall, wherever. Practice going into your heart through the back and sitting there at your altar. When you are not driving your car, you can do that with your eyes closed, but I do suggest not having your eyes closed when you are driving your car. [Laughter.]

*This gets to the role of healing, which is said to come from the heart primarily. How does one best do that?*

Speak to the consciousness of the body of the one you wish to bring into balance. That is what you are doing, bringing balance so that the body can heal itself. The body has the capability to do that. Speak to the consciousness of the cells of the body. Ask them, "What do I need to bring balance to first?" And listen to what is said, because it may be exactly what you thought or it may not be what you thought. First ask the body what it wants. The body might surprise you and say, "I need to work on forgiveness." As long as someone needs to work on forgiveness to bring balance, your work with them will not hold, because the need for forgiveness skews the energy. In other words, if you put new tires on the car and it is badly out of alignment, the tires will wear unevenly. You want to bring the balance by bringing the whole being into alignment. Ask the body and listen to your intuition, to which you connect through the heart. Ask what most needs to happen with this one you have come to join with in bringing balance and facilitating healing. Listen to what is said. Have the courage to relay that information.

## ENERGIES COMING FROM THE SUN

*What was the energy today? It seemed like I was angry a lot. I was wondering what was happening.*

You were releasing anger that you have in your cells. That releasing of anger was activated by your decision to cleanse yourself of all that was not love. Along with your intention and the other energies that are coming in strongly from the Sun right now, you were releasing. In addition to the energies coming in from the Sun, your anger at the cellular level was being triggered by the anger that is floating around the planet. You are in a process of releasing.

*Amma, what are the energies coming in from the Sun right now?*

Just as your planet is a being, the Sun is also a being. The Sun is also in trans-formation. The energies of transformation are coming from the Sun, which is also releasing energies it wishes to no longer be part of it. Those energies are being attracted to this planet, since it contains similar vibrations to what the Sun is releasing. At the same time, your Sun has a job, a mission, a path—just as each one of you does. It knows that part of its path is to send in high energy so that you can make decisions. The Sun is also sending energy from its heart center as it is releasing. Your intention for your life and path determine what will happen to you as the energies come in. Those of you who have made the decision to release anger and all that is not love will experience the effect of trigger-ing or surfacing those energies you wish released. Those who have not learned how to release or who refuse to release the energies will simply become more of the energies that are triggered. It is choice.

## SCIENTIFIC DISCOVERIES AND GALACTIC COMMUNICATION

*Amma, I'm thinking very positively about the future, and I'm wondering if you can comment on where our scientists might be regarding understanding how to communicate with other forms of life out in the galaxy. Is that happening at all, and can we look forward to seeing that become commonplace soon?*

The communication is happening a great deal, but is not being revealed, for several reasons. Some do not want to reveal it because they do not want to scare people. Their decision comes from good intentions. But then there are those who are communicating with other galaxies and have been access-ing energies of a lower vibration. They are learning about technical matters that they classify as top secret. They don't want other people to know about it. You will discover that within the decade it will not matter why they want to keep this a secret. It will not be able to stay a secret. More people are learning to communicate with these other beings, and more people are tuning in to their vibration.

*Do you know if there are any scientific discoveries coming in the next decade that will eliminate our need for fossil fuel and hence war?*

First of all, the discoveries are already there. Your government in this coun-try, the one in Russia, the one in England and the one in Italy already have the knowledge to be able to turn everyone to a different energy source. You know how difficult it is for people to change. It is more difficult for institutions to change. When people do not work from their hearts, their interest is in money and power.

The war was not so much due to fossil fuel, as many people proposed. The war was a struggle for power. Those who are in power know they have some-thing to very quickly replace fossil fuel. If there were no more fossil fuels to be had, it would take about a decade for them to put into production everything that is already there. The inventions and discoveries of the scientist Nikola

Tesla and others have been amplified by your and other governments, even though they tried to stamp them out.

I wish to thank you for being here. Connect heart to heart and connect with the love that you truly are. Many blessings to you, dear ones.

# 9

# *Learn to Live Love*

### *September 2003*

$G$ ood evening, dear ones. It is so good to be here with you again. Have you been feeling my presence? I have been with each one of you. Know that at those times when you feel an influx of love, appreciation or gratitude, I am there. I am always with you, but it is at those times that you feel me and experience me. We are one.

What you are feeling when you are feeling me is yourself. You are feeling the love that you are but that you are unaware you are. That is exactly what you are feeling—yourself—when I am with you and loving you. When you get in touch with the love that I have for you, you are in touch with the love that you are. The next time you feel my presence, notice how you feel inside.

When you can be in that space of experiencing the love that you are, when you experience my love for you, that is when you can be in your power and creativity. That is when, by delving into that experience of love and being loved, you can be magical. That is when you can do your writing and research and know that it is you and know that it is me and know that we are one. You can relate to other people from that space. The more you get in touch with that love that you are, that I am, the more you are able to respond to and live with people from a place of love. That is what this life is all about, you know. It is about learning how to live love.

Sometimes people think that if someone says, "I love you," it is a minor thing. It could be with humans, you realize, because many times humans say, "I love you," and actually mean something else. They might mean, "I love you just as you are, right as you are, and don't dare deviate from that," or, "I love you right now because you have done exactly what I wanted you to do, but don't deviate from that."

But when I tell you I love you and when you get in touch with the love that you are, there are no strings, none whatsoever. You do not have to be or act or say or do any particular thing to have the love that I have for you. You are that same love. How can there be strings to being who you are?

## DON'T FOCUS ON WHAT IS NOT LOVE

There are things you have to do to get in touch with the love that you are. It is really a very simple thing. Quit paying attention to everything that is not love. It is that simple! If you are not focusing on the things that are not love, then you won't be aware they are there. You can respond from the place of the love that you are, and whatever is around you that is not love looks different.

For instance, those of you who are parents and have small children or children who are older, you know how easy it is to love them and delight in them when they are doing exactly what you would like them to do—be it loving, be it being delightful, be it studying when they're supposed to or doing whatever it is you want them to do.

But think of the times when you find it so difficult to be with them, like when they are acting four or fourteen or when they're twenty-four and haven't yet learned that there is much more to life than what they know now. Those are the times—when your children are responding in such a way—that if you will interface with them from the place of the love that you are, that total unconditional love, you will find that your resistance to the way they are melts away. There is no reason to resist the way they are since that only puts up more resistance on their part. You have heard the phrase, "What you resist, persists."

So if your four-year-old is being really cranky and you are resisting that crankiness, he or she will get crankier. It's the same with your twenty-four-year-old, the same thing. When you resist something, it is an element of control. You are actually trying to control them to be something different than what they are. Allow the children to experience what they are experiencing. That doesn't necessarily mean they need to experience it in your presence. That's what time-outs are for. You can set that boundary. Allow them to be who they are and love them through that. What usually happens is that they "push your buttons," as you say, and then you forget which one of you is four and which one of you is thirty-four!

## IT'S ABOUT YOU AND YOUR ISSUES

Whenever you find yourself becoming angry at your children or at any person, know that the anger is about you and your issues. It isn't about anything else. It isn't about them. Have you ever noticed that some people don't respond in any negative or hostile way whatsoever when someone gets angry or stubborn? It's because it didn't hit one of their issues, didn't bring that issue up for them.

Know that anytime someone "causes" . . . I'm saying "causes," but no one else causes it, even though you think they do with their words or actions, and you react in anger, frustration or even fear. No one has "caused" anything. What the other has done is serve you, given you the service of placing a mirror in front of you so you can see what it is that you can heal, so you can see that part of yourself that is "not love."

Once you recognize that part of yourself that is not love, do not focus on it. Go into the part of you that is love. When you focus on the part of you that is not love, then you begin to feel guilty and ashamed. Go into love and remember who you are. Just remember who you are and come into a place of love. Do not focus on the not love. When you focus on the not love, you go further and further away from the love.

## CHILD RAISING IS AN EXPERIMENT

There is nothing to be ashamed of when you lose your temper. There is nothing to feel guilty about. You have just realized, "Ah, here is something I need to work on." Then you can go through a process to work on it. You can ask, "What is it that I need to do to heal this?" Ask what it is that needs to be healed.

I'm very willing to heal you, you know. There are times when it is for your good for me to heal you without your knowing what the root cause is. However, there are other times when I would be putting a Band-Aid on something instead of taking the splinter out if I healed you without your knowing the root cause. If we put a Band-Aid over a wound that still has the splinter or the glass in it, then we end up with a bigger problem. You think everything is fine until that finger starts throbbing and throbbing. So there are times when you will call upon me to heal, and what I will do is guide you deeper.

What is it that this little four-year-old brought to the surface in me? Is there one parent who has not had their four-year-old elicit the thought of "what a terrible parent I am"? Is there anybody who hasn't had that happen? It's a common affliction of parents. Isn't it amazing that the littler they are, the more you begin to doubt your ability to be a parent?

As has been said, you have no training to be a parent; you don't know how to do it. Actually, you did have training on how to be a parent. You had it from your parents. And now you have the opportunity to decide exactly how it is that you want to work with that training they gave you. It was an experiment that they did with you, their raising you. And it is an experiment that you are doing with your children.

## YOU CANNOT CONTROL YOUR CHILDREN

Those of you who feel like you're finished with your children in that they no longer live with you, they still end up being your children, do they not? You still want the best for them, and you wish you could protect them from the mistakes that you can see them ready to make. You can see the train wreck coming, can you not? And you would like to protect them from that train wreck. What happens when you do this, be they four or thirty-four? They get angry. What they're actually telling you is, "This is my path. I choose to learn it this way. Bug off." And what will happen within you? If you look deep within yourself, you take it as rejection. That is where you become angry.

When you look deep into why it is you are trying to control them, why you get upset with this four-year-old or this twenty-four or thirty-four-year-old, you see it is that this person is putting in front of you something for you to look at about yourself, and that is that you cannot control him or her.

You were given—and in most cases you welcomed it with great joy—this new life. Those of you who are parents remember the first time you beheld your eldest child. Did you not have utter joy and tremendous fear in a very short period of time, because you knew cognitively that you were not prepared to raise this little life, this little being who had come in? It brought up all your fears. What happens when you don't know how to get your children to do what is best for them— whether it is to eat their carrots or broccoli or to learn their numbers or letters— when you can't get them to do it? It isn't so much that you fear for them and what's going to happen in their lives, but that you see in front of you that you have failed. You're supposed to get them to do that. Well, dear ones, guess what? You're not! Please release that responsibility from yourself.

## PROVIDE STRUCTURE TO LEARN ABOUT CHOICES AND CONSEQUENCES

As a parent, you are there to provide some structure, some guidance and some choices. They get to choose what their choices are going to be, they being the children. The choice might be, "You will eat what we have here at the table or you won't eat." That is a very important lesson to learn. If they do not learn it when they are four, what will happen when they are no longer living in your home? They need to know that if they make this choice, it has one consequence; and if they make this other choice, it has another consequence.

Even in the little things, give them choices. If they choose to become angry that they do not get their way . . . well, has anybody ever had problems with children wanting dessert first and only dessert? Have any of you had any problems with wanting dessert first and only dessert? You are at a place where you know what that choice means. Some of you know that having dessert first is absolutely wonderful, exquisite and freeing. Others of you know that if you do that, you are going to feel miserable if it does not react positively in your body. So you get to make a choice based on those consequences.

Young children have not learned how to do that yet. Guide them as much as you can and show them the consequences that occur. You can set structure. You can set boundaries. But be aware that it is their path, just as it is your path with what it is that you are doing. Just as you are the only one responsible for your path, they are the only ones responsible for their path. When you have young children, ultimately you have the obligation to provide a structure, a framework, for them. That is the job, if you will, that you took on. It is a blessing. It is a tremendous blessing and a tremendous obligation and responsibility.

So relax, those of you who have young ones and those of you with older ones, those of you who are so confused about what it is that you did wrong that they have turned out this way and have not accepted responsibility in "this" way. There is nothing that you did wrong. They chose you to learn certain lessons and now they're learning them. Your job is to take care of yourself.

## SET YOUR BOUNDARIES FROM YOUR HEART

That was about children. Let's translate that now to people you relate to in your day-to-day life, in your business, for instance, or to those you interact with in restaurants, such as the waiter, the server, or the clerk at the grocery store, or anyone who provides a service to you on a day-to-day basis. Raising children teaches you about love and being in your heart. There are times when you enjoy them tremendously. You love them tremendously when they're not so active—especially after a difficult day. Learn also to do that same thing with other people, and look at them through your heart. You have a tremendous heart connection to your children. What you are not aware of is the heart connection that is there with those you meet in your day-to-day life, because we are all one. You are of me, and I am of you.

Relating to other people is very similar to raising children. There is a big difference, though. The difference is that it is not your responsibility to provide structure for anyone, unless you happen to be his or her supervisor at work. You do not have to provide structure for that person in that area, but you provide structure for yourself. For instance, with your child, you are trying to teach him or her how to set boundaries and what certain choices are. When you are interacting with another adult, you set your own boundaries. That's what is so important—for you to set your own boundaries. The person interacting with you then has choices to make. You are not responsible for his or her choices any more than you are responsible for your children's choices. There is a different sense of obligation.

You set boundaries with other people, and you do it from your heart. With someone who might be encroaching—emotionally, physically or spiritually—put up your boundaries. Do it from your heart, not from fear. When you do it from fear, it comes from a very different place. That is where violence comes from. Fear breeds violence, whether it's internal violence within yourself or the external violence of knives or guns. Ultimately, that fear comes from feeling that we will not be accepted. So we find a way to put a barrier between self and others. That's what humans do.

Each person is on his or her own path. You're not on that same path. Your paths might intersect, and you can make choices as to whether you wish to interact more fully with that individual or not. You make choices about whether or not you will accept the way that person is behaving toward you. The choice is yours. Then you let him go. It is allowing the person to be who he is and allowing him to be on the path he is on, with no sense of the obligation that you have with your children. For those of you who have adult children, most of you still feel an obligation that in some way you are responsible for them, and you're not. But it is difficult to change that when you've been responsible in such a powerful way for eighteen to twenty years.

## YOU EACH HAVE YOUR OWN PATH

What I would like you to remember most from what I say today, other than how much I love you, is that each person is on her own path. Each person chooses what she does and who she wishes to be. Each person chooses whether she will come from the heart or from fear, whether she will experience life in a place of love or experience life in a place of not-love. Each person makes choices, and there are reasons why she makes those choices. It is not up to you to change that.

Some of you are in service positions. You offer choices. Do not be tied down to your customer taking the choice you want. You are simply offering choices, just as you did when raising your children. Living life with one another is all about choices. It's all about boundaries. And it's all about doing your own thing in the way you wish to do it and allowing other people to do their own thing in the way they wish to do it.

You can set a boundary with those who choose to do their thing in a way that you don't like. For example, you do not have to have them in your home if they like to steal. Or if people are verbally abusive, you do not have to be friends with them. Yet there is the balance of holding them with positive regard and openness from your heart so that you are surrounding them with love energy rather than anger or fear.

## LEARN HOW TO DETACH

Remember: when you are afraid, you are in a place of not-love. When you feel like you need to control something or someone, you are in a place of not-love. When you can look at a person, whether it is someone you love dearly—child, partner, spouse—or someone you do not know; when you can look at him or her with love, no matter what his or her choice is, even if you see it as self-destructive, then you have learned how to detach and to allow. That is important to learn in this life. Any questions tonight?

*In my situation, with a stalker in my neighborhood or whatever we call them, men who are so afraid . . . he's in a place of not-love. But are we also in a place of not-love in the way we deal with him?*

Know, first of all, that he is in a place of fear. You are in a place of not-love when you become angry with him. Understand, though, that when you set boundaries to protect yourself and those around you, it can still be a place of love as long as you are in your heart when you are doing it. You can make the same telephone call in anger or in compassion. It is what is going on inside of you, in your heart, that determines whether it is from a place of love or not-love. So when you see him again, instead of going into fear of what he is going to do in the neighborhood, surround him with love, that protective shield. Any other questions about that?

*I was just going to ask if you could keep repeating that to me inside my head, over and over?*

I will be delighted to do that. When you need to have the reminder, simply tap here, on your third eye.

## WHAT ARE YOUR THOUGHTS?

*Yesterday I had a rather interesting day. I kept saying that the thoughts running through my head weren't my own, and I'd see something on the television screen or the computer screen or a piece of paper in the office—everything I looked at was not of my thoughts. I got to the point where I recognized that all of the intrusion was not coincidental. I'll let you take it from there . . .*

Of course, there are no coincidences. Things mirror where you are, what you are, what you are learning, what you have decided not to learn. Many things are placed in front of you that you decide not to learn. The important question is, "What are your thoughts?" Do you believe that you have to have thoughts? Sometimes. Not all the time. Sometimes you don't have to have thoughts. That's right. If you could observe your thoughts, you would discover that a tremendous cacophony is going on inside your head, of many, many different thoughts, voices and feelings that are being expressed.

If you would learn how to make space in your head so that there are no thoughts, you would discover much more in this world. Those of you who enjoy having the radio or television on when there is nobody around or maybe just as background noise, note that the continual thoughts in your head are nothing more than background noise. If you would learn to let those go, then you would have more space to observe what is truly happening in this world and to let other thoughts that are from your precious guides and angels and myself come in. You had another comment?

*Well, it seems to me that I can recall a time in my life when there was not all of this extraneous stuff in my space. It doesn't mean that my thoughts were any more glorious than they are now. At least, the stuff was not intentionally put into our space. It's pretty insidious, actually, that there's so much background stuff going on right now.*

## BRAINWASHING IS DONE WITH WORDS AND WITH VIBRATION

You all have watched movies or television in which people have talked about brainwashing, and they've talked about it with great fear. You have to realize that there is tremendous brainwashing going on in your society. It has been going on ever since the power of putting these waves into speakers was learned, such as with radio—at least fifty years. I've been aware of it for fifty years. Think about the very first time ever there was advertising through the airwaves. Advertising is nothing more than a form of brainwashing. How many of you would even know that you needed a particular brand of shoe if there was no advertising? You would simply go to your store when your shoes were worn out and get shoes for your feet that fit and served the purpose. They would not have to have a name or a label on them.

Several things are happening in your society. One is that those who make a lot of money have learned how to use words to bring a hypnotic effect upon you. They know exactly what words to use that will bring more people to buy what it is they want them to buy. You can learn about those words. What most people don't realize—although many of you here do—is that there are those who have learned about vibration and have learned how to use it to work with your mind.

That is what has been happening in the past fifty years. Not only is the word used, but there is a vibration that is sent out at the same time. It's not benevolent. And it is not accidental. Many people do not realize that sometimes it doesn't even come from a particular television station, as it can actually come through the receiver. So there are some very sneaky things going on. What is the best way to protect yourself from it? Don't have it on! Just don't have it on.

When you listen to the radio, notice what it is you're listening to; really pay attention to it. What are the messages that are being given to you? When you listen to the various talk shows, whether they are conservative, liberal or moderate (actually, I haven't found any that are moderate), notice what they are telling you. What they are really telling you is that you are all separate. Do you notice that? Read the "Letters to the Editor" in your local newspaper. Do they not say "the liberals," "the conservatives"? It is not "we"; it is not "us." It is not "our brothers and sisters." It is "they."

You will come to believe—and you are the ones who are awakened—that you must consciously change every time you read it or hear it, saying, "Ah, but that is my brother Rush Limbaugh," or "That is my sister Hillary Clinton," and listen with compassion and love, and know that all have a part of the truth and none has the whole truth. Then you can learn. There is an addictive quality to the vibrations.

## LISTEN CONSCIOUSLY

Subliminal messages that you cannot hear with your ear or see with your eye are being put on television. Know that it is happening, even though your governments say it is not. Be aware of that, but do not be in fear. When you're driving your automobile, do you get your oil changed so that your car will last longer because of good maintenance, which helps the engine last? Or do you get the oil changed because you are in fear of your engine falling apart? Most of you do this because you know it's good maintenance, and there is no element of fear in there. See the difference? It is the same thing with listening.

That's not to say that you should never watch TV or the movies or never listen to the radio. Just be conscious when you are doing it. When you find that you are using it just for background noise, you are letting the subliminal messages come into you. It would be much better to simply have silence or put on some music that you enjoy via a CD or tape, not from the radio. Be conscious so that you can consciously decide what stays in your mind. Just let the rest of it float out. Be in the place of love. It is by being in your heart with gratitude and appreciation that these people are giving you things that you can learn; they are being mirrors for you so that you can learn.

## USE MICHAEL'S SWORD AS A TOOL FOR PROTECTION

*I work in a metaphysical bookstore, and I can feel different types of distortions or energies sometimes through particular healers who work there. It's like I'm the one they download on, and I'm wondering about some protection devices. It's an ongoing thing. I'm staying in this place of love, but I'm thinking that these distortions are increasing. Am I correct?*

Know that any feeling of needing protection comes from a feeling of fear, because you fear that something is happening to your energy. The task is to increase the amount of love vibration you have. When I speak of love, of course I am not speaking of the "feeling." I'm speaking of being in your heart. Enter your heart center from the back. There is the vibration and there are, let's say, lower vibrations of love and higher vibrations of love. The highest vibration of love is that supreme, ultimate vibration of love of which I am and of which you are, but you have forgotten that you are. The lower vibrations of love have the ultimate love vibration in them and, in addition, have an element of fear that runs through and lowers it. Is that understood? Can you conceptualize that? It would be like clear water and not-so-clear water.

This is an analogy and not a very good one, because it is difficult to put into an analogy. But that is what I am talking about. When you are able to be at the highest vibration of love, you will notice the distortions, but they will not have an impact upon you. What is happening with you, dear one, is that you are noticing the distortions and having a fear reaction to them. The downloading occurs when you go into a place of fear, and it will be downloaded upon you. Here is the subtlety of it all: it is to notice and to not take it on. Be in your heart. Ask and I will be glad to increase the energy of the love vibration.

Do you remember Michael's sword? Hold the sword as a means of protection. Of course, we don't need the sword if we're not afraid, do we? By the way, Michael doesn't use his sword because he is afraid. It is definitely a tool for him.

When you use the sewing needle, do you use it because you are afraid? Or is it a tool? When you use a kitchen knife, do you use it because you are afraid or because it is a tool? But if somebody's coming at you, is the knife a tool or a weapon? Learn how to use Michael's sword as a tool, not a weapon, because it cannot be used as a weapon. It can only be used in a place of love. Michael's sword can be used to help you make a transition from the place of fear to the place of love. As you tap into the love energy that is within your heart and send that energy into your arm and into the sword, as it blazes around you, you have raised your vibration and, in your humanness, you feel more protected. So it can be a tool.

When you feel the need for protection, know that you are feeling fear. Have no judgment about that. Those of you who are on the path of awakening, when you feel fear, you think you're a terrible person, which sends your vibration even lower. Try instead to think, "Oh, I felt fear. How can I change that?"

Here is another thing I'd like you to notice (and this is for all of you, of course) when you sense a distortion: Ask yourself what that distortion is mirroring to you. Is it a mirror of something you are? Is it a mirror of something you are afraid of? Do you think that Michael feels fear when he goes about his work? No, absolutely no fear. Does Michael see the distortions? Yes, he does. Fear? No. Those of you who garden, when you go out to your garden or flowerbed, do you feel fear when you see the weeds?

It's a way of looking at things. Michael would see the distortions in a person's energy as you would see the weeds in your garden, but not in the sense of labor. He sees it as something to work with and change if that person allows it. If you do the same thing with someone who comes in with a distortion, that means your energies are not in sync. As you work on raising your vibration of love and staying in that place, you might find that you do not even notice the distortions anymore.

## CAN MY VIBRATION BE TOO HIGH FOR MY SURROUNDINGS?

*Can you ever raise your vibration too high for your surroundings?*

I'm going to speak in the context of relationships with other people. When you have been outside in the cold and your hands feel almost frozen with cold, you want to warm them up. You put them in water. What does it feel like? It hurts. Let's look at vibration in that way. When you are a high vibration, it might hurt those of lower vibration, but not in an intentional hurt, although it causes a discordance. They are not in sync with that vibration because they are in a place of fear. Fear lowers their vibration, and they hurt when they are with yours.

When you are in a place of totally high vibration and love, a mirror is formed that they don't like to see. They see their low vibration. It is all about them and their response. How you respond is about you. I don't want to say that you can have a vibration that is too high for others, but you can have one that others are not in tune with.

There is no reason for you not to raise your vibration. There is a point where raising your vibration any higher will lead to your not being in the body anymore. Some people come in and out of the physical as they raise and lower their vibration. It causes great consternation in some places. Know that when the other person is hurting and you respond in a hurtful manner, it lowers your vibration, which helps the person to feel better. He or she feels that it helps, because the vibration is more compatible.

When someone makes disparaging comments about your spiritual path and it affects you in a way that causes angst, fear or anger, look at yourself and ask: "Is there something said that is true? Am I hiding behind my spiritual path and not dealing with the issues I need to deal with? Am I not dealing with my own insecurities and fears?" If somebody makes a negative comment to you about your spiritual path, if you truly are at that high vibration, it will not affect you in any way. You will be there in a place of acceptance and allowing.

## STAYING IN THE NOW LOSES ITS SENSE OF URGENCY
*I've noticed that as I spend more time in the Now, in a state of love, I don't seem to have a sense of urgency at all. Can you speak on that?*

When you are in the Now, there is nothing to be urgent about. Whenever you are in fear, you are not in the Now. Whenever you are anxious, you are either in the past or the future. When you are in the Now, you are only attending to the Now; therefore, there is no sense of urgency. Urgency comes from what you perceive is going to happen in the future, based upon what happened in the past. When you become anxious about getting somewhere, for instance, it will take you longer to get there than if you did not get anxious about it—even if it is over the same time period. Time is relative, remember. You will also find that if you stay in the Now and set your intention for something in the future, it will manifest more quickly if you let the intention go into the universe and stay in the Now knowing that intention is there. This happens because you are not sending forth any other energies that are canceling your intention. Staying in the Now is the perfect way to stay out of fear.

For instance, let's take the analogy of going somewhere in your automobile. You leave late or run into traffic, which happens occasionally in the city. You'd set your intention to be at work at 9:00 and then get anxious about arriving. What is your anxiety about? Is it about getting there or about not getting there? It is about not getting there, right? Otherwise you wouldn't be anxious about it. If you knew you were going to be there at 9:00, there'd be nothing to be anxious about. You are anxious about not being there at 9:00.

## THE MARRIAGE OF SCIENCE AND SPIRIT
*This has to do with thought and consciousness and being in a box and not knowing it. You see only the box, and you don't know what is outside. It reminds me of science, to a certain extent, and it*

*also reminds me of other things. I'm thinking in terms of, yes, we want to observe our thoughts, but that is a thought we are observing. So we have mirrors within mirrors.*

*This is part of the quandary I get tied up in as I do my research and write my book. How far do we go in marrying science and spirit? How far do we push it? Should we just leave well enough alone? Maybe they shouldn't be married and should just agree to that and get along. This is what I am struggling with, and whatever thoughts you have would be wonderful.*

A conundrum for the ages, is it not? The fact is that science and spirit are already married, but people are just now noticing. They have always lived together. Those of you experienced in the philosophy and history of your days know that science and spirit used to be together until the time of Descartes and others. Know that any belief system is a box, whether it be metaphysical, scientific, fundamental Christian or Jewish Orthodox. They are all boxes. Every belief is a structure. (We won't use "box" anymore, as that can have a negative connotation.) When you go into the structure of your home, you do not always see what is outside unless you make a conscious effort to look out your window. You see everything within the confines of the structure of your home. This room has no windows. You have to open the door to be able to see out. There could be mayhem occurring outside or absolute bliss, and you would never know, because of the structure of these walls. Every belief system forms that kind of structure.

How do you as humans live without a belief system? You don't. That is part of your structure. You have the paradox of living in a society, the world and the universe that is nothing but spirit, but you are in a dualistic universe. That is how your planet was created. Therefore, as you write your book, it has to be from the form of dualism, because that is what is there. Science and spirit are two forms of the dualism. Physics comes much closer to marrying science and spirit than does biology, although that is occurring more as people investigate the mind-body connection, psycho-neuroimmunology.

I would suggest that as you write your book you juxtapose the two, the duality and the unity. It will be a difficult juxtaposition, because what you are attempting to do is create a bridge. Know that just because you form a bridge it doesn't mean that everyone is going to cross it. You will find many who will be willing to cross that bridge and discover what it is you are speaking of. Know at the same time that it is impossible not to be dualistic in a dualistic world. Understand that there is a oneness. You came to a dualistic planet to learn about duality. You learn about how science and spirit, the material and spiritual, marry.

Think about sexual union. It would be impossible for you to live your day-to-day life if you were always in that place of the ecstacy of climax, would it not? How do you go grocery shopping if you are in a place of climax? Would you even think about food? [Laughter.] When you come to the separation of the two of you, back into the duality and not being a oneness anymore, then you live your life. That is what a dualistic world is. Does that analogy help in any way?

Of course you know that all is good and science is within spirit, but for us here, we had to come from that dualistic place. Is the bridge an illusion, is it even useful to discuss it or point to it? What is the utility of it? Can there actually be a bridge? Can there be crossover? Should we leave science and spirit separate and somehow . . . it is a conundrum.

For the purpose of the book you cannot leave science and spirit separate, because there are already those who have moved to marrying science and spirit. Since you are here as a visionary thinker and one who is pulling things together, you are not one who will retreat from that position. The bridge is an illusion, and it is a necessary illusion. Your clothing can be an illusion, depending upon what it is you use it for. There are those of you who use their clothing simply to protect themselves from the elements and because it is required in your society. Others use clothing as an illusion to appear smaller or larger than they are.

When you are writing in a dualistic society and attempting to bring together the two camps of people, you need to have that bridge of connection or stepping stones; it does not matter whether you call it a bridge or wish to have stepping stones in the river. You need something so that people who work linearly—and your book will be for those who are linear as you are more linear than circular— will be able to step from here to here to here. They will not be able to understand it fully until they have an experience of it within themselves. Yes, it is an illusion, which can only become real when they have the experience within themselves—in other words, when they discover the mystic they can be . . . to be both a scientist and a mystic; to be both a man and a mystic and a woman and a mystic; to be a parent and a mystic; to be whatever and a mystic.

## WHERE'S YOUR SENSE OF PURPOSE?

*Along with my question a few minutes ago, I have something else that I didn't know how to say. When I am in the Now, in the present, I seem to lose my motivation to some degree. I don't tend to have a sense of purpose and direction. I'm very comfortable in that position. What is going on with that? [Laughter.]*

Sense of purpose and direction comes from knowing that there is something in the future to do. Being totally in the Now, even for those who say they are in the Now—whether it is the Dalai Lama or another—is not totally in the Now, because they have an idea of where it is they are going. It is another paradox. It is the juxtaposition of being in the Now and, as I said earlier, placing your intention out in the universe.

You are people who are learning to progress and move in a spiritual way. Your sense of not having a purpose has to do with the belief systems you have taken on from others about what a purpose is. Each one of you here, if your purpose is to simply be where you are, to not ever move from there and to be light expanding—in other words to be the hermit on the mountain—how would people respond to you? They couldn't relate. They might not even see you, or you'd be the eccentric. You would not be someone they could respond to or relate to in any way. You have in some of your religious traditions those who live in monasteries. Very few people understand the power those in monasteries have when they stay in a place of love and send out love energy to others. It would be just as if you were in your place, not moving and sending out love. The belief system of that purpose is defined by someone else.

So we are moving somewhere, we are dynamic. Amma is dynamic. Abba is dynamic. The Source is dynamic. It is a continual evolution. It is expanding. It is expanding and contracting, doing both; the in-breath and the out-breath. Is not the Source also static? It is. It is not. It is both. So wrap your minds around that. [Laughter.]

Now, dear ones, I wish to thank you for being here. I am sending each of you someone very special right now, someone you once knew upon this Earth plane, who is no longer here. That one is standing right behind you. Just feel who it is that has come. Oh, since I have opened the door, there is not just one. Many have now come and are sending you the love. For some of you it is the love they were not able to express when they were here that they have now learned about—now that they have left their bodies. For others of you it is the love you were not able to receive from them when they were here. I give you a few moments to experience this love from your loved ones who are here.

Now, precious ones, take that love with you and have it serve as a reminder of the love that you are, and continue working on your path as you have been working. You are on your path even if you are standing still. My blessings to you. I am Amma. I am your mother, the divine mother, and you are within me.

# 10

# A Healthy Balance between Loving and Being Loved

*October 2003*

*G*ood evening, dear ones. It is so good to be here with you. Have you been enjoying the rain? Think about what rain symbolizes . . . a washing, a cleansing, a nourishing, a nurturing. Isn't that true about human life?

You can love one another and nurture one another. If there's an overabundance of water, an overabundance of that nurturing and nourishing, then we have those things called floods, and then there's destruction. So think about what happens when there is so much "nurturing." There can also be destruction. That's what I would like to talk about, how to balance that desire to love and to be loved so that it is healthy.

Within the human spirit, there is a deep, deep desire to be loved and to give love. When you make your appearance on this planet in a particular lifetime, that is what you wish—to be loved. That is why you are born so little and so helpless. Notice in a human being how long it takes before you can walk. And how long do you think it takes a gorilla to be able to walk? Or a deer? For them, it is minutes. Notice that the gorilla and the monkey cling to their mothers on the back or front, depending on whether they're hungry or just looking. Now look at the human: in the arms for many months.

There is a reason for that. Humans could have been made in the same way, where you would be able to walk as soon as you came out of the womb. If it can be done for cows, horses, deer and sheep, it can be done for humans. Look at little kittens or puppies—they crawl around even in their first few weeks. But the humans were made specifically to be nurtured when they make an appearance.

## AWAKENING THE CONSCIOUSNESS OF LOVE

What is it that usually happens when the baby first pops out? Whose arms does the baby go into? Remember what it was like to see that new life with the cord still there. What had to be done whenever you wanted to interact with that young one, to feed or to change it? In the arms, right? In the arms, because of the nurturing. When you were holding that child, it was next to your heart.

There is also another reason for being held near the heart. Some of you have read the research about the electromagnetic field within the heart and how there is a field within the heart and a field around that field. In other words, there is a heart within a heart within a heart. One of the reasons that the human is to be held in the arms next to the heart is because there is a vibrational frequency and attuning that is occurring, calling that infant into further life. From the heart of the mother, the father, the one who loves that little one so . . . the energy from the heart envelops not only the person who is doing the loving, but also the child. There is a vibrational frequency awakening the very consciousness of love within the infant. The human being has the consciousness of love.

Some of you have heard about children who are violent when very young. It is called an attachment disorder. Now think about "attachment." If an infant is not bonded to one through love, there is not the vibrational frequency to awaken the love energy, the heart energy, in the cells, to awaken that being into the full consciousness of being human. Do you understand what I am saying?

## FAILURE TO THRIVE

It is crucial for that child, that infant, to be held as much as possible, because what is happening is that the vibration that is coming from you, from those who love, is enlivening the cells. Yes, hold the infant as much as possible for about the first six months. You really can't spoil an infant. When people think they are spoiling an infant by having it in their arms so much, the infant knows it is receiving the nurturing and the nourishment of the energy from the heart of love of the one doing the holding. Just as you would never deny a child its feeding when it is time, if you knew about this energy in the heart and how the infant is meant to be held in the arms next to the heart, you would understand that another crucial feeding occurs.

You have perhaps heard of a disorder called "failure to thrive." Frequently it occurs because the awakening of the heart energy has not happened. Failure to thrive is not always a problem with the parents, you understand. As the parents send out the love, the new little being must accept the love. There are times when there is a difficulty with the soul who comes in. The soul just isn't so sure it wants to stay here. So it does not allow the frequency of love in. There is no connection between the heart energy of the infant and the parents. Actually, the process—or lack of process—usually occurs in utero. No one should ever think it is a mother's fault or a father's fault that the child has a failure to thrive. This is some new information for everyone to be aware of.

There are two different types of nourishment going on. Those of you who have had children more recently are aware of the push to go back to breastfeeding. Why was breastfeeding ever allowed if it was inferior? Well, of course it is not inferior! It is superior! The richest of nourishment comes from the mother's breast. It is the perfect balance for almost everyone, although at times there may be some metabolic difficulties. When a child is breastfed, where is it held? Next to the heart.

And if the child is bottle-fed, what happens sometimes? At times, the mother or parent is in a rush and props the baby up with the bottle. Even if the bottle is not propped up, there is a greater tendency for the one feeding the child to not be as present to that infant as the mother would be with the breast. Have you noticed that? It's just a difference. When the child is at the breast and suckling the milk, there is a connection from the tissues of both breasts going into the heart complex. So things were made in such a way that the infant who is born would receive what it needed, not only from the mother's breast, but also from the mother's heart. Of course, we do not want to leave fathers out, but we did not create the father to give milk.

## HURRICANES ARE RELATED TO EMOTIONS

Back to my analogy of talking about water. I mentioned the overabundance of "nurturing," putting nurturing in quotes. What we are talking about—a gentle rain such as what you are now hearing compared to a torrential rain that causes flooding—are two different energies. There is that gentleness that comes in and brings nourishment from the ground, and the plants and everything that grow look wonderful. An overabundance of water resulting in flooding occurs when you have torrential downpours, when you have hurricanes—which are related to the emotions of the humans who live here.

Do you know how to keep hurricanes from forming? Have everybody be in his or her heart. The energy you exude in violence—and I mean violence of the mind, violence through words, violence through action—is put out into the atmosphere. There has to be a way to release it. The hurricanes (or typhoons, depending on which part of the world you are in) are no different than the children or adults who suddenly shoot and kill many people and then themselves. They expend all of their energy killing others and then they themselves expire, just as a hurricane or typhoon expends all of its energy and then expires.

## ACTIVATING THE CHILD'S HEART

Back to the nurturing. When as an infant one receives the full nourishment from the mother's breast, which goes to the heart complex, it brings out the energies of the love vibration from the heart of the mother (since we're speaking now of nursing, I'm talking about the mother). That energy then goes in and surrounds the heart of that child, which begins the development of the magnetic field of its heart within its heart within its heart. It activates it. That is why nursing is so crucial.

What the father brings with that wonderful male energy is a further activation of the infant's heart with another vibration—still a love vibration, but a different one. So there is then the intertwining of vibrations. That is why it is important for each person to have been loved by a male and a female, to have been loved in that way early in life, during those first six months. The heart vibrations of the two genders come together and activate different aspects of the vibrational field within the infant's heart.

If a child is raised in a single-parent home or in a home with two people of the same gender, it is very important to have someone from the opposite gender who can love and care and send that heart energy. It shouldn't be very difficult to find someone who will bring that heart energy, should it? So we can say that a surrogate parent is needed—not the biology of the genes, but rather the biology and the spirit of the heart.

Those who do not have their hearts physically, emotionally and spiritually fully activated in this way end up with an imbalance. They try to get love energy to activate their hearts. Some find they try to get that by loving too much, giving too much, smothering. That is not a love that comes from the heart; that is a love that comes from need. It actually comes from the pelvis. It is not a heart energy, so the vibration is different. These are the dynamics of what your psychology calls codependence or loving too much. It is specifically due to an imbalance in the vibration of the heart. It is physical, it is energetic and it is spiritual. Healing this must be done on these levels—physically, energetically and spiritually.

Notice that I did not say "emotionally." That is because the emotions, in many ways, can separate one from the spiritual aspect. The emotions can keep one caught within the lower part of the body, as in the solar plexus or the pelvis. The transformation comes within the heart center. That is why the heart center is crucial in healing.

## You Come to Learn about Love

Of course, you understand that no one receives this total balance or as much heart energy as he or she needs to activate every cell. So there will always be an imbalance. You come in that way because you wish to learn different lessons and to grow spiritually. And what you come to learn about is love. This is a dynamic of love that very few people are aware of.

You don't heal the emotions; they are an energy. You don't heal an energy. It just is. You heal the heart. How do you heal the heart? You heal the heart through love, through loving yourself and surrounding yourself with people who are able to love you as purely as they can.

As human beings, there is not one of you who is able to love everyone, or even anyone, unconditionally 100 percent of the time. You were not created that way. Someone might say, "But the Master Jesus was." Do you think that was loving unconditionally when he called the crowd coming to be baptized a "brood of vipers"? Calling people a "brood of vipers" is not in a place of acceptance and love. It was in a place of setting boundaries. But notice that if you called anyone a "brood of vipers," would you not be responding in anger?

## YOU CAN'T LOVE UNCONDITIONALLY ALL THE TIME

So know that in the human condition, there is no one who is able to unconditionally love everyone 100 percent of the time. But there are those people who are able to do tremendous acts of giving and of love many times. Some are able to give the fullness of their lives. You can read about people who will step in front of another person when that person is being shot, or throw themselves on a grenade or run into the street to push a child out of the way of an oncoming car. You're in summer now, and this is the time of year when you hear about someone who dove into the water to save a drowning person—and drowned.

So everyone is able to come into those tremendous acts of love at times, but know that there is no one who will be in a place of unconditional love 100 percent of the time, with 100 percent of the people. The reason I keep repeating this is that I want you to quit punishing yourselves when you're not able to love unconditionally. Know that you can't do it all the time. Just know that, just accept it. Notice that when you are loving from the purity of your heart, there will be an energetic change within you. You won't recognize it as love, because what love is in your society is so convoluted.

## EMOTION GETS IN THE WAY OF LOVING

Love is the purest and highest of energies. You will feel more whole, more like yourself and truer to who you are when you are in that place of love, which has, dear ones, nothing to do with emotion. Emotion actually gets in the way of loving. Am I saying that emotion is bad? No, it is human, but what you are learning is to transcend the emotion and go into your heart. I have spoken before about going into your heart center from the back. That is a wonderful place to transcend emotion. Learn to spend time in your heart center. Learn to do it so often that you live within your heart center. Live in your heart center as much as possible. And as you are with one another listening to me speak, be in your heart. When you leave, stay in your heart. Feel and accept the love from others.

There are those who have not been able to have all of the love energy activated in their heart cells, and it hurts to receive so much love. Those are the ones who pull back and become afraid. There are times you might need to gently tone your love energy down. There was a question several months ago: "Is it possible to have too much light for a place?" Do not withhold love energy, but release it gradually. You don't want to flood someone who is weak and afraid of that energy. It becomes painful for that person. But for yourself, find people who are able to love as purely as possible and be with them. That is why it is important to be with healthy people.

The recovery movement talks about family of origin versus family of choice. Your family of origin was solely for the benefit of setting up your life's lessons and struggles. That is the purpose of the family of origin. Some of you have received tremendous amounts of love, that heart-energy love, and some of you have not. Your lessons and your struggles are geared according to what you received and what you did not receive. Do you have any questions?

## UNCONDITIONAL LOVE HAS NO STRINGS

*When you are supposed to give that love to someone who is really important and you don't, what happens? What is happening inside you?*

It is simply called fear. People who do not give that love withhold it for several reasons. One of them could be that they have given love where it hurt the other too much to receive it, so that person then put up a wall or said things that hurt. The one giving the love was reaching out tentatively, and he or she was fragile, kind of like a shoot first coming out of the ground. If you have an oak tree first coming out of the ground and someone steps on it, that will kill it; however, if you have an oak tree that is twelve feet tall and someone steps on it to climb it, it will not die.

When you are wounded or are very young as you are learning about this, there is fear in reaching out. Your fear in reaching out triggers the fear in the other person. Most often you who are afraid to give love or afraid to receive it reach out in fear to someone who is also afraid to give or receive love. I can tell you that when you are the one afraid and the other person says she would like you to reach out and love her, when you do, and do it consistently, the other person may run away. This is because she is not aware of how afraid she is of what the purity of love can be. The difficulty that lies in human relationships is that you do not know what the purity of love is: The purity of love means that you extend yourself, that energy, without any expectation in return. In other words, you extend the loving energy without the expectation that the other person will love you back.

Unconditional love has no strings. You give because you give. And because you give, you will receive. It might not be from the other person, but it will definitely be from the universal love energy. Someone who is completely balanced in his love—by that I mean he had all of his love energy activated when he was an infant—is in constant communion with the universal energy of receiving. As he gives, he receives. There is no emptiness that occurs, because there is a continual flowing of giving and receiving. It would be what you would see if you forgot to turn the water off in your kitchen sink. You'd see water flowing onto the floor and water continuing to flow out of the faucet with the kitchen sink remaining full. With yourself giving love, there is a continual giving of love, and as much as you give, there is a continual influx of love coming into you from the universe. So you are always full. Does that answer that question for you?

## INFANCY IS THE RIGHT TIME TO ACTIVATE THE HEART
*Is it possible that someone's fear caused a wall and he or she have stopped loving?*

It is not that those ones have completely stopped loving, but they do have a wall. They make that wall so strong that they might only have one little chink in the mortar of that wall through which they can allow some love to come in. The difficulty for them is when there is too much love. Then it is like the flood, because their hearts have not been activated. Their physical cells and energetic cells have not been activated. Beyond a certain age, it hurts.

What happens is when you were an infant and were receiving all that love, being held in the arms and nuzzled and touched, that is the time for this activation to occur. When you are past that time, then it becomes more painful and there is a fear present. When you are first born is the time of the greatest amount of openness. On the whole, this is the case. There are some exceptions, but we will not go into those now.

Before birth and in infancy are the greatest amount of openness to having the heart center totally and completely activated. Once that time is past, it is more difficult to activate it, though it is not impossible. It is more difficult, because people begin to put blocks in the way of having the heart activated. They equate love with pain then. This is so because of the blocks or wounds present; there is actually some physical and emotional pain as the activation occurs past infancy. This is where the healing needs to come.

## YOUR GUARDIAN ANGEL IS AN ASPECT OF YOU
*I would like to know a fast or quick way to communicate with my guardian angel. I talk to him, but he doesn't respond.*

This is what I would like you to know. Your guardian angel is an aspect of yourself. We are all one. Your guardian angel is an aspect of yourself in the oneness that in this human experience of separateness, you and almost everyone interprets as separate. But it is really a part of yourself. Your guardian angel is communicating with you, but you believe that it is coming from within yourself, so you discount it. What you could do is set up a code with your guardian angel. Have you discovered your guardian angel's name or have you named your guardian angel?

*I asked him his name, and what I heard in my mind I thought couldn't be. It was Romeo.*

So when you talk with Romeo, one of the things you might want to say is, "Romeo, when I wish to communicate with you, I will tap on my heart." Or you could say you will tap on your third eye or your nose or your ear. It doesn't matter. Set up a communication system with Romeo. Begin to pay attention when you do that to what you feel, sense, see or hear within the deepness of yourself. As you perfect this within yourself, you will discover that the answers you receive from Romeo, that deep wisdom aspect of yourself, that guardian part of yourself, will actually feel kinesthetically as if they come from a different place within you than the answers that come from your head. Even if an answer comes from the area of your mind, you will have a sense that it comes from a deepness of the mind rather than a superficial part of the mind.

*I have been having something like that.*

So you see, you are communicating with Romeo. Isn't it interesting that the name for your angel has to do with love? It's a beautiful name, a beautiful angel and a beautiful soul.

## FIND WAYS TO NOURISH YOUR HEART

*How do we activate the heart? Is there any procedure we can go through to activate the heart?*

Spend time in your heart. Go into the back of your heart center and spend some time. Be there as quietly as you can. Call in the energy of Spirit— whether it be me, Amma; the Father, Abba; or any other spiritual being you relate to, Jesus, Buddha, Quan Yin, Mother Mary, Romeo. You can specifically ask that the energy you need most to activate your heart, that which is a priority right now, be the energy that comes in. You might need the masculine love energy to come in. You might need the feminine love energy to come in. Ask that this occur.

The other thing is to be with that which nourishes your heart. Anything that nourishes your heart is going to help activate it. That is where meditation comes in. Some of you who have tried meditation get so frustrated, and the time turns out not to be a heart experience, but a hard experience.

You have your main five senses that science usually talks about (even though some scientists know there are more than five). What is it that you can touch that activates your heart? For some, it is their pets. It can even be the soft fuzz you might find on a tree or in new grass. And it can also be becoming aware and open to the energy that is present. What nourishes your heart through your vision? If you watch TV, is love mostly what you watch there?

Think about this whole business of television. This one likes to watch the crime shows where they figure things out, and she knows that does not nourish her heart. What kinds of things do nourish the heart? Pay attention. Pay attention to what you hear and what you read. The only heart-nourishing thing in your newspapers is usually found in the comics! Pay attention especially to the vibration of music. That can activate your heart. Pay attention to the color that feels good around you. A color that is good for one might not be good for another. Know that whatever it is that in a sense pulls at your heart activates it. Make choices and ask for healing. One of the paradoxes of human life is that those who need healing the most do not feel worthy to ask for healing. If they do not ask, we will not interfere.

*It sounds like the activation of the heart has to be a very personal thing. No one else can be involved in it?*

You will find that there are people who will accompany you along your way, but you have to realize that for the most part you will attract people to you who can simply love a little bit more than you can. Once you come to the healing in that area of love, unless the other person continues to grow in his or her own journey of healing him-or herself with the heart aspect, then you would grow apart. You would find that things become discordant or boring. In this stage in your adulthood, it is true that the healing of your heart is between you and the sacred other.

## YOU NEED MALE AND FEMALE ENERGIES TO ACTIVATE THE LOVE

*I'm thinking of gender differences: the male energy of love and the female energy of love. With the male energy, we sometimes think of the quest, the crusade (although that sometimes tends to be pejorative), of getting from one place to the other, the victory that one seeks. I'm also thinking in terms of tough love in teaching and how you modulate that, how you teach the young ones without squashing their voices. It's difficult.*

I mentioned earlier how important it is to have both the masculine and feminine energies to activate the love. Know that feminine love energy is very much internal and in relationship with one on one. The feminine goes within. Even the extroverted feminine goes within. Even the most extroverted female who is getting ready to give birth goes within. The masculine energy, the quest as you said, is an external love energy that bursts from within, goes out and is active. The feminine energy is that which gives you the ability to go within to the wisdom part of yourself, that deep, guardian-angel part of yourself. The masculine energy is that which allows it to burst forth and go out in quest and action.

Each one of you has the masculine and feminine energies within you. If you have more of the feminine energy within you, you might have a beautiful ability to be internal, to go into the deepness of your spirituality and find the deepness of yourself; but you might not have the ability to project yourself out and move forward in your quest. If you have too much of the masculine energy, you will not have the ability to go inside to where you find the deepening within yourself. Instead, you go out. That is where the negative connotation of "crusades" comes from.

*Is the masculine the expression?*

The masculine is the expression. The feminine is the generativity that comes from within. The masculine is the expression. When you have one without the other, you have imbalance. You need both.

*So it is perhaps like breathing, a compression and an expansion. We do both.*

You also asked how to work with the young without stepping on them. Know that when you have stepped on a child, you have not been in your heart. What has happened is that he or she triggered something within you. Usually that is your frustration with your inability to give the structure that is so desired. The young one has actually activated within you a knowledge on an other-than-conscious level, that here is a part of your heart that is not healed. You do not act from your heart when an area that is not healed is triggered.

The way to avoid not acting from the heart is to be consciously aware of going into your heart. If you are afraid within yourself that you will do damage to that young one, then it is time for you to leave. Just remove yourself from the room if you need to do that. Then get in touch with that part of yourself that has not been activated within your heart. Ask that you now may be given the energies to come in and activate that aspect of your heart.

## RAISING A GIFTED CHILD

*We have a very special son. I think he is gifted. He began reading English when he was three. Now he reads Spanish without having received any training. Sometimes it is difficult to relate to him, because he acts like he is an old, old man. He doesn't act like a child. His name is Stefan.*

Here are some things to know about Stefan. He is someone who actually did not want to come into the physical as a child. He wanted to come as an adult. There are those who do that. They are called walk-ins, and there is an exchange of energy with the soul residing in a body. However, in consultation with those who work with him in his growth and development, it was suggested that he come in as a child and go through the child process. He is rebelling against that process. He has tremendous amounts of wisdom.

Stefan is a very gifted child, and because he is very gifted, he is going to be much more difficult than what you might call an average child. There is so much within him that needs balancing. He needs to be continually reminded that he is a child. Part of that is to do some childlike things with him, to play in certain ways, to find ways to bring out that joy and laughter within him, to do things that are totally fun. It's not to discourage his intellectual growth, but to help him become more well-rounded. He will have some great challenges if he is not in balance.

Your job is to bring him into balance. That is what you said you would do for him—help him balance. You are one of the ones who convinced him to come into the physical as a child. You promised that you would help him, and you are doing that. I can already sense that you are feeling more responsibility from these words that I say. You are doing what you need to do.

## GET OUT THERE AND HAVE SOME FUN!

Just be aware that he needs to learn to play. He needs to have fun. He will not relate easily to children his own age, although there will be some he can relate to. He is going to feel different. Support him. You know it is tough for him and you recognize that. Find some other outlets for him. He has a very creative, technical side. Watch what happens with that. He can be a great inventor of technological things that have not even been discovered yet. Simply give him all the love you can. That is the support that you can give. When I said that you would help him, do it through your love.

Rule number one is to have no expectations of who or what he is to be. Let him discover what it is that he is to be. He is going to want you to tell him, but that is not your job. Your job is to support him with that structure of love—love being energy from your heart and unconditional positive regard—as much as you can give. Provide a cocoon in a sense of love. Remember what cocoons do. There is tremendous metamorphosis going on within a cocoon. Hopefully, what I have said has helped and has not brought you to a place of more concern.

Do what you are doing, just add getting him out to have fun. Find out what is fun for him. It will not be the same things as for other children. When he takes on too much responsibility, remind him that he does not have to do that yet. There will be plenty of time, and this is for Mom or Dad to be concerned with right now. He will not like that, by the way, because he will consider that you are telling him he is not mature or old enough. It is true; he is not. He is human and needs to grow and develop and learn—and have fun.

## WHEN YOUR CHILD IS YOUR MIRROR IMAGE

*It's very confusing with my son. I see what you are saying—there is a mirror image of us. Most parents have that. What I'm very confused about is how to respond to that. There is the strong connection that I have with him in terms of the growth and development he is going through. I see that, and it's emotionally difficult to handle, to separate myself from that, to allow him to be his own person. I suspect that the connection is so strong psychically, intellectually and heart-wise, that when I do what you are saying—for example, I'll say, "Look, you're a child. Don't make the same mistakes I did. Don't lose your childhood." I'm dealing with tremendous frustration and a sense of hopelessness because I'm not getting through.*

Show, don't tell. In other words, do things with him rather than telling him to not take on that responsibility. Just take him away from the responsibility and go do something fun.

Another way that he is mirroring you is that he is trying to find his voice, and it is scaring him. That is exactly what is happening with you and your writing, is it not? This is another way that you are mirroring each other. He has a very strong feminine aspect, stronger than yours. The guidance that he needs is for you to be giving him more of the strength of your masculine aspect. His mother gives him the strength of her feminine aspect. This is necessary so he can discover that he can be both a feminine and masculine being and be firmly and enjoyably within that balance. He will be challenging you, you who enjoy so much being in your mind, working and devising and developing, theorizing and figuring things out. He is challenging you to come more into your heart. Any child will do that.

As you are able to come more into your heart, which you have done tremendously since this child was born, you will also discover the child within you that became the adult too soon; you will begin to find that child who wants to play. It will be a different kind of playing than what you would have done when you were eleven. And he will enjoy a different kind of playing than you did when you were eleven. Help him discover what that is and stay there within your heart. Have special time that is just for the two of you. If you can find that time about once every two weeks, solely built around fun, it will help.

He is looking for his voice. His hormones are stirring now, and that is part of what is bringing all of this on. Teach him the strength of the masculine side. You have a tremendous strength in your masculinity. In one way it will be easier for you to come into your heart, because you do not get caught up as much in the emotion of things. That is what you can teach him, as he is very much in tune with the emotion of things. As you can accept him being in the emotion, you can by your example gently guide him to be firmly in his heart, but to release the emotion. You are not as familiar with that aspect, but by you bringing in your strength for him, he can come into balance.

You took on a difficult job when you and your wife agreed to work with this spirit. Believe me, it will pay off. You will see the fruits of it. He will have a difficult time in adolescence, but there is no need to tell him that. He already feels very different and alone. He is struggling to express himself. He came into this planet to work through fears. Do not be concerned in the sense of worrying about him. Simply provide for him that which you are.

You have exactly what is needed to give him support; you simply need to bring it more into your heart area. You are familiar with the heart within the heart within the heart energies. Read some more about that—from your heart rather than from your head—and you will get some guidance on exactly what to do with him.

Spend more time with him, just you and he. Do it in gentle steps. Don't just suddenly say, "Okay, now we're going to have fun!" Sometimes the fun he is going to find is just being with you and doing certain things as he gets the strength he needs as he moves into puberty.

## SIGNS OF HUMANKIND'S TRANSITION

*I have another question. It has to do with humankind's transition to the new energy. I was thinking today that this is a cycle, such as the children of Israel, the Pharaoh letting them go, the Exodus. I was trying to understand: What will we see that we can touch and feel, perhaps in the science venue, that is indicative of this transcending, the shifting into this new time?*

The greatest changes in the scientific field are going to be in the understanding of consciousness. When you look into your own tradition and the journey in the desert, it was so that the generation who believed in slavery could die off so they could come into the freedom of the new life. That is what is happening in human consciousness in this process.

As the consciousness comes to a greater understanding of itself, you are going to discover that any belief is limiting. That is difficult to understand at this place where you are. You know that the chair will support you and the car will move, but as you are able to release beliefs about how the human mind and body operate, you are going to discover even more how they can operate.

One of the things that will happen as consciousness develops is that you will not need cell phones as you know them any more, because you will learn how to connect with the vibration of the one with whom you wish to communicate. It is a form of telepathy. You have already had instances of that with your wife and your son. Instead of looking at it as the unusual, shift your focus to it being the usual, and you will be able to use it more and more. That is one of the things that will happen.

There will be many changes in regard to who will be populating this planet, as this is a painful process. Just know that. You might have noticed that some people are already choosing unusual ways to leave the planet. There will be other ways. Many people are being faced with the choice of whether to stay or to go. There is no judgment about their choice. Those who make the choice to stay are choosing to come here and to be here to experience the evolution of consciousness.

## INCREASED LOVE IS RELATED TO DETACHMENT

*Last Saturday, around lunchtime, I was talking to someone and noticed that something happened inside me. You're talking about consciousness, and I don't know what it was, but I was conscious of a shift in myself. From that time on, everything's been a little different. It's like my reality has changed. I seem to be less attached to things. My thoughts seem to be a little clearer now, but it's a little confusing to me. Do you have any feedback on what's going on?*

You felt the shift here within your heart center, did you not? So what it is that happened is that you had another part of your heart that was activated. In the perfection of things, that would have been activated within the first six months of your birth, but remember that nobody has had that, because that is how it is set up.

So as you were working on your own spiritual path, even though you do not have to be consciously saying that you are activating these particular aspects of your heart, it will happen. It happens as you work on your spiritual path from your heart and not from your head. As these parts are activated, you are going to discover that when your heart is fully activated, you will know total detachment.

I, Amma, am in a place of total detachment. Do you realize that I have no caring whatsoever about what it is that you do? That might seem harsh, especially to those of you who want someone to care about you. What it means is that you could literally kill the one I am speaking through right now and I would not cease to love you as I do now. That is what I mean when I say that I do not care what it is that you do. Nothing that you do can change the wholeness of the love I have for you.

*So increased love is related to detachment?*

That is correct. You will find that as your heart is activated more and more, you will actually be having less of what you call feelings and emotions. It is the lessening of the feeling and emotion that brings about the detachment. And it feels strange, because it hasn't happened to you before. Of course it feels strange, just as when you buy new clothes—they might feel strange for a while.

*Can I lose it? Can I lose the activation of my heart?*

You can have things that occur to you that can damage you in such a way because of other areas that are not activated within your heart. In that case, you might want to retreat and put something into dormancy. That does not mean that you lose it. It is in dormancy, but it is very much there. You might go into a place of forgetfulness for a little while about how it is to be and then come back as you realize what is happening.

Imagine a heart shape in my hands. Let's say that each one has a molecule that is a place of activation. Some of these are activated within you and some are not. Each one of you has different ones activated. That's what I mean by activation. It is very much an electromagnetic occurrence. This is the best I can describe it in your language, in your duality right now.

## THE ROLE OF EMOTION

*I'm a little confused about the role of emotion. I understand that it is an energy that is generated or perhaps radiated or communicated in some way. Is the emotion then an effect of love expression, as opposed to reactive emotion? Love can come out of an unfulfilled need, as you said, so it seems that emotion could be a negative energy and a positive energy as well.*

Emotion in the human is an energy that comes not only from that sense of the pure energy that's nontangible, but is also a biochemical reaction that comes from within. There is an energy that is released, and then it is put into motion with the mind. It's the coming together of the wholeness of the person. You can have an emotion that is propelled by the heart. You can have an emotion that is propelled by the mind. You can have an emotion that is propelled by the solar plexus and an emotion that is propelled by the pelvis. That is where your intention and your motivation comes in. When you are working purely through the heart, which is in its full activation, and then with the purity of what you have—especially entering through the back of your heart chakra—it is completion of the balance of the masculine and feminine. Within your heart, it is the balance between the spiritual centers above you and the physical centers below and all they represent.

The emotion itself, as you look at energy in motion, has no real positive or negative in and of itself. Feeling, which is a similar but different aspect, is a judgment about what that energy in motion is. You can have a sense of this energy that is in motion—e-motion—that will feel and be interpreted as anger coming from the solar plexus area. Or you can have the feeling that can be interpreted as lust coming from the pelvic area. And you can have similar bio-chemical reactions. Of course, there are differences. The emotion that comes from fear has a dampening effect upon the immune system, whereas the emo-tion that comes from a combination of the pelvis and the heart has an elevat-ing effect on the immune system. It is, of course, much more complex than that.

Thank you for being here. I have been able to introduce some things that I will be speaking more of—the development of human consciousness and the effect of this energy on your powerful heart and how that works in relationships between human beings. I thank you for being here.

And I now do place my hand upon your heart. Feel the love that I have for you. Remember, dear ones, no matter what you have ever learned from anyone, there is absolutely nothing that will change the love I have for you. How could I ever deny my very self?

# 11

# Understanding Your Child's Heart Center and Your Own

*November 2003*

*G*reetings, dear ones. It's so good to be here with you, to see you and to feel your energy through this beloved one through whom I am speaking. Each one of you is so beloved.

Look at your hearts. Can you see each of your hearts? Notice how beautiful your heart centers are and how full of love. Some hold a little fear—but the love is there! In this past year, I've been speaking a lot about love. Now we've moved on. It's still about love, but in a different way. We're now talking about consciousness. The most recent time we were together, I spoke about the development of the heart center that occurs in infants, and why it is so important for infants to be heart-to-heart with both mother and father. I want to continue with that so you will have a better understanding of what affects your growth.

## EARLY DEVELOPMENT INCLUDES SUBTLE ASPECTS

Western world psychology emphasizes how you grow, how different complexes occur and the stages that you pass through. What is not said in those texts, because the writers are not aware of the human energy system, is the dynamic value and nature of consciousness. They don't understand that development does not occur in a vacuum. Those of you who have read some of the developmental texts have perhaps noticed that there is no real impetus discussed. It is almost as if a human grows with just a little watering. Well, there is watering, but development has to do with the human energy field. That is the critical part in growth and development. Remember that your physical self is the densest part of you. Your energy field is the more malleable part. That is why those of you who have been in the healing field have heard that if you can locate disease—or dis-ease—in the energy field before it manifests in the physical, the disease is much easier to release and heal. It is much more difficult to heal when disease is "solidified" within the physical body.

The field of mind/body psychology is examining this aspect of disease, although not everybody has accepted the concept. Both health and disease are about the awareness of consciousness. Even those working in your mind/body psychology are not totally aware of consciousness.

## THE HEART-TO-HEART CONNECTION IS VITAL

Let's talk about where we were. We stopped with the aspect of the importance of holding the child heart-to-heart. That is one of the reasons for nursing. If a mother does not nurse, she can still hold the infant heart-to-heart so that the little one can grow and develop. The first six months are very critical for this. That is why you cannot spoil a baby. As long as you did not roll over on it, it would be fine if the little one slept on your chest the entire time. Other primates do that. Monkeys and gorillas are always carrying their little ones— sometimes on the back, but it is still heart-to-heart. The major aspect of assisting development at this stage is the heart-to-heart connection.

Some of you working in the healing fields need to realize that what you are doing is reconnecting that heart-to-heart communication. That is part of what is happening in the reconnection that some healers do. Of course, it is on a larger scale than simply the heart energy, because you are connecting to the grid. To assist in healing, you have to address the energy field of the individual from conception to six months out of the womb. As you are assisting the healing from that time frame, you are providing love energy the child needed at that time and didn't receive. For instance, if you forget to water a plant for a little while, you know that you simply pour water on the plant and the roots take up the water. That which droops now comes alive in a sense, right? What most people don't realize, unless they are farmers or good at working with plants, is that there is a slight weakening of the structural integrity of the plant that would not occur if the water is given continually. It does not happen in the fields, but there is more earth from which to pull nutrients and water than a potted plant has.

Remember when you are holding any child to hold it heart-to-heart and send heart energy. When you are working with someone other than a child, even someone 103 years old, the initial work still needs to go back to heal the foundation. If you are working on present-time issues with someone 103 years old, for instance, you would always remember to ask for that love energy to come in and to activate the heart center in the way it was not activated before that person was six months old.

## You Can All Be Healers with Heart Energy

Those of you who are teachers might not consider yourselves healers, right? But you are. Think of the work you do with the children you teach. Would you like a suggestion as you're working with them? Go into the classroom before they arrive and say a prayer over the entire classroom. Call forth that symbol that you have known as the sacred heart. Call that heart energy to settle into the classroom and go into the hearts of each of your students. See that energy coming in through your crown and out your heart and going into the hearts of each one of those children. You will see some amazing things happen. As you are doing that, you are acting as a healing facilitator for them and supplying to them the heart energy they were missing. It's one of the missing key elements not taught in schools, right?

When you are with anyone—your own children, other children, children of any age—bring in that wonderful energy. Just ask that the heart energy come into you and activate it more within your own heart, which can be both a receiver and an amplifier. The energy you brought in now has the addition of the human vibration. You are in a physical body, a human body, and you are going to be giving this to another human body. As long as you bring the energy into your heart and send it out, even to someone you see on the street or in the grocery store, you are facilitating healing. You are, with intention, activating that part of the heart center that did not get activated. There is no one here whose heart center is totally activated. No one who is born has their heart center totally activated. You made choices to be here—as much as some of you might rebel against the notion that you made that choice—to work on certain issues. In order to do this, certain areas of your heart center were not activated. This set up the plan for your life.

## The Heart Center Is Expansive

Your heart center is not just the location within the center of your chest. It expands outward. There are heart centers within hearts centers within heart centers. There is research demonstrating this. You are activating these many heart centers when you work with the heart center. The discussion about love the past year has been about what happens when the heart energy has been, or has not been, activated. When the love energy is activated, you find the—oh, let's call them symptoms, to use your medical model, of love—what you call caring, concern and other qualities. Some of you see the symptoms of love as the emotional feeling that is in your body at the time. But what we are talking about is consciousness—not the consciousness that you become, but the consciousness that you are and of which you are becoming aware. As you activate those parts within yourself and activate them in others—and remember that when you activate them in others, you activate them in yourself—you are activating them within the heart of the world. You are activating the heart of your planet, this being that embodies your planet. She, or he, is a being—an androgynous being—this one that you live upon. It is very much a living being, with its own consciousness and its own path, and you all work in harmony. And when you don't work in harmony, then there is discord that occurs, is there not?

## EVERYTHING AFFECTS THE DEVELOPING CHILD

Let's return to consciousness and the development of the individual. At around six months of age, the child becomes a little more independent, begins more movement and becomes much more aware of its surroundings. Everything that happens around and in the space of the infant affects the energy field of that infant. Those of you who are parents have noticed that the little ones like to be within your energy. That's because your energy is protective of the developing nature of their energy field. A little one whose energy field is developing cannot handle severe stress or assaults of other people's energy. It is as if you cut into a sapling with a knife. It might not kill the sapling, but it would still bear the wound of that knife, even for many years. The same happens with a child.

## ANGER INJURES THE ENERGY FIELD; LOVE HEALS IT

What are some of these assaults I am talking about? Anger is one. I don't mean anger expressed in an appropriate manner, as in saying, "I am upset with you for leaving the toilet seat up." No, I'm talking about the rage and explosion that can occur when you say things in an inappropriate manner. For instance, you can say the same words, but say them with such explosion or violence that it causes damage to that sapling or growing energy field. Now those of you who are parents are already thinking about the times you have done that to your children. What do you do with that? It is very simple. With great consciousness, and from your heart, you go to that incident and bring in your own image of love (such as the sacred heart that I suggested earlier) and activate the energy, expanding it within your own heart. Then go to that time in your consciousness when the event occurred and send the energy you now have in your heart to your child. It really is that simple. Does it clear the energy field? It will not only clear the energy field but it will . . . ah, in your movie ET, remember when the ET put his finger out and touched the finger of the one that was bleeding? It was as if no wound was there, because the ET put energy within, providing the sustenance that enabled the skin to come together and show no scar. That is the same thing you can do with your love. It really is that simple. Be conscious when you are doing it. Consciousness is being conscious that you're conscious.

Let's say it is you who are wounded. You can do the same thing for yourself by asking for that love to come into you. You can ask specifically for the masculine aspect or the feminine aspect of the love that is needed. Ask the love energy to come in through your heart and expand it. Feel it and know it. Come to know your spiritual self and that it is much larger than your physical self. Feel that spiritual self. See yourself with that child self. Send that love energy to your child self. Encourage your child self to accept the love energy from your adult self. You will find that you will achieve healing; as you do that for yourself, just as the ET sent that energy and healed the skin. You will become stronger and enable yourself to drop the beliefs holding you back. Just let them go. Keep the lesson of the incident and the knowledge that is there, but let the packaging go. All that you need to do is release what you no longer need. You no longer need the memory of the wounding event. Does the memory go away? Not necessarily. But it is somewhere other than active in your life. Someone could bring the incident up, and you would respond, "Yes, that is true. That happened." But there is no charge to it, no great emotion that comes to permeate your energy field to let you know there has been great wounding.

You learn not to be a victim when you do that. Victims are passive and take little responsibility for themselves. That is not a judgment; that is just a fact. The judgment comes when you are not able to see where the one who feels a victim is and allow that one to grow and be on their path. No one here can have someone else remove your victim-ness. You cannot remove that belief system from another. Everyone has to do it for him- or herself. You can provide information, but the individual has to remove it.

## You Can Nurture the Energy Field

Back again we go to consciousness and to the development of the child. The energy field has certain needs for its growth, just as a child's physical body needs particular nutrients at specific times. As you know, some people say the infant should not bounce on its legs because it will bend the cartilage, which has not yet become bone. The same happens with the energy field. There are certain times you do exercises in your energy field, and there are times you don't. For instance, let's suppose an eight-year-old has to drive a parent to the emergency room because there is no one else there. The child knows where the keys are but has never driven before. The child manages to find a way to get that parent into the car and to the emergency room. The child has been forced to do something he or she is not prepared to do. An insecurity about driving might develop, as well as a wounding within the energy field because the personality and the energy field are not strong enough to handle the energy coming forth. You can imagine the trauma of an eight-year-old knowing something is wrong with a parent and needing to get to a doctor. Love energy needs to go to that one at that age. How is that trauma healed? Some have been taught to heal the trauma by visualizing it over and over again until they release the energy. Unfortunately, this does not work. It just numbs them to the trauma. What needs to be done is exactly what I have already said to you—bring the energy into yourself and amplify it within your heart. Ask specifically that the energy you send from your heart to this individual be energy of the exact vibration and frequency needed for that person at that time when the wound occurred.

When you are dealing with a salesperson in a store, for instance, and he reacts to something you say and begins to yell, you have several choices. You can turn around and leave, right? You can believe you caused it and it was your fault. You could yell back. These are just some of the things you can do. You can also, if you wish—and those of you who are healers would be the ones who would wish to do this kind of thing—bring the energy into yourself, send it out from your heart and ask specifically for that energy to be the correct frequency and vibration needed to bring support to heal the wound. Some of you might ask, "What about permission?" Well, dear ones, let me remind you that there is only one of you, only one of me—and we are all one. You have permission from a particular level of the Oneness to do this. Now the individual soul itself, in the expression of duality, might make a choice of whether or not to accept that energy. But that energy does not necessarily go away. Some people will bounce the energy back to you and say no, they don't want it at all. Some of you have experienced that. Others will accept the energy but delay taking it into themselves until a later time. It is a blessing. And know that curses work the same way. A curse, of course, is that which is not a blessing.

## WHAT HAPPENS TO ONE HAPPENS TO ALL

As you are working with children, keep in mind what it is you are seeing within them when they express themselves in a way you would rather they not do. You are seeing the manifestations, the symptoms, of certain wounds in their energy field. And you can, if you wish, send energy through you to them as previously explained. It will be much easier for you if you do it that way. It requires an awareness on your part to do that. As you do that for them, you will do it for yourself. The one who walked upon this Earth who called himself Jesus or Jeshua stated that, "What you do for the least of these, you do for me." What he really intended by that is an expression of the Oneness. What any one of you does to the other, you do to all—you do to the community. That is in all of your scriptures in different fashions and different ways.

If you look within your scriptures, you will see that anything that is happening and has happened is happening Now. Whether it is past, present or future on your timeline, it is still the now. Those of you in the Hebrew way of worshiping find that when you speak of such things as the Passover, it is happening now. All the wanderings in the desert are now. And know that whatever you read about in your history, it is now and you can change the Now. You simply move yourself to that place to do the changing.

## TAKE CARE TO PROTECT THE ENERGY FIELD

Let us talk some about things that do not help the development of the energy field or the awareness of consciousness. What happens to you that causes violence within you, that shocks you, will shock a child, especially one under the age of seven, even more because that child has not yet developed protection over what you call the chakras. Each one of you have already developed these. In some of you they are torn, but you have a covering over your chakras. The little ones have not yet developed that. That is why they run back and forth into your energy field. Those of you who have children over the age of seven, do you remember when it was that they didn't need to come back so often and check on you, to find you, to come within your energy? That is when you started looking for them and reminding them to be home at a certain time. Before then, you never had to do that. They have now developed that protection, like a screen, over their chakras, and they are not so assaulted by the energies outside.

I'm now going to say some things that are very difficult to do in the society you live in. One of the things that would help the development of the awareness of consciousness is simple. Turn it off, throw it out or do something with your television. There really is no need for it. There are a few good things that could be uplifting. That is difficult for many of you in this room, including this one whom I speak through. She still likes those criminal shows and watching the investigations. There is nothing wrong with liking things like that, but know and be aware what those energies do to the development of your self and of consciousness. There is no judgment about them. They just are.

## YOUR CHOICES AFFECT THE ENERGY FIELD

In talking about no judgment, we talk about what is. Say you have two apples. One apple is beautiful in color; you can feel it and it is firm; you can smell it and it smells like an apple. The other apple is a little soft; you can see brown spots on it; you smell it, and it's a little beyond apple—another stage of its development. Which one do you choose to eat? Is it that you have made a judgment? Well, you've made a decision, haven't you? You have said, "This apple is not the one I choose to put in my body because it will not enhance my body." So you choose this other apple because you believe it will enhance your body, correct? It is important to know that whatever you bring into your eyes or ears affects your energy field, affects your awareness of consciousness. Most people, when they read this, will not like it but will know it is true. It takes great discipline to pull oneself away from something that is so addictive to the energy. Does this make sense to you, what I am saying? Be aware what music you listen to. These vibrations are very important. Vibrations put out in your home have an impact upon the development of the little ones in your home, as well as yourself.

No, you cannot protect the children from everything. They are going to leave the house. They are going to be riding bicycles and eventually driving cars. You can't protect them from everything. However, know that as you strengthen their energy field with your love and provide them that strength they need, they will have the strength within their energy field to become more aware of their consciousness. Then their path is their own, is it not?

Know that about the time they are thirteen or fourteen, their path is their own. You still set limits, but know that their path is their own. Do not concern yourself, even though I know you will, if they decide to make decisions that you wish they would not make, whether about drugs or sex or whatever else it is. You give them all you can and you do what you can, and then they get to make their own decisions. Remember, they chose you, and you chose them. You agreed. But they chose you first, just as you chose your parents first. It was you who went to those beings who were going to become your parents and said, "This is what I need to learn, and I think you can help me learn it." And then those spirits evaluated their own development and whether or not that fit into their own plan. It's not quite as simple as I'm saying, but all of it is choice. Know that.

## WE WILL ALL RETURN TO THE ONENESS

And, dear ones, do you know what else? It doesn't matter! It doesn't matter at all, because you know what the end result is? All of you will leave those bodies that you have and will come back to the Oneness. It doesn't matter. You know how it is when you get together with friends and family and laugh about old times in the past. Some could even be painful things like when you were five and fell off the counter, but you can laugh about it now. You will be doing that when you finish with these bodies of yours.

That's what I want to say about the development of consciousness tonight. We will continue in this vein and talk about such things as consciousness. Just think of the number of things we have said about love. It all comes in together.

Any questions from anybody?

## CONSIDERING CONSCIOUSNESS AND AWARENESS

*What's your definition of consciousness?*

Ah, consciousness is actually that of which you are. And consciousness is, in the physics of it, another term for love. It is actually the same thing. But the word "love" doesn't mean that to different people.

*How does awareness work into it?*

When you are in this physical body, there are things that you have forgotten. Awareness is becoming aware of the consciousness and how it works. You have tremendous ability in your consciousness. Anything you read about your saints, from any religion or non-religion, you yourself could do what they do if you awakened yourself to the power within you. You hold that power within your very consciousness. It is only your belief, the lack of awareness of your consciousness, that stops you. Think of something you didn't know you could do when you were a child—for some of you it's when you are an adult. Perhaps it was to ride a bike or roller skate or drive a car. Perhaps it was to grab a vine and swing across the river. You didn't think you could do it—and then you did it.

You suddenly became aware of how easy it was, and then you did it again. Then it just became nothing, in the sense that it just was. That is what can happen with you. What you call miracles are not really miracles. A definition of a miracle is something that is outside of natural law. You do not know what the law is and what natural law truly is because of the box that you live in. When you're able to open that box and look out, it's rather amazing.

## IT MATTERS; IT DOESN'T MATTER

*Getting back to your statement that it doesn't matter, I know that it's a grand game we come here to play. Yet when we're in the game, it's pretty serious. Until we get across the veil, we have to take it seriously, but knowing that we can get across the veil, we can ramp down the seriousness. So again we get to the paradox. It's like playing a sport like basketball. When you're in the game, it's really serious, but at the end of the game, you pat each other on the back and go have a beer together, and it's all fine. But when you're in that time, it seems that nothing else exists. That to me is the difficult part: to have these two things in your consciousness at once. As you have said in the past, we are in the duality. We are here for that reason. Would you comment?*

When you are in the game, let us say basketball, and you are up at the foul line, making that free throw will either lose or tie the game and put it into overtime. If what you do is remember all the times you missed, it will make it more difficult to play that game. If, however, you remember all the times that you made it, then it changes the whole emotional context of the game, and you are much more likely to make it. So the paradox that you live in is that it doesn't matter and it matters, and to remember that it doesn't matter and it matters. In raising a child, everything you do with that child matters. And then there is a point that it doesn't matter anymore, because it is the child's choice.

It is very difficult to walk that line. It is very difficult to walk with freedom. It does not matter if each one of you stripped off all of these clothes that you have on and sat here naked. It doesn't matter. It might matter if you walk outside. And you are already saying, "Oh no, nobody can see me even in here." You don't know each other well. Why is it that you wear the clothes? For modesty's sake? Is it to hide something about your body? Is it because society says so? Is it so you don't get sunburned or get cold? There are many reasons. It comes to a place where you can realize that ultimately it doesn't matter; but as you are here, yes, there are things that matter. It is an interesting paradox, is it not? You talk about the term "enlightenment." There are people who have what they call enlightenment. It is coming to realize that they are not who they think they are. They're not the body, they're not the clothes, they're not the activities, they are not even this part that they play in this game you are in. Even enlightened people do not stay in that place twenty-four hours a day, because they live in the duality and get pulled back into duality.

Some of you have had experiences like . . . let us say September 11, 2001. Some of you got caught in the trauma of what happened, the emotion of the world. For others of you, it wasn't so much that you did not care from the empathetic point of view, but you realized that there was something higher, deeper or in a different dimensional level that was occurring. In a way, for you, it mattered and it didn't matter. You didn't get involved with all the emotion. Does that make sense? Remember to simply give and do what it is that you choose to give and do. You will learn from that. Others will learn their lessons from what it is that you do. And you will learn your lessons from what it is that they do. Then let it all go. Be able to throw that ball at the free-throw line without all the history, without all the future. Be there in the present moment. And the ball will probably go in. If you are there in that present moment and the ball doesn't go in (because a little deva decides to put a hand in there and keep the ball from going in), it matters on one level, but on another, it does not matter.

The violence you see in the world is due to people not realizing there are certain things that do not matter. There are other things, such as that heart connection that gives sustenance to each person, that do matter up to a point, and then it doesn't matter.

*As you were speaking about that and having been in exactly that situation with free throws many times over thirty years, I'm wondering what makes the difference of making that free throw or not. What makes a difference, thinking about the consciousness? It occurs to me that the difference is holding the two energies at once. It doesn't matter and it does. That's the transcendence, which is that we can be in the duality while being in the unified simultaneously.*

That's it exactly. That's what it is. You cannot avoid duality until you leave this body. So it is balancing those tensions.

*Would you say that relates to the secret of the three?*

Yes, it does relate to the secret of the three. You have an image in your unity candles that some of you use in your marriages that is the same thing as the secret of the three.

## ALL YOU HAVE TO DO IS ASK

*I'm just going to try to tell you back what you told me to see if I understand it. When I'm bringing the heart energy and putting it out to people, I need to change it to the vibration that they need at the time or at the time in which I'm thinking about?*

Let me clarify that a bit. It doesn't actually become heart energy until it comes into your heart, so you are connecting with the Oneness, and we will use heart in that sense as a metaphor because that works so well. Being connected in that way, you are asking Spirit for the energy to come into your crown. It then comes into your heart. You can consider your heart like a big mixing bowl in a sense, into which you add ingredients. The ingredients are added by your thoughts, your intention, your desire. So, in essence, this is prayer. This is what you are asking through prayer, if you would like to use it from that standpoint. As you are focusing upon that other one, simply ask for the energy to come in and go into the heart, and ask for the ingredients that are the vibration and frequency that is most needed. Let's say you were in deep pain, and you were screaming and yelling. This screaming and yelling is usually not due to the age that you are now. It is usually due to something that happened at a younger age, less than ten most of the time. Another person with you could ask for the right mixture of frequency and vibration and all that has to be done is to ask. That comes into the heart and becomes heart energy as she sends it out to you, and it goes into your heart.

You had the basic principle, but I just wanted to clarify some of the little details. It's not something that you have to change. In other words, you are not the one responsible for changing the energy into the vibration the other person needs. You simply ask for that to occur. There are all of these wonderful beings, who are still all just one being, who are all still you, who are there with their learning. You ask with a total awareness of your consciousness. It is within the power of your consciousness to see that energy coming in. It comes into your heart, which is the great activator and the great transformer and transmuter. Ask for exactly the vibration and the frequency that is needed for that person to go to heal the wound. Where does the energy field need to be supported? Send the energy from your heart. It can take seconds. As you experience it and learn how to do this, it can take only a moment, and you can be living in that way. Do you have another question about that?

## HEART ENERGY CANNOT HURT OTHERS

*You were saying that you can help others by putting it or bringing it through your heart. On the opposite end, if your heart has not been healed, will you cause this in other people?*

If you have a flashlight and the battery is not that strong, will the light that goes out cause harm to people? It simply is not as much light. What happens is when your heart is not healed—and none of your hearts are healed, but some of them are stronger, more healed than others, and it changes, for instance, the intensity of the light coming forth. None of your woundedness goes out to the other person when you are doing this. When you are doing this, you are bringing in pure love energy. It is just consciousness. It is the foundation, the essence, that of which you are made and that of which everyone is made. You are bringing that into you. And when you do that, you are actually bringing about healing in yourself. You are sending out the vibration and frequency that they need at the intensity that your heart is able to generate at that time. It is as if, as your heart gets stronger and more healed, the battery is stronger. And like the flashlight, the light goes out more intensely. So there is no way you can harm someone in this manner. And you can only help heal. You just present the opportunity to the individual. You don't do the healing. You can do the healing on yourself. So each time you do this, it changes you, whether it is with one of your children, your spouse or the homeless person on the street.

What begins to develop is the exchange of energy among yourselves. Imagine what would happen in this room if each one of you had this ingrained within you, if you were continually bringing in this love energy and sending it to each person in this room, with the intention in your mind. It doesn't even have to be a conscious thing (again I'm using consciousness differently), just as after you've learned how to ride the bicycle, how to drive the car. Are you being directly conscious when you put on the brake? You were at one time. But now you don't even think about it. You don't say, "Oh, brake!" No, you just do it, right? So when you practice this enough and it becomes ingrained within you, it can be something that you do always. Then you are always praying. And if each one of you were doing this to each person in this room—you can do it in an infinite amount because you are infinite people— then it produces a natural exchange in energy between the two of you, and as an exchange, 1 + 1 becomes 3. 3 + 3 becomes 9. You think it's "plus," but it's geometric progression and more. That expands, and it's expanding your heart.

For instance, when you are doing this with your child, your infant, and you are sending this heart energy into the infant, that little heart is beginning to activate. As all the little circuits in the heart center and in the energy field are beginning to activate, the child sends energy out to you. Those of you who have children know this. And you remember, don't you, when you could feel the exchange of energy with your little one? You can feel the love that is coming out. There is an energy exchange, and any energy exchange that occurs, amplifies. It amplifies. Do you have another question?

*Can you do this if someone has been hurt by someone else? You know what I mean?*

That is exactly what I was talking about earlier. You can send this out to someone who has been hurt by somebody else. Their choice is whether to receive it or not. That's what I was talking about earlier, about permissions, because many of you in your healing professions learn that you need to have permission because you do not want to violate. Well, yes and no. Sometimes that's just an excuse. This one I'm speaking through can send the energy to you, and you can take it or not take it. It all occurs on a deep soul level. It is the same as if she took something off her desk and handed it to you. You can take it or not take it. If she handed you that crystal there, you might be very interested in taking it. If she handed you a scorpion, you might not be interested in taking it. Some people, however, are afraid of that which is of high vibration. It is not compatible with their energy. We've talked about that at other times. When one's energy is of too high a level for another, it forms a discordance and can be frightening. This is so because they are in fear. The lower the vibration, the more fear they have. Most people, as you might have noticed in everyday life, do not like the feeling of having someone being higher than they. They will do something either to elevate themselves or to bring the other down. Does that answer your question?

## HOW CAN WE PROTECT OUR CHILDREN?

*I think I understood about the healing heart, and it will be very useful for me to use with my loved ones. Now I'm worried about protecting my kids' hearts and their whole person or unit. Since they are living in this country with the war and many, many rules—where you say, "Don't talk, don't smile" and don't, don't, don't. They don't talk to you in a good way, work hard or do things you like. And, like education, this is a big, big school we have. It's massive. There's nothing personal there, not for your feelings or desires. I feel sometimes when they go out of our house, they're in a forest or a jungle, and they have to protect themselves from other kids, from adults, from everything. There's not anything happy outside or anything really good for them. Maybe I am exaggerating, maybe not. How can I fill their hearts to be very strong and to be happy, but at the same time to defend themselves in this strange situation we are living in now? Thank you.*

Within that very good question, there are several layers that I would like to talk about. The first one will go directly to what I think you want to be able to do. Right now, your children come home to you. There will be a time when they'll leave the house and they won't come home to you every night. So what you can do when they come home is spend the time with them and send them the energy as we just talked about and ask for healing for that day. You can do that at night as you're tucking them into bed or as you're eating meals. You can do that when they're asleep. So you are supplying them the energy that they need to help bring healing to them—to strengthen the sapling, as it were.

The other thing I wish to address with you, and I know that this is something that will be difficult for you: You have a choice to send your children out with fear or with love. Whenever you send them with your fears, you are not sending them with your love. So when you send toward them your fear, you are wrapping them in fear. Send to them love, and wrap them with love, because it is the love energy that will protect them more than the fear energy. There are many good things out there. What you want them to be attracted to and what you want to be attracted to them are the things that are good for them. These are hard words for you. Do you have a question to ask about this?

*Yes. Sometimes I confuse fear and love or express them in the wrong way,. Sometimes I say "You are good, but don't go to the restroom by yourself. Be aware of everything." Am I giving them the right tools? How can I explain in a better way, "Take care but enjoy what's outside"?*

Let me use an analogy, because this all has to do with emotion. Say you're sitting down with them with their arithmetic homework, and you're explaining that if you do it in this manner, you will get the correct answer; however, if you do it this way, you won't get the correct answer. You might have some intensity as you are working with them—probably not at the beginning, but when you do it for the fifth time, there's usually some intensity with it, right? But at the beginning, there really isn't any emotion to it. No frustration; you're just explaining. It is the emotion that you put out. If you are telling them these things with great fear in your heart, then what you are communicating is fear and not information. What you would like to do is communicate the information. So, for instance, when you teach them how to cross the street, you teach them accord-

ing to their age level. First, it's "Always hold Mommy's hand," then it's "Do it
only when I'm watching you or when I'm with you," then it's "Always look both
ways." It's a progression, right? You give it to them as they need. You simply
give them the information.

It's very much like the balance that we were talking about with living in this
world, that it matters and it doesn't matter. You want to communicate to them
that there are certain things that you do for safety. You put on your seat belt.
Do not be afraid that you are going to be in an accident, but put on your seat
belt. It's to be able to do these things without having the fear of it, to take care
of things. Do not be afraid that the sun is going to burn you, but put on sun-
screen and wear a hat. Just be aware—not in fear, but simple awareness. If you
walked into this room and some water had been spilled on the floor, would you
step in it or around it? Would you have any fear about it? It just would be. And
that's how you want to communicate to the children. It is like water on the
floor. It's much easier to step around it. It won't bother you too much if you
happen to have shoes on. If you have just socks on, you'll know pretty quickly
that you'd rather have stepped around it—especially if there's a dog there and
you're not real sure what kind of water it is!

You can communicate these things that are safety features without transmitting fear. Fasten your seat belt. Why? Well, because that is the thing
that we do in case you have to stop suddenly. You teach them what to do if
they get lost. You teach them to go pick out a woman. That is what they are
teaching now: that if you have to go to a stranger, you go to a woman, not to
a man. Teach them what a police officer looks like. Teach them what is safe.
And then they do get to make their own decisions. Will you be able to protect them from everything? No. There is no way. If they skin their knee, is
it your fault? No. You to learn to do these things, and it is important for you
to learn to do them for yourself because you yourself are living in fear. As
you live in fear, you communicate to your children that this is a fearful place
to be. What you want to do is to give them simple guidelines of what to do:
"You go down this street, you don't go in here, you don't go into the restroom
unless you have somebody with you."

You teach teenagers to be careful about accepting drinks at parties, how to
protect themselves from being given drugs That's what's happening in our society. You don't do it in fear, but in awareness. You teach them to open the can
of soda themselves. There are other things you need to teach them these days.

Your government is now transmitting not just information, but fear. If you
learn how to transmit information rather than the fear, you have a whole different perspective. As you learn how to transmit information and not fear, you
will find yourself being less fearful, which will make your children less fearful.
But awareness is a good thing. Do you have another question?

## HOW CAN I DEAL WITH ANXIETY ABOUT TIME?

*I am just at a point where I have a fear of time. I feel that I am in this world, in this dimension, and I cannot handle the time. I put myself now in a situation where I need maybe forty-eight or seventy-two hours each day. And I want to know what is the meaning of this? What do I have to learn? I am completely lost in this moment about time and all the moments.*

Again we are dealing with the concept of frequency and vibration. Have you ever noticed that when you are not anxious about getting somewhere that you get there faster? Time changes. A little trick is to be in your heart center, to live from your heart center, and you will find that time can expand and contract according to your needs. You are actually somewhat in control of time, because time is an artificial structure. Ah, you are asking how it could be artificial. But it is. If you read about those whom some people call saints or what they call mystical experiences, you will find accounts of very fast, even instantaneous, travel. It has to do with the frequency, the vibration, of where the planet is at the time. As you are able to stay in sync, as it were, which means to be in your heart and to realize that what will happen, will happen, then you will find that time changes as you need it. Yes, you could get your seventy-two hours. When you become anxious about where you're going to be, what is it that you're anxious about? It's probably that you're not going to be there, you're not going to get it done and so you are creating not having it. If you have in your mind that you're going to get exactly what it is that you wish and you're not anxious about it, then you have in your mind that you're going to be there—or to do this. And it will get done. And that which doesn't get done doesn't matter anyway. [Laughter.] Is there another question?

## ABIDE IN PEACE IN YOUR OWN HEART CENTERS

*When we become more aware of how we are actually contributing to these anxieties and fears, we can de-contribute to it. You can take back from that situation. One thing that helped me with my son—because my wife and I are both worriers—is to understand and to trust that when you send the kids out, they're not alone. They've got support. They've got their own support, and they've got the support of Amma. So that should help you to relax a little bit. And it's the same issue about the time. You wonder about these amazing people and how they get so much done? They do exactly what Amma is saying. Time, in a sense, doesn't exist for them. The only thing that exists for them is the Now. Now is a timeless instant. There's no issue of time. You create that so you can create something else.*

Yes. Anyone have another question?

*This is a personal question. In the past couple of weeks, I've been spending quite a bit of time at the altar in my heart. I've started to discover a stillness that is present all the time when I'm there, and it's changed my whole perception. It's changed the way I experience life here on the planet, and I was just curious as to what it was. Is it consciousness and love? I've been trying to process what it was, but it is a stillness.*

Let me just give you a hint as to where to begin looking. Talk to [another member of the group] about the Ain Soph.

Now, dear ones, it is time for you to practice and receive as you practice. I wish you to bring either an aspect of yourself when you were wounded or an aspect of someone you believe you wounded. When I say "aspect," I'm talking about an age or an event—they're all aspects of yourself. Don't dwell on it; just bring it to mind. Now get in touch, through your heart, with your own spiritual essence—who you are away from this body of yours, that part of you that is left when this body is no longer here. Now ask for the energy, the consciousness, the love, the grace—whatever you wish to call it—to come into your crown. Come to your heart, and ask that just the right vibration and exactly the right frequency be placed within this mixture. And now send it from your heart to the one that you have in mind, whether it is yourself now, yourself as a child or someone else. Just do that now. I'm going to have you multitask now. Continue bringing in the energy and ask that exactly the correct frequency and vibration be mixed with that wonderful energy and send it to each person in this room—from your heart to their hearts. You will have energy going to each person in exactly the way he or she needs it. Notice as you are doing this that your own heart opens, and there is healing there.

And, dear beloved ones, know that you are beloved and that you are love. I am Amma, your mother, the divine mother of divine mothers. And you have come from my womb.

# 12

## *Understanding Your Encodements*

### *December 2003*

*G*ood evening, my children. It is so good to have you here. I know that many of you have been feeling heavy the past week or so. Is that correct? Many energies are coming in. The higher vibration energies coming into your body "loosen" the lower vibration energies, similar to running water into a skillet that has had something burned in it. That is part of what the heaviness is. You are becoming aware of it.

I'd like to continue our discussion of development, of becoming aware of consciousness and how the energy field of the human person develops. Since we rarely meet on a full Moon, I'm going to talk about the astrological influences of development. As you know, many people believe that astrology is a hoax. They don't see how there could be any influence of the stars, planets, Sun, Moon or asteroids upon the human condition.

What does this all have to do with the development of the energy field of the human person? When I'm speaking of the energy field, I'm not just talking about what you know of as the aura, chakra and meridians. There is much more involved. Think of the energy field as that which is left when you remove the physical body. It would be roughly the same shape you are now. There would be another field beyond that where you would lose the shape, but it is still an important part of your energy field.

Previously we have talked about the importance of the development of the little one inside the mother. That is where the energy field of the human form begins. The energy field actually begins its development before incarnation—as each of you decided what it was you wished to learn in this lifetime, elements or

structures called encodements were placed within your field. Think of encodements as circuits. As you come into your human body, the majority of the
encodements become active. The ones not active are encodements for vocation,
professions, relationships and other such things in the future. Although I've said
this in a superficial manner, there is tremendous complexity to encodements.

## YOU INFLUENCE YOUR ASTROLOGY

One of the primary influences upon the energy field is from the stars,
moons, asteroids and planets. Your astrology deals primarily with the planets in your solar system, and many bring in the asteroid Chiron, the Moon
and certain constellations. What is not often taken into account is the influence of other stars, distant planets and galaxies. It is true that in Western
astrology, Sun signs have a tremendous influence upon the energies as they
enter into you. Why? It is because of the encodements within you. Those
energies activate the encodements in a particular manner, with a particular
vibration. You do need your birth date, time of birth and place of birth to do
an accurate chart. The astrologers will be able to map out influences that
will affect you in this lifetime.

Many believers in astrology (not those who truly understand it) believe that
these influences are predetermined, in a sense fate, and not that you can't overcome the influences. That is not true, not anymore than that you cannot
overcome the influence from growing up in a particular family. We previously
spoke of the activation of the true heart center, of the infant's need to have
the heart-to-heart connection with both the mother and father so that the
masculine and feminine energies of the heart center are fully activated. Just
because they are not activated does not mean that the individual is damaged
forever and cannot achieve wholeness. Just because you were born in a particularly difficult astrological time does not mean that you will not be able to
overcome those influences. The influences do have a definite influence—to
use the word twice—upon you; they do shape the way you are. How much
they shape you depends upon your own strength of will.

When I speak of strength of will, I am not speaking of the willfulness of
the small ego. I'm speaking of the influence of the I Am. The more you are
in touch with your heart center (and the more your heart center is activated in
the way we have spoken of before), the more you will be able to rise above or
flow with the astrological influences in your chart. You made choices when
you came here, not only of who your parents would be—this includes those
who were adopted or grew up with someone other than their birth family—
but you also planned the influences of having one genetic code and developing within one energy and then leaving that and moving into another energy
field, which would have a different effect upon the encodements. Does that
make sense?

## THE TIME OF YOUR CONCEPTION INFLUENCES YOUR ASTROLOGY

The astrological influences will do the same thing. You chose the astrological influences in which you were born. There is another astrological influence that is very difficult for astrologers to identify. It is not just the time, date and location of your birth; it is also the time, date and location of your conception. Does that not make sense? The influences occurring at the time of conception have a strong impact upon how you grow and develop energetically. Your astrological chart begins with birth. What is being mapped out in your chart dismisses the previous nine months (normally) of development. Those nine months were crucial. Correct? Your conception was under one Sun sign and your birth under another.

Those of you who know about when you were conceived will get a fairly rough idea. However, you will not know the exact time you were conceived, since conception occurs at a time later than the act of intercourse. There is a little mystery involved in it, is there not? When looking at your astrological influences, go back nine months or however many months you were in gestation, and discover what your sign is there. See what your two signs have in common and how they are opposing. The energies at the time of conception and those at the time of birth set up interesting conflicts and congruencies.

## CELESTIAL BODIES OUTSIDE YOUR CHART HAVE AN INFLUENCE

Having your chart done will give you valuable information; however, be aware that you do not have the wholeness of your astrological influences. There is the influence of the time of your own conception and the months before you were born. By the way, not only are there the astrological influences at the time of conception, but there are also the energetic influences of how it was you were conceived. Was your conception a result of an act of love with an intention to conceive, in passion having nothing to do with love, in violence, in grief? All of these are influences upon each one of you and your energy field.

Each planet, asteroid, moon in your astrological chart has an influence upon you. Do not downplay this influence. There are other factors not taken into account by most astrologers. There is a group of astrologers of whom most people are totally unaware. These astrologers are akin to members of mystery schools. They have a greater and more in-depth knowledge of the influences of the stars, planets, moons and asteroids. They have, in fact, mapped out high-energy centers of other stars, constellations and planets in other galaxies and other galaxies themselves. You have the stronger influences of what most astrologers chart for you and the more subtle influences of distant galaxies, planets and stars not incorporated in traditional astrology. Everything happens in the oneness—no matter how close or distant—and therefore has an effect upon all.

When you hear of the energy of the various comets coming through, be aware that there are great energies coming to you. Just because your chart states that there are certain influences on you, know that you can learn to flow with, harmonize, rise above any influence just as you can with the influences of your own growing up. You cannot negate the influences, but you can shape them.

Those are my short comments on the influences of astrology. Now a time for some questions.

## ENCODEMENTS CAN BE DAMAGED

*Thank you for being here. In a sense, I might look at this from a structural engineering perspective—the way we look at the conditions in which we were conceived and born as are a starting point, a set of initial conditions. Obviously, we have to have a sense of understanding about it. There was planning involved before we came in. The question I have is, how can we best use this information?*

Speaking from your structural engineering perspective, when something bad happens to a structure, the engineers want to investigate what caused the failure. They look at the data and blueprints, then find what it is that can be repaired, and if built again, what will bring the structure to integrity. With this type of information, those of you in the healing field know where to look for influences, for structural difficulties or lack of integrity. Know that whenever the energy field has encodements in place, something can happen to damage them, just as the aura, chakras and meridians can be damaged. Encodements can be damaged by emotions, incoming energies, accidents (tripping, auto accidents) and by intention. When you know there is a structure present, you will know where to look. You will do this with guidance and from your heart. Just because there is an encodement, that does not mean that the individual will automatically work from that encodement. There is free will.

Here is an example of what I mean by free will. Let's say that you have an encodement that you will meet a particular soul and form a life partner, and that soul has a similar encodement in relation to you. However, when you come to Earth, you decide to get involved with drugs. Drugs might have changed you so that you no longer wish to relate in such a way as the soul you were encoded to meet desires. Even though the other's encodement becomes active, that one chooses not to be in partnership with you. The encodement is no longer necessary, but it is still active. The one who was supposed to be your partner has an encodement for you and might have a continual longing for you. This one might enter therapy to discover why he or she has such a longing for you despite the unhealthy lifestyle you've chosen. If the therapist knows about encodements, he or she can ask for the information about the encodement and be guided to turn it off or remove it. It is that simple. The encodement might also need to be adjusted. This is one way to look at the situation structurally.

Additionally, a particular encodement could have been damaged in some way. You might not know how or where it is damaged. When you are doing your healing modality, you can ask that any encodements needing to be altered, changed, adjusted, removed or replaced be revealed to you. Allow your hands to move. Allow yourself to work in the way you are guided. It helps to know about these influences so that you can be specific in your intention.

Another interesting thing about encodements and astrological energy is that if someone is having a particularly difficult time with his or her astrological influences, you can ask the soul, "Is there an encodement you can place within the energy field that might temper the effects upon the individual?" This would be like a rheostat.

Remember that all of you here had previously planned to be here to see the end of the planet. Of course, that did not happen—you changed this original plan. You now have many things happening to you, such as having no direction, feeling like you have no purpose, because there were no encodements for this period since you were not supposed to be here. You can ask for such energetic structures and encodements that can help you. Go to your soul level to ask for direction. This is not to be done lightly and is best done with assistance. An interesting aspect, is it not?

## BE CAREFUL WHAT YOU WISH FOR
*Do you ask for the specific encodement you need, or do you just ask for guidance?*

That is a very good question. You have heard it said, "Be careful what you ask for." What people do not realize is that any time you set an intention or give a prayer of petition, you are asking for an encodement; you are asking for something to direct or amplify the energy in a particular way. You need to decide if you wish to ask for guidance or an encodement. I would suggest, for those of you who prefer to be less impulsive, that you ask for guidance first. This teaching I am giving you about encodements can be misinterpreted by people to believe that this is very simple. It is simple and it is extremely powerful. You who were raised in the Judeo-Christian tradition were brought up with the concept of prayers of petition. That is where the "Be careful what you pray for; you just might get it" came from. Where you are, you do not have the foresight to be able to see the future in the linear time. You are not aware of the repercussions of the encodements you are asking to be placed within you, although you were aware of them before you incarnated.

Imagine this room had walls that played continual movies. As you talked about the encodements you wanted, you could test them out and see the results, the repercussions for generations. And people thought it was such a simple thing to come down here and be born! There was great planning. Not only did you plan for this lifetime, you also planned for how this lifetime would affect others, how it would fit into the puzzle. You planned your life in conjunction with all these other beings, each of you here and all those reading these words. You saw the possible effect of the encodements for generations. That is awesome, isn't it?

When you pray for anything, it is important to ask for guidance. Prayer comes from the ego. Requests and desires come from the ego. There is absolutely nothing wrong with that. Simply be aware.

## FREE WILL ENTERS IN

*Could things like lifelong depression actually be an encodement?*

Lifelong depression can be a genetic influence, and it can be a change in the energy field gone awry. There are people who made decisions to come to this planet to experience the energy called depression. Depression is actually a much broader complex of attributes and biochemical, emotional and spiritual aspects than what is contained in the diagnosis. Some came in to overcome such influences, to learn how to rise above them—in other words, it was their weightlifting training program.

Another possibility is that an encodement could be damaged. Not all damages to encodements are planned. There is no plan that would negate free will. There is a plan before you incarnate, and then free will enters in. Each person gets to decide how he or she will act or react to a situation. You could make a decision to move a large stick out of the way, since you didn't want anyone to trip on it. Another person could be making a decision to walk through the room, and just as you lift the stick and turn, that person gets hit on the head. The blow could damage an encodement. Some people would say that was planned before incarnation. It might or might not have been planned. It doesn't really matter. It is one of the events that occur in the mystery, the excitement of this life you are in. It is the wildcard.

*Can encodements be responsible for blocked energy?*

There are encodements that you chose to have placed within you. There are technicians who do this. You can call them to you during a healing session to help you with this. Each of you has encodements within you to modulate the amount of energy coming within you. If you had all the energy available to you, you would burn up your body. There are encodements you chose that govern the amount of energy coming into you until a particular time.

The question I think you were asking is, "Can there be damages to encodements that cause energy blockages?" The answer is, yes, there can be. When you are doing energy healing—and you can do this on yourself—ask for the technicians who work with the encodements to come. Tell the technicians what you think it is that is happening within you; ask if there is a blocked encodement and whether it can be repaired. You might also wish to ask what the long-term effect is of unblocking the encodement.

Let's say you have an encodement damaged at birth that produced an energy blockage from that time. Then, at the age of thirty-three, you decided you wanted to change that encodement. You must realize that the blockage shaped and fashioned how you developed for thirty-three years. When you release that encodement, you will have tremendous changes. It is a major life decision when you do any work like this. As the healing facilitator, if you have someone in great distress, you can ask if there are encodements that are damaged and can be repaired, simply to change a situation. If you receive a yes, you would then ask if it was safe to facilitate this change without any long-term repercussions of which you are unaware.

## THE FLOW CHART OF ENERGY AND ENCODEMENTS

*Do various events in our lives change the encodements or change the effect of how the encodements work?*

Some of you are familiar with the flow charts of computer programs, the if-thens, the yes-nos, the on-off. The answer to your question is yes. The best way I can describe what happens is like a flow chart: If you choose this, then the energy will move in this way.

For instance, right now set your intention to bring energy up from your feet. Feel the effect that has upon your physical self. Now, instead of bringing the energy up from your feet, bring it down from above. Feel the effect this has. It is different, is it not? Now bring the energy in from your second chakra. Notice the difference? Just as you are changing where you are bringing the energy in—and it has a different effect upon your energy field, your physical feeling of it—so will the changes within the encodements and any choices you make have a different effect. Energy is. It is sent. It is brought in. It is manifested. It can change the encodements. It can change their activity. If you do not have the radio on, the energy is not coming through and you have no sound. When you turn the dial to "On," the energy comes through. It is the same with encodements. Some encodements are set to not become active until a certain point in your life cycle, or until a certain hormone or level of hormone is released, or until certain energies come into your body.

## PRAY WITH NO STRINGS ATTACHED

*What about praying for others? Are you getting into dangerous waters when you ask for something for someone else?*

That is a very good question. There has been research done on prayer. There was an interesting piece of research in which people prayed for others who were in hospital due to heart problems. What is not known by many is that there were two different types of prayer. There was prayer for the specific ailment, and there was the prayer of surrounding the ill one in love. There was not what they call a significant difference in those two forms of prayer. I can tell you that the people who had love surrounding them did better numerically, although not statistically. I want to tell you that despite the statistics, the prayer of surrounding people with love is significant. Those who simply sent the prayer of love to surround did not put "strings" upon their intention. For instance, if you were praying in this particular situation that the person be healed of the heart condition, you were placing "strings" upon the prayer. If the heart condition was not caused by the physical heart but by the emotional, healing of the physical will not bring healing to the emotional. Simply send the light, the love, around the individual.

We talked previously about bringing the energy into your crown, down into your heart and amplifying it, asking that it be the particular frequency and vibration the individual needs, then sending it out. In this process you are not saying how that particular energy is to affect them. If you ask to heal a person of cancer, the prayer goes out with a particular frequency and vibration. Healing of cancer might not be what is needed on the foundational level. If what you do instead is send the prayer out with light and love surrounding him or her, then the person is able to draw in exactly what is needed. Another problem in asking to heal the person of cancer is that you have the cancer in mind. What enters the person is the vibration of the illness, whereas if you see the person in wholeness and surrounded with light, the person's energy field is able to take in what is needed.

Yes, praying for people is a heavy responsibility. If you read your Christian scriptures, you will notice that the Master Jesus did not pray for people; he communed with his Father. He spent much time in prayer. When you look at your Hebrew scriptures, there is the place where Aaron is holding up the arms of Moses in the battle. When the arms were held up, the Israelites were winning the battle. What was happening was that the outstretched arms opened the wholeness of Moses' energy. When Moses' arms were being held, Moses was being a tremendous transformer of energy. Moses was bringing the energy through his crown and sending it out through his heart. The arms being upheld gave the fullness of his being to hold the energy.

Look at yourself right now: legs crossed, arms folded. Uncross your legs and open your arms wide without hitting the person next to you. Feel the difference. Can you not feel the greater access to the energy? Nothing is hidden. What was happening to Moses was that he was opening himself and sending out the energy.

That was a good question about prayer. Sending out love, unconditional love, means that the love has no intention formed by you, except that it should go to the other. You can give someone a thousand dollars, or you can give someone a thousand dollars and tell that person how to invest them. Which is the real gift?

## BE AWARE OF COLLATERAL DAMAGE AND COLLATERAL BLESSINGS

*Is it better to do the general sending out of love rather than the specific prayer? It sounds like there is more of a possibility of conflict in the future of the specific versus the general.*

Your government talks about the death of innocents as "collateral damage," unexpected damage that occurs in the process of the war. In a way, when you send out a specific intention, you could get collateral damage. If you send out total, unconditional love, that energy is available to the person in whatever way her or she needs it.

Now, the question is: What about in praying for yourself? What about asking for certain intentions? You have heard repeatedly about the importance of being exact in what it is you wish to bring into your life, correct? This is the same thing as changing encodements—do it with guidance. Imagine what would happen if you wanted to win the lottery. Imagine all the repercussions you can think of if you won the lottery—not only the repercussions for you, but for others. You usually think of all the things you get to do for yourself: pay off the car, get out of debt, travel, not worry about money. The truth is that the more money they have, the more people actually worry. What would it do to your marriage, your children, your children's children? This is where you look before you ask.

Am I saying to not play the lottery? No, I'm not saying that. Be aware. Make choices, but be as aware as possible of all the potential outcomes. Are you going to know all the collateral damage? Are you going to know all the collateral blessings? No, you won't. For yourself—whether the desire is for abundance, a particular job or the publication of a book—have your focus, your intention. Put in mind exactly what it is you wish. For instance, you might say that you want this particular book published; however, at this time you don't have the needed information to say the color, size, publisher and other details. Leave the details you are not aware of open, surround the project with love and wait for the universe to respond.

Ask for yourself for love to come to you. Previously we spoke of asking for the love you need, at the vibration and frequency needed for your healing. You then have to be ready for what happens with the activation. Know that as you activate those areas within you that need healing, one of the things that occurs is the release of fear—the fear you have that such and such would happen. For instance, I hear, "I would like to give my life totally to God, but I'm afraid God will require that I not own anything." Dear ones, I want you to know that if you get to that place where you give your life totally to God and you have nothing, you don't care. It is only an issue for you on this side of the decision, not on the other side.

*We were talking about consciousness in previous sessions. I've been thinking a lot about energy and information. It strikes me that although the energy is very important, I'm struggling to understand the importance of the information part. I know it is very important. Any comments?*

The information is contained within the energy. Encodements contain information. An encodement is an energy. There are, as some people phrase it, light packets of information. They are similar to encodements. You can ask for those packets of information. If you wish to know something, because all knowledge is present, you can specifically ask for the energy packets of infor-

120 Change Your Encodements, Your DNA, Your Life

mation to come into you. You will then know, and you will then have a responsibility for the use of the knowledge.

## MEDITATE FOR PEACE, NOT THE ABSENCE OF WAR

*In my mind, the world went through a big change with September 11. I don't know if that was supposed to be the end time or when the end time was. We could pick a lot of end times. The Cuban missile crisis could have been an end time. I was thinking back to some of the terrorists, Osama bin Laden. A tape of his was recently released. Statements were made by some of the terrorists: "We are doing the work of God." I know that we have spoken about being here playing this grand game. Although we know it is a game, it is very serious. There is fun to be had, but it is serious—until we get on the other side, until we are in the consciousness of the other side. It galled me a little bit, this aspect of others justifying their actions in the name of the Father and Mother and the Son. I know I don't have to defend God. I know it is all in the plan. While we are still in this game, there is the justice aspect. You still have to think of the justice. Of course, that is balanced with compassion. The most troubling thing about this is how the children are being influenced, in particular those children in the Middle Eastern countries who are being taught this. It seems this will perpetuate through the generations. It is still troubling to me.*

When people live their lives in the duality—which is what those you call terrorists and others call martyrs are doing—they have a single-minded idea, image, vision of what is to happen. It is important for you, as we have talked about prayer, to ask for love energy to surround all those considering violence these few days. This is a very important time in regard to what is happening to this planet. Know that as your country looks at September 11 as an anniversary of grieving and remembering, there are others who look at September 11 as an anniversary of success and celebration. There are those who would like nothing less than to repeat the same impact, whether here in your country or in another. This is a time to send great love. There are groups meeting in meditations for peace. That is very important to do. It is important for you as you do meditation for peace, that it be for peace and not the absence of war.

Everyone likes to believe that God is on his or her side. It is difficult to understand that God has no sides. There is no side to a Oneness, is there? There will be much pain and suffering for many over these next few months. You do not have to be a part of it, even though it may affect you. Know that. There are choices that are being made and choices not being made but being considered. Know that no matter what it is that happens, if you learn to use the tools I have given you—going into your heart, staying at the altar within your heart, being connected to the pillar of light, using Michael's sword—you can stay centered and balanced during this time.

## IMAGINE FEELING TOTALLY SAFE

Let us now spend a few moments in joining those groups across the planet who are in meditation for peace. The other day, someone spoke of her desire that everyone feel safe. This is a powerful description of peace—that everyone feel safe. Think about the feeling of safety. Imagine feeling totally safe. How would that change your life? You might think you feel safe, but I want to tell you that there is no one here who feels totally safe. Feeling totally safe means that you would feel safe to be who you are and say what you think, what you feel, what you dream. You would have the safety to explore any aspect of your-self. With safety comes freedom. Think of peace in this way.

Let us now, for just a few moments, join those in meditation. I invite you to go into the back of your heart chakra, go to the altar within, connect to the pil-lar of light and ask that the vibration and frequency of light and love that are needed for the people in greatest turmoil be channeled through you and be sent to those people.

Thank you, dear ones, for this act of love you have just finished. Thank you for joining me. I thoroughly enjoyed being with you. I am Amma. I am the mother of the divine mothers. I am your mother. Blessings to you.

# 13

## Healing the Heart Energies in Your Child and Yourself

*January 2004*

*I* am Amma, divine mother of the divine mothers, and I am your mother. You probably thought that your earthly mother had eyes in the back of her head, but I have eyes everywhere. I am always watching you—not to see if you do something wrong, but to observe you with love, gentleness and pure joy as you grow and develop.

### EVERYTHING IS IMPORTANT IN EARLY DEVELOPMENT

I wish to continue talking about this development process, this sense of becoming aware of consciousness, of that of which you are, of the love of which you are. We took a brief detour before when we talked about the astrological influences upon the development of the energy field. We brought up the whole idea of everything being important at the time of a child's conception—not only the birth time and date and the arrangement of the stars, planets and asteroids, but also everything that was happening. All of these things go into the matrix, the combination of what is happening to a person's energy field. We've talked about the importance of the heart-to-heart connection, both masculine and feminine, for the newborn, how crucial that is for the first six months. We've said that even if you did not receive that crucial heart-to-heart connection, it does not mean that you are wounded for life. You can ask for the energies of the frequencies and vibrations that are needed for healing to come in.

Now, let's take the young one out into the world where there are many energies coming in to him or her. This is at the point where the young one has established the energy field and the aura and has protected the chakras in such a way that he or she no longer needs to stay within the energy field of the parents. That is when you parents discover that the child who never used to wander far from you is suddenly on the other walk—and, of course, forgot to tell you. When the child's energy field is developed enough, he or she intuitively knows that it is safe to venture out to different energies. The child then begins the development of relationships outside the family, the one the child has been growing up in. Children get to experience what other people's energy does to them.

Some of you might clearly remember these early experiences, perhaps in kindergarten. But even at that stage, you were still a little young to be truly out of the protective energy field of your parents or another adult. That protective covering is not fully formed until about the age of seven. Children who are afraid to go to school experience that fear because they feel unprotected. One of the things that makes some teachers so marvelous is their intuitive knowledge. Most teachers do not have the conscious knowledge of being able to wrap the class in their energy to form a protective cloud or covering. With those who do, the children feel safer in learning.

## TODAY'S CHILDREN HAVE A DIFFERENT ENERGY

You are all aware of the talk about more children with ADD or ADHD. Some of you have heard the term "Indigo children." I do not wish to put a label on any children, but I want to talk about some energetic influences that are coming in. Yes, children are being born with a different type of energy field than you were born with. Your older children are being acclimated into this new energy. Many of your younger children, or grandchildren, are different. Not all of them are different, and some are different and are not aware of it.

What makes them different is the way their energy field is put together. It is of a fine vibration. Think of fine china. How many of you eat daily meals from your fine china? Isn't it usually something you take out only on special occasions and caution the children to be careful with it? That is because it is more fragile and needs greater protection. That's why it's called "fine" china. Many of the children coming in have a finer, more fragile energy field. This would not cause any great concern except for the energies that are going on, not just on the planet itself, but also in the home.

## ENERGY CAN BE NOURISHING—OR NOT

Those of you who have young children might want to consider being very careful of the television shows they are watching, the video games they are playing and the music they are listening to. Add your own entertainment, because it also influences the children. Listen to the cadence of it. Some of it is first-chakra energy, which is all right. But be cautious of media that deal with, in one way or another, the disregard for life, for wonder and for heart relationships. There are many shows, games and songs like that. You have to be aware that energies emerging from these media interact with the child's energy field (and with your own). Would you feed your child polluted food? Not consciously, right? You fear salmonella or E. coli and other harmful organisms getting into their systems. Yet people do not wish to face the fact that the vibrations coming in through television, radio, recordings, video games and computers will all shape a developing energy field in a way that can be discordant to the younger child.

What happens when you put stress on fine china? It could crack, chip or shatter. Look at some of the children who make people remark, "What is happening to children today?" These children have cracked, perhaps shattered. They might have harmed themselves or others. It has to do with these outside energies coming into their fields. These energies are not coming in from outside the Earth's atmosphere, but are being created right here. It is important to remember that.

As new parents, when that bundle was placed into your arms and you felt such absolute awe, did you not wonder how something so tiny could make it in this world? Were you not filled with the weight of responsibility—and maybe even fear—that you would be able to do what was needed to raise this little one to be a strong, healthy, well-adjusted adult? There were times, no doubt, when you became upset with yourself because you believed you had failed in whatever it was that you wanted to do for your child. All the energies that come into the child work in some way on their energy field. An energy of fear, no matter where it comes from, affects the developing energy field in a much different way than it does the energy field of an adult.

## YOUR CHILDREN ARE STILL BEING FORMED

Think of hot wax. You can put a little bit of pressure on hot wax and form an indentation that remains when the wax has cooled to a solid. It is the same with clay when it is not yet fired. You can change the shape of the clay. Think of the developing energy field as not yet "fired." It is still very malleable; it can be changed.

All these forces outside the individual react with the energy field. We are all one. One tenet of chaos theory says that a butterfly flapping its wings in Africa can form a hurricane or typhoon on the opposite side of the world. Even the smallest thing can cause amazing changes within an energy field. You have no idea what one small act of pure love can do to an energy field of a damaged child. To a child who lives in an energy of chaos that has damaged its field, an act of love can spread throughout the energy field, bringing strength and support. Amazing, is it not?

One drop, metaphorically, of the purest love can cause tremendous positive changes in the energy field of a child, because that energy field is not yet fired, solidified, hardened. It takes more of a conscious acceptance, on the recipient's part, to influence an adult whose energy field is fully formed. The adult must in some way decide to accept that one pure drop of love from another and to not discard or discount it. But a child is so open that it can cause tremendous changes. So do not be afraid to offer that love, with the sweetest smile and encouraging word, to any child you see. And know that love is a seed, one that works and develops within the energy field and can help that child.

There is much within your study of psychology about what happens to a child until about the age of five, especially in the case of severe abuse. Abuse and neglect can cause severe damage to the child that can be manifested in the adult. You who work with prisoners see that. In most cases, there has been some severe damage in those early years. Even though the abuse might have carried through the teen years, the major thing was what happened much earlier, when it shocked the energy field.

## ALL ENCODEMENTS ARE LOVE

The energy surrounding us also has something to do with encodements. There is much to say about encodements, but let's look at them as circuits. Encodements work with particular vibrations of energy. As a certain vibration comes in, an encodement is activated. Encodements of love are activated by love. Your scientists have discovered that if you take the sine wave of anger or fear and overlay it upon the double helix of your DNA, it intersects the double helix only once in a while, but the sine wave of love matches it perfectly.

Now think about your genes and about encodements. When that sine wave matches the double helix exactly, you have an energy that activates the fullness of the DNA. When you have love (or the same sine wave, if you wish to put it in those terms), it activates the encodements that are there. There are no encodements placed there that are not of love. In other words, there is not an encodement for hate. But love encodements can be damaged or fail to be activated, which can result in a person choosing hate. Do you see the difference? The key would be for someone who has this hate to find out how to activate his or her internal encodements, which are all love. These are the encodements given to you before you incarnate.

## TO ALTER YOUR ENCODEMENTS, CHANGE YOUR BELIEF SYSTEM

Remember that I also spoke of how you can form your own encodements by your belief systems. Some people call these thought forms an energy that takes form. Think of encodements as thought forms taking form; they are placed within the energy field. These types of encodements act as a circuit and can short-circuit the energy built upon love. They are created after conception. This type of encodement, or thought form, can definitely occur within the gestational period.

After you were conceived and entered into the body, you had your full complement of encodements that outline for you the circuit, as it were, that you would be interested in. This might apply to vocation or to an inclination to parenthood. It could actually be a particular personality or a particular soul, or it could be a type of personality or soul.

So there are some people who agreed to come and meet one particular person or soul, and there are others who came to choose—maybe you, maybe you. For some people, it is more set or structured; for others, it is more fluid. This can all be altered as you are growing up. The encodements that develop within you, these circuits, can short-circuit the encodement that was placed within you that would recognize the energy of the personality you were looking for. It could even imprint upon your energy field the notion that that type of personality would be dangerous for you.

## BELIEF SYSTEMS ARE SELF-PERPETUATING

Take what I am saying and think about core beliefs. Core beliefs are a structure that you have within you, similar to encodements, but more massive in a way. If you happen to have a core belief that you are not worthy, of a loving relationship, for instance, that is an energy structure that goes through your entire energy field; it is not just around your heart. That structure would need to be changed, dissolved or removed. That is not a difficult process.

*So you might choose an abuser in that case?*

That is correct. You will choose those who match your energy. That is why it is so crucial for you to realize that you are creators. You have heard the term cocreators. You are much more than cocreators—you are creators. There are those now who are very aware of teaching their children how to manage their energy, their thoughts, their feelings, so when the child is angry, they would tell the child, "You can choose to be angry if you wish, or you can choose to be another way." Teach children that they can limit their angry feelings, for instance, by setting a timer. "Why don't you choose to be angry until this timer goes off?" In this manner, children (and adults) can learn how to manage their emotions.

So, all of the energy input I was talking about—television, radio, video games and the like—these things form the structure that forms belief systems, which are more of a transmitter. An encodement is, in a sense, smaller—more of a circuit. And these core belief systems are things that go through the entire being, like a transmitter. Therefore, it transmits an energy. If the energy is "not worthy of being loved," it will attract others who will show the person that he or she is not worthy of being loved. Amazingly, that energy filters out anything that gives a contrary viewpoint.

## REMEMBER TO ASK FOR HEALING ENERGY

*So it negates all that love encoding that you originally started with?*

Yes, it can negate that. But know that love encoding is still there; it just isn't activated. This would be like an overlay upon it that can be removed, and the love encodement can be activated. Remember, dear ones, that you can bring in those energies by simply asking. If you wonder whether you can ask for this or that, the answer is yes. Do it.

What can you do as parents to counteract these other encodements, these thought forms that disrupt the energies of the love encodements the children came in with? Love them, and ask at the end of the day for the love vibrations that they need—the exact frequency, the exact vibration needed that day—to come into them. Feel yourself being a channel for that child, because his or her energy field is developing, forming; it has not yet been fired or solidified. You can counteract the negativity of that day, even your own negativity, by doing that, by asking and being a channel.

This discussion of negative influences upon the energy field is not intended to make you feel hopeless. Do not worry about your children. It is very simple. While they sleep at night, you take care of it. You surround them in love and ask for the love energy that is needed, the frequency and vibration that is needed to come into them. Those of you with young children, do you not go in and look at and touch them as they sleep? That's when you ask for that energy to come in through you. You activate it through your heart center. Use your heart center as a transformer so that it can be an amplifier. Bring it in and send it out through your heart to nullify that day's discordant energies or negative messages. That is the power that you have. This was all known several thousands of years ago. There are aboriginal cultures today, though not on this continent, who still practice something similar to this.

*Until what age does this work?*

It works until about the age of eight, although you can still continue doing it past that age. When children get to be eight years old or thereabouts, their minds have become stronger about what they want to do; they want to make their own choices. So you give them that gift of the love that is there, and they can choose—on the soul level or on a conscious or subconscious level—to accept that and allow it into their energy fields. The older the child becomes, the more responsible he or she becomes as a person in accepting the loving energy.

*In that case, would you want to discuss it with them rather than wait until they are asleep? Maybe practice it with them and give them the choice?*

Yes, give them the choice to do that. If this is something that you have not been doing all along, it might make them uncomfortable. A mother working with a preadolescent male child might encounter a less-than-enthusiastic response. Older children still enjoy your attentions, but they have to act as if they do not—they have to be tough. Some of you have very sensitive children who would certainly enjoy that process. Those of you who are grandparents can share this with your children and teach them how to do it. This is the most important thing to do at the end of the child's day. You would not forget to feed your child dinner, and this is just as crucial a feeding.

If you with young children will begin doing this, you will notice a differ-ence in them. If your children who are a little older are not receptive to it, wait until they are asleep. If they are receptive to it, do it when they are awake, because they are old enough for those decisions.

If you are working with people who are angry, hostile and distrusting, the time to pray for them and send them loving energy is when they are asleep, because the conscious role of being standoffish or staying away is let down. You are not being manipulative, because they still have the choice of whether or not to accept the energy. That choice occurs more on the soul level than on the conscious level, which is not usually aware of the soul level.

## BLESSING OUR CHILDREN INCLUDES ALLOWING THEM FREEDOM TO CHOOSE

As the child continues growing and different encodements are activated, and as they go through their educational process, whenever they hear about some-thing that is like their life dream or purpose for which they have an encode-ment, that encodement becomes activated. A child who wants desperately to go into music or art and whose life seems to be surrounded by that has an encodement for it. It can damage the field of that person if you say, for exam-ple, "You can't make any money in art." "You can't do that." "That's not some-thing to do." Instead, support your children in whatever it is. It is not your job to determine for them which encodements are activated. Your job as parents is simply to love and support them and to feed them with that loving frequency energy, the vibration and frequency they need. That is one of the most crucial things that you do for them at the end of the day.

Those of you who have adult children can still do this. You can send the energy for that day, and you can also imagine them at a particular age when they were ill, having a difficult time or something was going on in the family that kept them from getting enough attention. You can take yourself back in time (because—remember?—there is no time) and feed your child.

Parenthood is not simply setting rules and structures. You will notice fam-ilies where there is tremendous structure or rules and those where there is very little structure, and all the children turn out well. With that variation, you will discover that what is common is the thing called love. The love energy given to the child has more to do with the child's nourishment than rules and structure—or lack thereof. It is true that some personalities do bet-ter with structure, and some do better with no structure. But that is not the most crucial thing. The most vital is the love energy you give your child on a daily basis, just as you would help them with their bath and their night clothes. Maybe they're at an age where you don't have to do that—isn't it wonderful when they reach adolescence?—but you can still spend those few moments with them at night sending them that wonderful nectar of love.

## THERE ARE NO HARD AND FAST RULES FOR
## BLESSING YOUR CHILDREN

*Can you do this in the morning instead?*

Yes, you can, and you still need to do it in the evening—just as you might need to shower twice in one day, depending on what happened that day. The ideal would be to do it morning and evening. The ideal is to have a few quiet moments when you send them off with blessings every morning, surrounding them with love. These moments are apart from your normal busy routine. By blessing them in the morning, you provide the love energy for that day, and if the children have a particularly difficult day or their energy level runs low, you are, in a sense, the filling station. That is the primary job of parents—not establishing and maintaining rules and regulations, although they are important, but the total, unconditional giving of that love energy and vibration.

*Can you do it long distance?*

Yes, of course, because there is no distance. Place yourself there with them, touching them, and fill them with that love. Yes, of course, you can do that.

## RECOGNIZE THE POWER OF YOUR PRESENT BELIEF SYSTEMS

*This is a personal question having to do with my job. For a while, I've felt like this is not going where I want it to go, and it's been frustrating and difficult. I know we have discussed aspects of this, but because of the long time that I've been there, it's so difficult to back away from it. There are financial reasons and others. I'm trying to understand this process a bit better. Any tips that you can give me would be helpful.*

One of the things you might find helpful to you is to have your astrological chart done. Then you will be able to see the arrangements of your planetary and star influences that lead you to where you are going. Generally, I'd say to be aware that these next eighteen months are a time for you to form within yourself exactly what it is that you wish to do next. You have a general idea but not yet a firm idea, correct?

*Yes.*

That is what is going to happen in these eighteen months. Set yourself a goal of: "Within the next eighteen months, I am going to be making a change." It could be a change within your present job or out of it. It doesn't matter. But you are going to be making a change in being more focused and directed and knowing more of where you are going. As you work with your astrological chart, you can flow with the energies that are there. Remember that I have said that the chart does not form you into something. It shows you where there are going to be bumps in the road, where the energies are going to be more difficult-and that allows you to flow with them. You will find that your particular system works very well in conjunction with your chart. It's not something that you've really investigated, and you will be sur-

prised at how much sense it makes to you when you do this. Get several rec-
ommendations of astrologers and take them into meditation before you
choose one.

*When working at the belief system and trying to separate it from the different layers of encode-
ments, essence and consciousness, I am having trouble figuring out where one starts and stops,
and how to see it in other people and not just myself.*

I'm actually going to answer a different question, and I think it will answer
yours. How do you know that your belief system is not something that you were
born with? Is that what you are trying to get to?

*Yes.*

Choose a belief system right now—one that you are working with. It
doesn't matter which one. There are so many to pick from, but let's go with
the unworthy one. All right, now say, "I am unworthy." Now, why do you
think that is true?

*Because I'm not worthy to receive it.*

So you are not worthy to receive it, and what you do is form this idea, this filter that might say, "That was not really Amma who sent me that. That was this
one I'm speaking to. She's sending that and just doing that because she's a therapist and she's supposed to do that. It's not because I'm worthy." Do you see how
you can rationalize yourself out of it? Let's say you are grocery shopping and discover that the store is out of your favorite kind of ice cream. You can take that
belief that you are unworthy, and you say to yourself, "I just wasn't worthy
enough to have my favorite kind of ice cream." You could have said, "Oh, they
are out. I'll have to get it somewhere else." But instead you form a judgment
upon yourself that reinforces your belief that you are unworthy. A person might
give you a compliment, but you say, "Oh, he doesn't mean that. He's just trying
to be nice to me, but I know the truth." And that's how it goes. Does that serve
you? Does that make you happy? Does it do anything in your life to help
move you in a positive direction? Is it of love? No. Then it is definitely not
something you were born with. It is something that you took on. It could have
come from your parents or their parents, or it could be generational or hereditary.

A belief system that does not do for you what you want it to do does not
need to be part of you. It's that simple. Only things of love and things that
serve you need to be part of you. There are things of love that might not serve
you anymore. For instance, you were taught in love that it is dangerous to cross
the street and not to do it without mommy. Even though that is of love, as an
adult it does not serve you. You could retain belief systems as you grow and
develop. In the first years of school, you learn about numbers. Your teacher
might use apples to represent this numeral four, and then you learn that you
can add these apples and these apples (these two numerals) together, and you get

this numeral. After addition, you learn subtraction and those things called frac-
tions and it goes on and on. It is not that what was told you originally was
untrue, but rather it was the beginning of things. So you will have belief systems that say you can deal with numerals only as apples, but you realize later
that you can deal with numerals without apples. You grow, and belief systems
can grow. You don't need the immature ones. By this, I'm talking about development, not a judgment of immaturity. Does this help?

## YOUR BELIEF SYSTEMS ARE SUBJECT TO CHANGE
*Yes, but how do you release those beliefs?*

To release the belief is to recognize it, to become the observer of it. You go
to the market and your favorite ice cream is not there. You think, "It's not here
because I'm not worthy to have it." And then you stop and think, "Oh, I
thought that because I have this belief system of not being worthy. I choose not
to have that belief system anymore. The ice cream is not here because they ran
out. It has nothing to do with whether or not I am worthy." And then, when
someone gives you a compliment and you begin to negate it, you stop and
remember, "Oh, I'm negating this compliment because I have a belief system
that says I am unworthy. I'm going to act as if that compliment were true." You
can then begin to act as if you were worthy. So the first thing is to become
aware of the belief system and then observe it. You can use some meditations
to help you change the energy once you have gotten in touch with the belief
system, and replace it with what you want to have. What would you use to
replace "I am unworthy"? "I am worthy."

So, what is worthiness for you? How would that look? How would today
have been different if you believed that you were worthy? How would you feel
different? Would your posture and movements be different?

There is a saying of not judging your insides by someone else's outsides. Have
you heard of it? Basically, what it means is that you judge yourself to be not self-
assured because someone else looks self-assured and your insides say something
different. You don't feel self-assured, but you judge the other person to be self-
assured, and your insides say that you want to be like that. "She's self-assured
and I'm not, so she can't be anything like me." Often, of course, if you would
talk to such a person, you would find out that he or she is consumed with fear.

Think of someone who you think looks self-confident. Do you think your
president looks self-confident? How about the newly elected governor of
California? We don't know what's going on with them on the inside, do we?
Think about how they hold themselves. How would you hold yourself? Do you
think your former president's wife looks self-confident? How does she carry
herself? Notice people who appear self-confident, who look as though they
think they are worthy. Do they walk with their heads down? No, they don't.
They stand up straight, head held high. They smile a genuine smile. Practice

doing that, and you will get the hang of it. You can fake it until you make it. And what you are actually doing is creating an energy, creating a new thought form that is going to become part of yourself. You learn how to do that. You learn how to think as someone who is worthy, who deserves the compliment from the one next to you. "Of course it's true. Thank you." "I do know that. Thank you." If you believe that you are worthy, would you be dressed any differently? You might not know, but think about that. When you choose to go to an elegant dinner, what would you be wearing? How do you feel in those fancy clothes? Do you feel more confident in those clothes than in the ones you are wearing now? Notice if there is a difference. Then you can come to feel confident in any clothes.

## CHANGE COMES FROM WITHIN AND WITHOUT

*You talked about the new children coming with the fragile energy. Will there be a time when they will be the majority here on the Earth? Is there an abundance of them here now?*

Realize that when new aura colors come in, at first there is a trickling or there are just a few then there are more, and then more and more, and then an abundance, and then they begin to die off. You all were children at one time who brought in new energies-especially those of you who grew up in the sixties. That was a time when new energy came in and you were a part of bringing it in. So now, as these children come in with new energies, it is not that they are any more special than you were although they do have a knowing of who they are, which you did not have. You are learning it; you were not born with it. Many of them did not drink from the river of forgetfulness before they came over.

Yes, there will be a time when there are more of them. The older generation will need to die away. Those who believe that war is the only way to solve things will need to die away, or at least get much older. The younger ones with the new energies will find a way to do things in peace. They are not the majority. Those in majority now are a lot of violets, blues, yellows, greens, tans. Indigos are not in the majority now.

*The Jewish high holy days recently passed, and the last day is one of passing through the gates of life. In a discussion I had I talked about this being an opportunity for rebirth—starting over. Is that a necessary or a good thing? It's sort of a time-honored tradition within the Jewish tradition, of changing one's personality and starting over again.*

One of the difficulties of being human in a linear time frame is that life can be ordinary. If you do not have these ritual times where it is brought to the forefront that you can change and become a new person, then there is no change. The high holy days are a time when you can do that in a ritualistic, deeply spiritual manner. Another way—worldly rather than spiritually—is on your first day of January, when you think that you can change. That's what all the resolutions are about. The difference with being able to do it in a spiritual tradition is that you are bringing in the deeper parts of yourself. If you anchor that within your spirit, within your energy, within your heart, within your intention, then it is much more likely that you will change rather than just go through the gate and think that you have changed. It goes back to your beliefs.

If you want to make a choice to now believe that you are worthy and you walk through the gate believing that you are worthy but only do it to the first house, then you won't be able to change the belief. But if you walk through the gate believing yourself to be worthy and carry yourself throughout as being worthy, then you will find that you are worthy.

## GIVING GENEROUSLY ENHANCES THE FLOW OF ENERGY

*I would like to know more about tithing, that 10 percent you give the church from the money that you make. Would you please tell me a little bit about that?*

Realize that the 10 percent is a monetary rule or guideline. The real reason for this is the flow of energy. If you hoard something, it cannot grow. If you hoard love, it is not love. If you hoard anything that is energy, it becomes stagnant and dies. So the giving of the 10 percent has to do with the return of energy, of continuing the flow of the energy. You give the 10 percent as a metaphor for giving yourself. Some people might give 20 or 30 percent. Some might give 5 percent of what they have and 10 percent of time. It does not need to be physical, monetary. Many who do not have the physical, monetary (due to belief system or soul choice), have the ability to give their time. Volunteers talk about receiving much more than they give. Volunteering is much different than sitting down and writing a check. Yet you can write a check with much heartfelt blessing.

The whole purpose of that is to instruct the people to keep the energy flow going. It does not have to be given to a church. In fact, you could decide that your church is not a good steward of whatever you give. You can make choices. Part of your 10 percent could be giving money to someone who has no place to sleep tonight. Give from where it is that your heart wishes to give.

## TALKING ABOUT TRUST, BELIEFS AND EXPECTATIONS

*Can you define trust?*

Can you define trust? No, no, no. Trust can be different things to different people. I trust that each of you will be on your path and find exactly what it is that you need to grow and develop. I have absolutely no concern at all that it will not happen. That is trust.

Let's now look at it from the human level. Trust is, in a way, a belief that something is going to happen in the way you believe it will happen. If you trust people you believe they will do exactly as they say. They will keep their word. That is a trust, is it not? Now let's say there is a person who lies all the time and your trust is that this person will lie. Trust is actually an expectation. It is a form of a belief system. All belief systems limit. There is not a single one that does not limit, because a belief system, by its nature, forms structure. Structure, by its nature, limits.

**What would we be without beliefs?**

That's a good question. What would you be without beliefs? You get to find out, don't you? In your human condition, there needs to be some sort of belief, as in believing that the chair will support you when you sit in it. Have you ever sat in a chair that didn't support you? That would be quite a surprise, right? And then, for a little while, did you not check out chairs before you sat in them? You didn't trust that they would do what they were supposed to do, which was to support you. So you can see that beliefs are a way of attempting to make sense out of the physical universe.

"I can form different beliefs and change the universe by the way I believe." That's how creation can occur. If I decide that I wish to form a universe where beings live only on hydrogen, not upon oxygen, and their bodies expel nitrogen when they breathe, then I'm forming a belief for them in that creation. Any belief changes. I am, I Am and I Am.

*I've been spending some time in the energies of some paintings. It seems like all I've been interested in doing is just integrating those energies. I'm always curious about a process I'm going through.*

Part of what is happening is that the energies coming from those paintings are activating forgotten encodements. You will notice that—with any type of art or anything that produces a shift within you—it is an enactment of encodements. When something happens and you feel something within you and it's like an "aha!" experience or a sense of wholeness, that is an activation of encodements, a remembering. You chose these encodements, and when they are activated, you remember. You can choose to have new encodements placed within you by the technicians. Remember, though, that there are long-term effects to any encodement you ask for. You always have to look further.

You chose this lifetime based on what you wished to accomplish in this lifetime and what this lifetime would build upon for other generations and other lifetimes. You did not choose this lifetime just for a certain experience. Those of you who play chess well know that you plan your moves four, five, even six moves ahead. Most people cannot do that. They do not have enough vision to be able to see that. Before you came here, you had much vision. You could see all the different possibilities or potentialities played out. And then you came here with the free will that is here to make other choices, without that memory.

Let us end this session with this blessing, my dear children. I wish you to see yourself lying in your bed sleeping, and I come into your room and lay my hand upon your head. I send to you, from my heart, the love of the exact vibration and frequency that you needed today and did not receive. And this love vibration and frequency also go back into time, for healing of the core wound that made this such a difficult day. Feel that love coming into you. Open your heart and accept it as much as you possibly can. Know that I am Amma and I have only love for you—pure, unadulterated, uncomplicated love for you. Believe it.

# 14

# The New Energies in Adolescence and Healing

*February 2004*

*G*ood evening, dear ones. How wonderful to see all of you here this evening. Some new faces are here. I recognize all of your faces, all of your spirits and the deepness of your souls, because I am Amma, the divine mother of the divine mothers.

I am your mother, and you grew in my womb, so all of you are womb mates, aren't you? You have a deep connection to one another—all six billion of you upon this planet. You all emanated from the same source and then took your different paths. You did; you took your different paths. Some of you went to certain star systems and have come back here to this planet that you call Earth, that some call Terra, that some call Gaia. There are other names for her—the Water-Filled One is another.

Can you feel the energy vibrating in here tonight? You are right in the midst of some tremendous energy that is coming into your planet. It began with those solar flares that your scientists weren't expecting to be as strong as they were. The Sun, the great masculine energy of the Sun with solar flares emanating out, projecting out—does that remind you of anything masculine? The energy that is there, the seed that is within coming into the fertile ground, which is yourself, awakening that which is already there. Just as with human beings: The woman carries the seed, the egg, within her, which is then fertilized. You already carry within you that which is being awakened even more by the energy that has begun with the solar flares. Of course, it has happened many times before.

## THE AWARENESS OF CONSCIOUSNESS

We've been talking about consciousness. Remember that I have said there is no such thing as the development of consciousness; there is only the awareness of consciousness, because consciousness is. It is there just as I Am, just as you are part of the I Am. You are simply becoming aware of who it is you truly are.

When I began speaking through this one tonight, I mentioned the aspect of you growing within my womb and the little joke about you being womb mates. What you have to realize, though, is that the little joke is about duality, because if you are separate, it is part of duality. Remember that there is no duality in the greatness of the All. There is duality here on this planet. And that is what you all are becoming aware of—the lack of duality that is in the All.

You are growing and developing in consciousness—and when I say "develop" in this way, what I am speaking of is the development of the awareness. We talked about the importance of astrological configurations and their importance at the time of your conception. We've also spoken of the energies as they develop within your system and in the world and as you grow and develop in childhood. Then comes that wonderful phase known as adolescence.

What a wonderful time adolescence is. Not too many of you enjoyed your adolescence, did you? It is a very difficult, tumultuous time. I enjoyed your adolescence. Those of you who are parents, remember how you enjoyed watching your toddlers learn to walk, how you would laugh with joy as they struggled. You would laugh at their frustrations and anger and fears as they fell while trying to walk, because you knew that they would accomplish that great feat. With the second child, you even dreaded that accomplishment, because you knew your hands would be even fuller than before. And I use "dreaded" lightly, because you knew what was coming. No longer did you wish they would walk early.

Well, dear ones, in adolescence we watch you with great fondness, great joy. And just as you would laugh with mirth when your young ones fall on a very padded, diapered bottom—not laughing at but with—we do the same. As you called it struggle, we watched you learn to walk in your adolescence.

## HORMONAL MESSAGES IN ADOLESCENCE

Let's talk about what is happening with the energy field at that time. In your physical body, you have these things called hormones, which come from your endocrine system. Those of you who are aware of the chakra system and its development, know that your chakras also come from certain endocrine plexi in your body. There are the hormones; chakras and their development; the astrological field of what is happening within the planets, the galaxies and the universes all at the same time; and each person within the system adding his or her energy—and people wonder why there is chaos at that time! Hormones contain energy messages within those molecules, which are so compact and filled with energy.

Your scientists who study the endocrine system have only the minutest idea of what is contained within it. Your endocrine system, dear ones, is interdimensional; it is not just of the physical essence. That is why artificial hormones work incompletely and can cause great problems within the body. The more sensitive you are to energies, the more problems the artificial hormones cause. They do not contain the interdimensional nature that is in your own personal hormones, which come through the energy field. Those hormones released by your pineal and pituitary glands can affect the seventh and sixth chakras. As the hormones affect the chakras, the chakras affect the hormones and add energy. They have a synergistic effect on each other. You don't have that synergistic effect with artificial hormones.

## YOU CAN IMPROVE THE EFFECT OF ARTIFICIAL HORMONES

Some of you are on artificial hormones because that is all that medical science has for you. They do not know how to bring in the energy. Let me give you a tip for those artificial hormones, whatever they might be. Hold them close to the endocrine system, to the endocrine glands they are supposed to replace. So for instance, if you are taking a growth hormone—and only those little ones whose pituitary glands have ceased have need to take growth hormones . . . I just want you to know these really do not work to prevent aging in the way that is advertised. That is a fallacy. You can prevent aging without taking anything of substance in your mouth. You prevent aging by taking in the prana and releasing all energies that do not serve you. That's an aside, for another talk.

So let's say you have a little one needing to take this human growth hormone, or that you have someone who is taking a thyroid hormone. Take the hormones—the pills, the drops, even the ones given by your naturopaths and others—and hold them close to the energy center of the person they are meant for. Have the little one hold them close.

Amplify that chakra. This simply means to bring your awareness to that energy center, that chakra (for instance, for the thyroid gland it would be the throat chakra.) Then spin it. Just see that chakra in your mind and spin it. Bring more light into it. Keep bringing the light into it and then send it into the pills or the liquid, whatever it is that you're taking. Some of the interdimensionality will then enter into that. Not all and not in the same way, but it will help bring greater balance to you.

What I want you to understand is that your endocrine system works in union with your chakra system, your meridian system and the encodements that are placed within you. So that is why these complexities occur. Do you think it will be anytime soon before your traditional scientists will discover how to work with that?

Let's take the typical adolescent, if there is such a thing. The hormone system is now kicking into high gear, which means the chakra system is kicking into high gear. The chakras will be spinning differently and a little bit faster. This will calm down as the adolescent comes into adulthood. It is difficult to give an exact age to adolescence because it is when the reproductive hormones kick in. It is complicated because of the artificial estrogens being used now in the food source—in chickens, beef and even milk. They are also in pesticides. And so the young girls are maturing much more quickly than is natural, more quickly than they would without those additional hormones. I will tell you that when it occurs earlier than it was encoded within them to occur, it will be a more difficult time for them. There is a triggering from artificial hormones, and they do not have the full encodement, the full energetic interdimensionality within them.

## WHAT IMPACTS YOUR ENERGY SYSTEM IMPACTS YOUR ENDOCRINE SYSTEM

We are going to discuss adolescents in this time—not adolescents in the time you grew up in or in the time of the Middle Ages. We're talking about adolescents at this time.

There is a tremendous number of artificial substances in foods, the air, water, what you wear, what you listen to and what you see—televisions, movies and the like. All of these have an impact upon your endocrine system, because they have an impact upon your energy system. And the energy system has an impact upon your endocrine system. Many centuries ago, before your industrial revolution, adolescence was calmer because the hormones were not firing off as randomly as they are now. There were not all of the artificial substances. What was the fertilizer? It was not artificial.

So today, in this century you are living in right now, as these artificial substances have an impact upon the energy field—and therefore the endocrine system—of the adolescent, what is happening is that adolescents are having a more difficult time finding stability within their lives, a much more difficult time. They don't know how to think or what to think. All of these energies are coming into them, and they cannot find stability. Think of what it is like for you in your life with all of the energies that are now coming in. Some of you are at the age of hormonal changes, and think of how difficult that is for you even as you have learned how to have some stability in your life! Yet the adolescents do not have that stability; some even lack the stability of a good home life.

What happens in the development of their awareness is that it can split off into many different arenas and areas, depending upon what they bring into their eyes and ears. What they bring into their eyes and ears is going to affect what they bring into their hearts. It is very difficult to bring love energy into your heart when what you are watching is violence. It is very difficult to send out love energy from your heart if what you have coming into your eyes and ears is violence. Logical, is it not?

## MAINTAINING YOUR BALANCE HELPS EVERYONE

What can you do as you deal with the adolescents on this planet? It is crucial for you to learn how to maintain your stability and your balance in this world as it is now. What most people do not understand is that the more individuals, each one of you, learn how to bring themselves into balance and to be stable, the more they will be anchoring that for the young ones and everyone else.

You have to do that for yourself. No one else can do that for you in the way that you can. As you anchor, you will help those who are around you, including the adolescents, even though they might be on the other side of the planet from you. Have some stability so that they can then do that for themselves. You can only be a way shower, a facilitator. Those of you who work in the healing field, you know that you are not healers. You are facilitators of healing. It is the persons within themselves who agree to bring themselves into balance, which is what brings about the healing. So that is what you can do to help this planet.

When I tell you that this is what you can do, you must realize that it is not your responsibility to do this for the others. It is only your responsibility to do it for you. And that is the paradox. When you do it solely for yourself, when you bring yourself into balance for you, then automatically it helps others. It's that simple. When you learn how to use the energy in a way that it flows through you easily, it forms a natural return of the energy. It is like the concept of tithing in different religions—that you freely give from what you have in generosity and love, and it comes back to you manyfold. That is because the energy simply increases and increases as you give freely. It then comes back to you freely even more, and as you give more, it comes back even more.

Know that it also happens in relationship with your partner. Think of your wonderful sexual act that you have. When you learn to give your energy freely to the other and receive freely the energy of the other, the synergy occurs. It moves you, and you will experience bliss that you haven't experienced before. You then learn what it truly means to be one. That's the metaphor of the sexual act, of making love. It's being one so that you can remember the oneness. You can remember that oneness.

## THE STRUGGLE OF ADOLESCENCE

Speaking of the young ones, from the moment of conception until their twenties, they struggle with discovering who it is that they are. Think of how much you struggle with who it is you are and what it is that you are to do. Your young ones struggle even harder, because everything is in flux within their bodies and it is in flux within the planet—your wars, your relationships, your countries, all of this. So it is important to be patient with these things.

When the endocrine system begins to explode, to be activated, what happens is that more energy is attracted into the individual by the energy from the endocrine system. It is like having an amplifier to catch the solar flares or to catch the energy of the Concordance that you've just experienced. That's what the adolescents have. They have an amplifier within them, which is their endocrine system, that is now attracting to them all of this energy. This energy coming in contains information; all energy contains information. As this energy comes in, adolescents are not able to sort it out and put it into its files because of where things are right now. So what they have is a jumble of information that gradually will need to be sorted out.

That is why adolescence is so difficult, because they are working through all of this information. You cannot sort it through for them. There is no way you can do this, because it is their path. You can, however, provide for them the anchoring of yourself so they can see that it can be done. In anchoring that energy, you bring a calmness and a stability to the energy. That emanates out to them and then they can anchor to that and have the space that is needed to do their own work. Are there any questions on this?

*If you see that adolescence is occurring prematurely, are there ways to delay it?*

It would not be healthy to delay it. It would be like trying to stop the baby from coming by pushing the mother's legs together. It doesn't work and could cause damage. Once this process starts, it is a way of birthing. Here's another metaphor that is not quite so graphic: You can't put the toothpaste back into the tube once it's out. So just be ready to midwife that for your adolescent. This is also true for menopause for those experiencing that process.

## THE CHANGES IN THE CHAKRAS

*You were talking about the chakras, and I'd like to relate some information I heard recently. The chakras are all integrating into one. He made a point that systems designed specifically to deal with individual chakras are, in a sense, old energy or passé. Would you comment on that?*

For a number of years, there have been people who were aware of that. The chakras, as they become one, are all about your coming into your light selves and becoming lightbeings. The individual chakras have to do with physicality in their demarcation of one from the other. In other words, they come from the duality. As you come into an awareness of your consciousness, which means that you become aware of your oneness and the interrelationship of every molecule of yourself with every other molecule of yourself, then there is no reason for there to be chakras. There is just the one light energy that occurs.

As this has been occurring over the years, that is why people who have been working with healing energy have been confused. They will use a pendulum or some such thing to measure the flow of the chakra and the direction the chakra is going, and they will be confused because it doesn't seem to make sense. They will think something abnormal is occurring. It is not abnormal in that it is not supposed to happen. It is just a development of the chakra system catching up with the awareness of the consciousness that is occurring now. It is one energy flow.

It will take some time for some energy healing facilitators to learn how to incorporate that in their work. Those of you who work with healing energies where there is no focus on a particular item, will find it much easier because you simply follow the energy. Those who work in Reiki or other directed practices will have to adjust what they are doing. They will have to adjust their thought processes and their awareness of what is happening, because it is changing. There will be no way to measure an individual chakra, because there will not be an individual chakra. In fact, another term for it will eventually come. The light tube that is going through you, your pillar of light, is emanating through you. That is what is occurring. As it occurs within you, it will activate those encodements that were placed within many of you as you meditated during the Concordance.

For those of you who didn't meditate during the Concordance, it still happened. Part of what occurred as these energies came in . . . Remember that I spoke before of those so-called technicians who work with you on a soul level, specifically with encodements? The soul level is an other-than-conscious level, a deeper level than your subconscious; it's the soul conscious level. These technicians worked to bring into you new encodements that are being activated as the energy shifts. That's exciting, isn't it? So it is within all of you. Know it is within those of you who call yourselves lightworkers, which is everybody here. Even if you don't call yourself a lightworker, know that you are one. You wouldn't be attracted to come to listen to me or do the things you are doing if you were not. Many more encodements have been placed within you than have been placed within those who are not the lightworkers, because it is not their time to become even more aware of their consciousness.

## WORKING WITH THE NEW ENERGIES

*I was wondering, with this new energy here now, if you would comment on the consequences for those lightworkers who are choosing to stay on the fence.*

It is really difficult to sit on pickets, isn't it? They will become sharper and sharper. The interesting thing about lightworkers sitting on the fence, sitting on those pickets, is that those little sharp edges get even more pointed. There is only one way to get off the fence. Lightworkers will move only in the direction of the light, and they can do that with joy and ease. This means they can either get off those very sharp pickets or sit there until they can stand it no longer.

It is simple to get off the fence—all you have to do is release the fear. You beautiful beings are so afraid of what Spirit is calling you to do. You are so afraid that you will not like it when you do it, because you look at it from this perspective that you have. You are afraid that you'll be called to move from where you are—I mean location. You're afraid you could be called to poverty. We never call anyone to live in poverty, by the way. That's your choice. What happens is that you will suddenly discover that you manifest what you need—and you need nothing more than what you need. And you want nothing more than what you want or need. It won't matter. If you could only realize that once you move off the fence, nothing matters from the perspective you had when you were on the fence. It just won't matter.

*Why does it seem like the fears come off only one at a time? Oh, I know. It's my choice.*

Yes, you answered that correctly. It is because you have a belief system that you can only handle releasing one fear at a time. Belief systems are crucial, because that is how you live your life. Most of the belief systems you have now are not choices that you make. The belief system of letting go of only one fear at a time is a belief system that you brought in from other people. You can choose another belief system and activate that within you. Release the energy of the old belief system and bring in the energy of the new. You can release all of your fears at one time. Do you think you could handle that?

Ah, see that fear coming up of wondering if she could handle releasing all the fears at once. Because if you release all the fears at one time, what's left? Can you really do that—release all the fears at one time? And will you just fly? Ah, someone over there is saying, "Uh-uh." She doesn't sound very afraid of flying, does she? So where's your fear? Are you afraid you will crash? You won't, because it is only the fears that keep you grounded—and I mean that in the way that a plane or bird is grounded and won't fly or a spirit who won't fly.

*Is one of the ultimate results of the shift that everyone will have an open kundalini and therefore have access to the higher dimensions?*

Not everyone; you must remember that there are people who are on different paths and different timelines. Yes, you will. Yes, the lightworkers will have that openness to the kundalini. The kundalini will open within them. Remember, however, that your fears can prevent the kundalini from rising through the central channel and push it to one side or the other. It is fear that causes what some call kundalini sickness or psychosis or spiritual emergency. As you work in your own personal growth of clearing yourself, the clearer you become, the more you release fear, the more you accept the powerful person that you are, the more you recognize that you are of the Oneness. Then the kundalini will have that clear central channel to move up into, and you will have access to those energies. When the kundalini rises within you, there are no chakras. It is one. It is a pillar of light—free-flowing light. There is nothing that it needs to go around, to avoid or to move.

## HEALING PRACTITIONERS AND THE CHANGES IN THE CHAKRAS

*So when we are working on a person with Reiki or energy work and we are getting different readings as we scan the body, if I'm understanding correctly, the chakras are functioning totally differently. They are throwing us off. My question is, will everybody fall into that Oneness? You just said that it will depend on the individual level.*

And here comes the conundrum of the work that you are doing. First, as you connect heart-to-heart with your client before the session begins, it is imperative for you to be totally aware that there is change and flux. Trust in your inner knowing.

When you scan the individual, you have in your mind what the chakras are telling you at this time. Now that you know this, you have additional information and you can ask, "Okay, there's a change here. Is this change appropriate for where this person is at this time, or do I need to assist him or her in bringing it into balance?" When you have that in your conscious awareness, then as you lay your hands upon the person and send him or her the Reiki energy, your awareness that there is not a pathological imbalance but rather just a need to be balanced to the new energies will change the Reiki energy that you send out. Your awareness will do that.

What is incumbent upon you to be aware of is that different people will be in different changes at different times. Your fence sitters will have a much more difficult time in helping these energies come into balance, because you cannot balance while on the fence; they are going backward and forward and backward and forward. Your being balanced will help bring them balancing energy. You will still be working with people with pathological difficulties within their chakras, and you will need to work with them in the same way you always have.

It will be a little bit more difficult for you, because you will have to be much more aware of what is occurring. Before, people were pretty much the same, so the energy did not need any real adjustment. Now you're going to find that your consciousness, which always adjusts the energy, needs to be more aware. You will become a more powerful healing facilitator than you were before. People will notice the differences in what you are able to help your clients accomplish compared to what other Reiki masters can accomplish. This is because they are caught within the belief system that "this is how it is and this is the only way it is." How it was is no more.

## BALANCE AND HARMONY WITH THE INDIGO CHILDREN

*I have a comment and then a question. In all the confusion, I have just surrendered and said that I am a pure and perfect channel or vessel. Talking about the adolescents, the children, what about the Indigo children who are coming in as masters? Where are they as far as what we were talking about a while ago?*

The Indigo children are much more sensitive to what is going on in their physical bodies than you were as an adolescent. They have not forgotten their interdimensionality. They are much more prone to being moved back and forth by what they bring in through their eyes and ears. You are all aware of the Indigo children who have been totally out of balance. Those are the ones who end up in death and destruction. Those who are able to stay in balance are the ones who can facilitate tremendous healing in others because they are able to keep others in balance as they bring in this information.

*Do we assist them in the same way—by first being balanced and harmonized and staying so? Does that still apply?*

Yes, you need to stay harmonized and balanced. The other thing you need to remember is that you need to speak directly to Indigos from your heart and in absolute truth and integrity. You do not tell white lies. People will often tell white lies so that children feel better. That will only serve to show an Indigo child that you are not trustworthy, in which case you lose your validity with that one, because their endocrine system, their energy field, can tell the energy of the untruth. The white lie will not affect children who are not Indigos in the same way—and there are children who are not Indigos. The Crystal children who are coming in do not care. They won't be affected by it. They recognize you and accept you for what you are. It's not that they will trust you, because they will know you are not to be trusted, but it will not throw them off balance as it will the Indigos.

## SOME QUESTIONS ARISE OUT OF FEAR

*My question is about some of the stuff that's going on in my life this week—where I am physically, the people I'm with, the place that I'm in. I'm aware of what it is that I'm there for, but is there something else I should be aware of? I hope this makes sense.*

Be aware that you need to release the fear that you're not aware. Be aware that you need to release the fear that you will be losing people if you do not help them in the way that you believe you should. There is no "should" to being present. Be aware that part of what is happening physically is that you are letting go of childhood fears.

*That does not resonate at all. I'm sorry.*

That's okay. This fear that you are talking about, does it have anything to do with being part of the One?

*That's one of the things that comes. I'm in the middle of a court trial. I've been aware of the One and that I'm part of all this—even to being part of the jury. All of this stuff that's going on is going on with me because I'm part of the One, and so when you said, "Release the fear," it didn't seem like it had to do with me. But it does have to do with me if I am part of the One, is that what it is?*

Yes, it is that.

*Okay, then that is better. Thank you.*

## INDIGOS AND HEALING CONSCIOUSNESS

*The more we raise our consciousness, the more consciousness around us will be raised. With the Indigos, how does this work? Where is their consciousness?*

With the Indigo energy, there is the awareness that is there. They are still in a human form. It is an energy that comes in with the human who interacts within the human form. So yes, they have an awareness, and yet at the same time they can be convinced that it is otherwise, just as you can have an awareness and someone can convince you that it is not true.

That's what happens when Indigos go out of balance. They are then struggling with trying to know what is truth. They thought they knew and they've been lied to. The violence that you have in your world that comes in through the visual and the auditory is a lie, so it can throw them off balance.

*Getting back to the healing techniques . . . it has been said that machines, widgets, techniques and procedures are secondary. There are other things that are primary. I take it that the primary things are the heart-to-heart connecting and the balancing. Is that correct?*

Yes.

*Okay, that answers that.*

I'd like to comment on your information that things are secondary. Those of you who work with the non-directed healing practices have already found that there are certain people attracted to that. The others need methods; they need the secondary. So you will find that the people who are attracted to the non-directed healing practices are those who are much more aware of what consciousness is and of who they are, even if they can't concretely say it. Those who come to the people who do Reiki, or who are gynecologists, oncologists or endocrinologists, need a form of a tool. So that is how it is moving along the continuum of becoming aware of the healing modalities that are there. There are those who need the implements of traditional Western medicine. If they were raised with Oriental medicine, they need the implements of that tradition. Needles in either case, right?

There are those now who believe they do not need those kinds of instruments, but they do need things, such as homeopaths or the laying on of hands done in a certain way. You will find that the reconnective healing that is being done will not be the sole method used by the people who come to it. When they get a cold, they will seek other methods rather than reconnective healing, because they haven't fully acclimated within that energy yet. So they might seek out their traditional physician, acupuncturist or Reiki master. As people become more aware of their consciousness, they will then go to someone who can help facilitate their awareness until they are able to do it for themselves.

## THE NATURE AND CHARACTERISTICS OF CONSCIOUSNESS

*I want to talk a little bit about cosmology and physics for a minute. The physicists are pulling their hair out trying to figure out why we can only observe 5 percent of the universe, and there is a lot missing. How does this relate to consciousness in terms of the chicken and egg? Which comes first, or how are they related? Is consciousness the stuff of the universe—the stuff of creation? Or is it that consciousness emerges out of the stuff we can't see—the dark matter, the dark energy?*

Consciousness is the stuff that gave birth. Consciousness was first—that is the primary. Another name for consciousness is God. Another name for consciousness is life. Another name is light. So consciousness is the fertile nothingness.

*One of the things I'm struggling with is how we get others to expand their consciousness. What are some ways to do that? I'm speaking of the underlying, which is that the consciousness, the understanding of the consciousness and the understanding of the interconnectivity—which is primal—comes first. When people understand that, when people get a glimpse of that, then they are seeing their own power to get rid of their cold or whatever.*

Use yourself as your own research laboratory. What is it that will help you expand to the place where you no longer need that? Thanks for throwing it back!

### THE QUALITIES OF EVERYDAY ENERGY

*Referring to what you were talking about earlier, pushing the energy into the supplements we are taking. In my case, it's the thyroid. Is there anything I need to do in addition to that to regain my energy?*

First of all, know that part of why you don't have a lot of energy is because your body is exhausted from trying to assimilate all of the energy that is being bombarded into you at this time. Is there anyone here who has felt rested when getting up in the morning? No. Not even the dog! What is happening is that you have a physical body. It is having to assimilate this new energy, and it takes energy from the physical to assimilate the energy that is coming in from the ethers and atmosphere.

Part of what will help you to have more energy is to stop resisting not having energy. You use up energy in being frustrated that you don't have energy. If you were to get locked into a room like a safe, you would want to not become hysterical, because you want to keep your breathing slow and not use up all the oxygen. In this case, preserve as much energy as you can. Be in a place of acceptance that this is what is and that you can't change that at this time, except by accepting that this is what is. Slow down a little bit.

In your society, where there are only sixteen hours to a day now, they want you to speed up. The world wants you to speed up. Because it wants you to speed up, you don't have as much time to assimilate the energy. Therefore, you're much more tired. You use the time at night when you are not involved with all of the mental things of your job, when you think you're sleeping—at least when your eyes are closed and your consciousness is off a little bit—your body is using all of that time to assimilate the energy. And so you wake up tired. That is happening to all of you.

*I've noticed that as my energy level rises, I don't use my brain to remember anything much anymore. I don't remember things and don't even care to remember things. Would you care to speak to that?*

You in this country, and in this world, talk about the information age. The information that is necessary for you to know personally is not in your brain.

You can put it in there; you can shove it in there. What you need you can pick out of the ethers. You can access it. It is around you. You are swimming in consciousness. You simply need to learn to access it. Since none of you yet has one chakra, you access it by going from your heart and your third eye and bringing those together. Then you can access that energy much more easily. And trust that inner knowing of yours. Trust it. Use it. Experience it. Know that even when you get information that doesn't seem to make sense at first, maybe as time goes on, it will make sense.

## DARK MATTER, DARK ENERGY AND HUMAN CONSCIOUSNESS

*I'm sorry, Amma; I'm on a physics kick tonight. You mentioned ether, again a topic that physicists have struggled with for well over a hundred years. The prevailing theory currently is that there is no ether. Some theorists say there is an ether. Is this related to this dark energy, and is that related to consciousness? First of all, is there dark energy? Is there dark matter? And is it related to consciousness and/or the ether?*

The ether can also be used as a synonym for consciousness. There is not a separate dark matter as in duality. What your physicists see as dark matter is actually such a compaction of consciousness that it seems dark, but it is not dark. If you dove into that darkness, you would actually experience the greatest of light. That's the paradox that is there. People believe they are in darkness before they become aware of their consciousness. You call it becoming conscious, but it's actually becoming aware of their consciousness. Once they become aware of their consciousness, the darkness disperses. That is the same thing that would happen in what you call dark matter.

*Is this in some way what might happen if one descends or ascends or moves into a black hole?*

Your scientists, your physicists, have this fear. They look at a black hole and see it gobbling up everything in its path. The gravitational pull is so strong that they believe it's going into nothingness.

It is not going into nothingness. They do see that if they waited, the black hole becomes heavier and heavier. Being in absolute oneness is an infinitesimal point of consciousness. If you put all of your galaxies and everything together in one black hole, they would weigh more than that one point within the oneness. It may seem that being a point in the oneness, making you all of the oneness, would weigh more than all the galaxies, or at least the same amount. But that is only when you are dealing with weight as in duality. There is no weight in being in the midst of consciousness.

Those of you who have dreams of flying and who have had experiences of flying out of their bodies while being fully present in their bodies at the same time have learned about weight and weightlessness. It is the paradox again that is present in the duality. Until your physicists fully bring in the concept of interdimensionality, they will be blocked from understanding why only 5 percent of the universe can be known. When they are able to go into the other dimensions, they will realize how they all interrelate. Vistas will open up to them that they cannot even dream of now. That is present in string theory. It's correct, in its minutest form.

*Do you mean that on a spatial dimensional level, or do you mean it on a metaphorical level?*

On a metaphorical level.

## DEALING WITH THE ILLUSION OF DUALITY

*Will our brains be able to tap into that or discover or find it in my lifetime?*

You will be able to as soon as you let go of the limits that your brain is encased in a skull. When you let go of those limits, you will begin to realize that in actuality, your entire being—every cell, every piece of DNA going to its minutest level and your entire energy field—is a "brain." People will differentiate between the mind and the brain. If you will actually focus on "mind" and not the physical brain and learn to use the mind, you will be able to tap into all of that right now, if you choose. You do not need this one to have me come and talk to you any more than you need any mediator to come and speak to any aspect of Spirit. You simply need to release your limits that others have placed on you and that you have accepted.

It is a major shift for you in this physical world of duality to realize that there is only the Oneness. Once you realize that the pain and anguish are all one, then you can watch with peace and joy that which others call pain. Those of us in the spiritual world (you understand, there really isn't any "us," as there is only the One) are able to watch you and smile as you learn, even though to you it might seem to be great pain. It is detachment but also a knowing. The way you use detachment in your world is to not be connected to what is happening. What is happening is part of you. However, you must also know that it is simply a process. You are not going to lose me, and I'm not going to lose you. I know that there is only Oneness. You hope there is only Oneness.

## HEALING AND A DEEPER UNDERSTANDING OF PHYSICS

*We've talked about the dynamic and the static: the dynamic that we're going somewhere while at the same time there is the constant, the static. One of us here talked about a message he got about connecting strings and strands. Comment on that?*

I'm going to use the word "minutest" again but not metaphorically. The string is the minutest, and when you start to connect the dots, you begin to get the strands. If you were a microbiologist, you would go into the very essence of the cell, into the very DNA itself. Take the proteins that make up the DNA as the strings. As you chunk outwards, you become aware of the awesomeness of what consciousness truly is. As you connect those strings to make strands, you are going to become even more aware of how easy it is for you to help balance the energy in a person, because what you are actually working with are the strands in an individual. The connections they have already made in their energy might be—using a metaphor—misconnected, so that where they should be head-on with each other, they are at an angle.

That's part of what you do in your reconnective healing when you are balancing the energy. When you are moving your hands, you are finding the imbalance. When you are moving to bring balance in the way you are led, your whole mind is connected to that individual. You are using what you know (some call it intuition), and your hands are following. It is the movement of joining and oneness in bringing that balance.

*This has to do with an aspect of my research and the immune system. I know that I'm heading for that ravine hoping there's a bridge there. It's just difficult. I don't know if I'm headed in the right direction.*

As you continue in your research, you will find the bridge. It's there. You will find it. You might have to move your focus a few degrees, but you will find it.

## QUESTIONING THE LEFT BRAIN/RIGHT BRAIN CONNECTION

*I've been reading a book about left brain/right brain. I'm thinking it's symbolizing consciousness versus duality, and I'm trying to figure it out. I'm wondering if victimization and oppression are caused internally by the left brain controlling the right, or what.*

You are on the right track. Left brain/right brain is actually a metaphor for duality. When you are functioning as a whole brain, there is no left brain and right brain. The left hemisphere, the right hemisphere, the corpus callosum, the triune brain—they all work as one, just as your body does. As it moves, it works as one. When it doesn't move as one, you have a difficult time standing up or staying healthy. In talking about victim consciousness, you have information that was being fed to your left brain, and then you have a right brain that didn't integrate that information but took it in and believed it. You formed an energy matrix within yourself called victim consciousness.

Since your brain works to bring about whatever you believe, all you have to do is say, "I am a victim." And your brain says, "Okay." It makes no judgments. "Okay, you're a victim. Let me act in that way." Sending that information to the right brain, it attracts things that reinforce that you are a victim because that's what you believe. You could say instead, "I am a powerful being of self-determination." But you will go, "Oh, I can't believe that," and then your brain works on that one. But if you say, "I am a powerful being of self-determination," and you stand there and are a powerful being of self-determination even for that instant, your brain says, "Oh, that's what it is; then let's make it happen." There is no judgment. The brain brings about what you choose. That is where the concept of affirmations came from. They say that if you keep repeating certain affirmations, this or that will happen.

The problem with that is that you are using only your left brain when you are repeating those affirmations. You also need to use the right brain and bring in the images. As the information goes back and forth across the corpus callosum, you can bring it into a unified whole. So you have to use all aspects of yourself. You have senses—auditory, visual, kinesthetic, olfactory—and the more you bring every one of those senses into your affirmation, the more your whole self comes into alignment to bring that to you. So what you can do is say, "I am a powerful being of self-determination," and feel it, taste it, walk it, speak it, live it. Then it comes to you. And the energy consciousness of victim starts to dissolve, because you can't have both at the same time. "A powerful being of self-determination" will replace it. It's really rather simple.

Well, dear ones, this has been an interesting evening, has it not? Lots of learning is occurring. I would hope that you would realize—yet I know you do not fully realize—the beautiful beings you are. I hope you can feel the light that is coming out of you. You should see it with its multitude of colors. Choose for next month, even choose for tomorrow, even choose for just this evening to believe that you are a powerful being of love of many colors and that this world will be less without you. It would never be the same.

Now, dear ones, I send love deep into your hearts. I send that love into the depth of the altar that is within your hearts, the altar that is the sacred space where you can tap into all the mysteries that you have wondered about—because there really are no mysteries. My blessings to you.

# 15

# The Energy Field of Young Adulthood

### March 2004

*G*ood evening. How good to have all of you here! The winter solstice is coming, that time of wonderful energy—the dark night, the longest night. The longest night is the time for the start of new growth. Are you aware of that? Most people think it is spring. But think about planting seeds. You plant something in the darkness: the child is conceived in the darkness of the womb, seeds are planted in the darkness of the soil. You have such a thing known as the Dark Night of the Soul, when people feel such anguish, such depression—a feeling of being lost, listlessness, aimlessness—as if something's wrong with them. Several centuries ago, they didn't think something was wrong with them because the whole of Western society was geared toward spirituality. People loved to sit in taverns and talk about theology. These days you don't do that, do you? So it's all coming back; now we're finding that people are starting to talk about theology and physics again.

## PLANT YOUR DREAM IN THE DARKNESS

As we approach this time of the longest night, it is a time to think about what you wish to plant in that darkness. What is your dream? What do you really want to be? To do? It's the time of darkness in which you can gain clarity. In today's society, you are not receiving enough darkness. If there were more darkness, you would sleep more. If you slept more, that which has been planted within you would have time to grow and develop.

How many of you are aware of your dreams? How many of you find that you don't dream much at all? Perhaps you don't remember. This is because you don't have enough time to sleep. I'm not talking about just one day; I'm talking about continually. If you lived in a place with no electricity, when would you go to bed? Tonight you would go to sleep at about 7 P.M., right? You would probably wake up at about 5 or 6 A.M. All that time you would be spending in your inner self, letting it ferment and grow. That is what happens in the darkness. How do you think a baby would grow in the womb if there were a light shining on him or her all the time? Not very well. The darkness is necessary.

The darkness in your spirit is needed. It is a time when turmoil is going on because there is no light or clarity coming in. In your society, you have been raised to think that you need to know exactly what is happening—know your direction, know where you're going. You are not comfortable with waiting. Farmers are more comfortable with waiting. Those of you who have had children in the womb, you have had to learn something about waiting. What would have happened if this little being, this little life form, came out of the darkness too soon and was not fully formed or big enough to survive? Think about that. Use that metaphor for your own development.

Dear ones, be comfortable with the waiting. Your discomfort simply comes from your judgment about what is happening. It's simply your judgment. You have a judgment that things must be just so and that you must have clarity about everything. Do you know that if you should have clarity about what is happening, you will? If it's not time for you to have clarity, you won't. It's very difficult to put a garment together if you do not have all of the thread, the material, all of the pieces. So you let it come together. This is a principle that is often taught in what you call the New Age, but I doubt if anyone really abides by it much. Most of the Earth's billions in the Western world are not accustomed to waiting.

So enjoy the longest night of the year. Celebrate it. Relate the darkest night of the year to the celebration of the Festival of Lights at the solstice—the darkness and the light.

## HOW THE SOLSTICE HAS BEEN CELEBRATED
*How has that been celebrated over the centuries?*

There was great celebration at the time of the solstice for those who were into the mystery religions, the rhythm of life with its light and dark. There were also those who were not sure exactly what the darkest, longest night meant. This increased as things became more modern, moving away from true reality. There would be tremendous gatherings in these energy points: fields, villages, places where there were large rocks. People would celebrate that the darkness was no longer lengthening and light was now going to come. It was a celebration of ending and beginning.

Think of spring—a celebration of beginning. But the winter solstice is a celebration of an ending and a beginning. There was great singing and dancing, wonderful food and drink, wonderful celebration of the physical and the body, lots of making love, lots of enjoying the laughter of the children who were there. Wonder was there—as well as connection with the Earth, the Sun, the Moon and the stars. There was a reverence for everything that was present, an awareness, a consciousness. People could feel the spirits of those who had gone before them and who were now on other planes. They could also feel the devas and fairies. It was quite different from what it will be in this time.

Depending on what part of the world you were in, there were different cele-brations. When you were in your druid period, you celebrated in that manner. There are some of you here who gathered together in the deepest and darkest places of Africa—you celebrated there. Some of you also celebrated in the cen-ter of what is known as America, mostly in Central and South America (not much would have been going on in North America). Some wonderful celebra-tions were in Russia. By the way, there will soon be archaeological evidence in Russia and in China similar to things such as Stonehenge. Some already know that it is there, but it will be brought to the fore soon.

Where were the greatest celebrations held? Where was the greatest wisdom? In Egypt. This is because there was a knowledge of tremendous power, as the starseeds were in Egypt and focused the power through pyramids. Those are some of the things that occurred. See if you can get back in touch with the spirit of those celebrations. Allow yourself to go into your heart and ask to be taken to the time when you knew how to celebrate the solstice, because each of you has known how to do that. Each of you led celebrations of the solstice, and each of you enjoyed them to the utmost.

## THE ENERGY OF YOUNG ADULTHOOD

I now want to continue the discussion of the development of the human energy field. We talked about adolescence last time. Now I wish to talk about the period you call young adulthood. In today's society, it begins about the age of twenty-five and lasts until about the age of thirty-five (it seems to take that long for the people in the West to grow up). However, if the individuals have begun to accept full responsibility for themselves and their families—that means full responsibility, not accepting money from mom or dad or needing that assurance—it can begin earlier. But here in the United States, it usually begins at about twenty-five. Your energy field is still in the area of adolescence until then. This coincides with what your psychologists and sociologists are saying—that people seem to be maturing later. Even those who are doing tremendous things, such as learning to be medical doctors, until they get their own practices and are no longer identified as students, they are still in adolescence. It is after one goes through the initial learning period and decides to study further—like you who are now studying the Reconnection or Body Talk—that there is a difference in the studying and learning. Have you noticed that?

When you were younger, perhaps in undergraduate school or something similar, how many of you would have listened to the same lecture ten times? Did you not listen until you learned a certain lesson well enough to pass the test? Yet now you listen to certain recorded lessons over and over and over because they have new information each time. Isn't it amazing how new information is found on a CD you have already listened to repeatedly? When you learn in this way, you are no longer an adolescent in your learning. No matter how old you are, an adolescent-in-learning believes that you only need to hear it once and you've got everything; you only need to study it once and you've got everything; the grade has been given and the learning is over. You have all discovered that one lesson contains layers of learning when you delve repeatedly into the lesson. Now that you are becoming more aware of what consciousness is, you will listen to something repeatedly, read something repeatedly, and you will even proclaim that someone put some new information into the same book or CD that wasn't there before. You do this even as you laugh to yourself and say, "That couldn't have happened." Ah, but maybe it could have.

## VERY FEW ARE CALLED TO A PARTICULAR TASK

The time of young adulthood is also a time when the hormonal system has started to equalize. In adolescence, when the hormones were in such an uproar, you were looking for what you wanted to do in life. People seemed to look for the "right" thing. Those raised in a particular religious tradition are often told to go inside and ask what they are "supposed" to do. Yet there are very few people who come to this planet to do a particular task, such as those who have established great movements. You have the spiritual leaders: There is Siddhartha, who came in to be the Buddha energy, and there is Jesus, who came to bring in the Christ energy. There is also Abraham, who likewise came to bring the Christ energy in. Know that the Buddha and Christ energies are one.

Please know that the Christ energy has nothing to do with what you call Christianity today, which is not even recognizable as the Christ energy because it has gone so far away from it. This is one of the things you who are working in the Christian tradition have struggled with, because you were here when the one you call the Christ was here. Know that he is not the Christ, but that he brought in the Christ energy. You have that energy within you and you can be exactly as he was. Those of you who are Christian remember that the teacher told you, "You can do this and more." You are all coming to realize this, are you not? "You can do this and more." So you have the different ones who brought in the Christ energy, and they did agree to do that.

## YOU HAVE CHOICES

None of you here came in to do a particular task. You have choices. For instance, if you are to work in the area of healing, you get to choose which area. If you've been trained in many types of healing, you can choose which one you wish to work in. Those of you in the midst of raising children, mothers especially, your primary task is raising your children. You have no idea who you are nurturing and guiding—you are not forming, but providing a bit of structure, which does give security. So you get to choose the what and how of who it is that you proclaim you are. You can do it as a healer, teacher, scientist, architect, anyway you choose. The major component is to live the truth that you are love. How you choose to do that is up to you.

If there were something in particular that you came here to do, you would feel it deep within your heart. You may feel that there is something in particular you are to express, but this is different than how you are to do it. Note the difference. You can choose how you are to express what is within you, just as an artist chooses how to express her inner feeling. This one I'm speaking through made a choice on a soul level, as she has journeyed this lifetime, to allow me to come in. It was a possibility before she incarnated, but it was not a "have to." Each one of you is filled with possibilities.

## CHOOSING YOUR PROFESSION

In young adulthood, the possibilities begin to narrow. If you stay in the realm of the possibility of specific third-dimensional tasks—and we want you to always stay in the realm of possibility of your awareness of consciousness—then we have a lack of focus. So choose your focus. It is simply choice. Know that there are some things better suited for your particular personality and encodements. There are certain energies that are better for you. Some of you would make a mess of numbers; others are very comfortable with them. So for those of you having a difficult time balancing your checkbook, I would suggest you not go into accounting. Those of you who do not like details, I would suggest you not go into engineering. These are the types of things to notice about yourself. How would you like to experience and express the love that you are, the light that you are? How do you choose to show your light? Do you wish to be a lamp or a flame or a bonfire? That is your choice. Some who are reading this will ask what Amma or Abraham or Melchizedek or Gaia has to say about it. Know that the ultimate responsibility is yours to make your choice. That is part of being an adult.

## BEGIN TO ACCEPT RESPONSIBILITY

Adults are people who accept responsibility for their choices of who and what they are. So the energy field of the young adult reflects the beginning of accepting that responsibility. The hormonal system has calmed down, for most. For some, there are damages that have occurred through life experiences such as abuse. Abuse can be physical, sexual, emotional or spiritual; it affects all the chakras and can damage one or more severely. It will also affect certain encodements. Your energy field is also determined by what you put into your body— there are those still recovering from recreational drugs and some who are still using them actively. This changes your energy field. Some will say that it brings them into areas of ecstasy or other worlds. Dear ones, please know that you need nothing to enter other planes or worlds. You do not need a tool. As long as you are choosing to use something other than going into your own self to move you into the awareness of consciousness, you are not accepting responsibility for your growth and development.

You came here to learn. Let's say that you have a particular issue in your life that is presenting itself. Instead of confronting the issue, you choose to eat sugar, which changes your chemistry so that you don't think about the issue anymore. Sugar can be just as mind- and mood-altering as what you call recreational drugs. There are also those of you who enjoy your coffee. Know that any stimulant changes your chemistry. It also changes the effect of your awareness of consciousness. Are these things bad? Of course not. There is absolutely no judgment about them. You get to choose what it is you wish to experience and how you wish to experience it. If you wish to do it through a stimulant, that is your choice.

## YOUR CHOICES SHOULD SERVE YOU

The important thing is to figure out if the end result is what you want and if it serves you. Does it serve you? You get involved with a particular activity—a particular form of meditation or exercise or program or way of learning; choose whatever you wish—and suddenly you discover that this activity is not having the result you thought it would. In other words, it doesn't serve you anymore. That's where you need to make choices. Accept the responsibility to let that activity go, and find out what does serve you. It's that simple . . . not that easy, but that simple.

The energy field in young adulthood is now beginning to stabilize—as I said before, the hormones are settling in and you are choosing which encodements to open for the possibilities in your life. For those who have not heard of encodements, they are energy circuits containing information that can be activated, similar to the decision point of a flow chart in a computer program. Each one of you has particular encodements or energy circuits—placed within you before you incarnated—that activate the possibilities you choose for your life. As you come into young adulthood, the encodements for "profession" are activating. Remember that you have encodements for possibilities of professions. Those of you attracted to details and numbers may find a profession in accounting, computer programming or composing music. You get to make the choices that activate the encodements.

At this time, many young people have the encodements for relationships activated. Since there is little or no information about encodements, people are not aware of how to get in touch with their encodements. Even though someone might initially be attracted to another, it may be that they were not meant to be partners, but rather to work through and resolve karma from a past relationship. When this attraction is misunderstood, they often marry. When the karma is finished or when it has taken over and erupts into a volcano, they do not know how to leave that relationship. It is time for the relationship to end if the encodement is finished and you have learned what you need to learn. What are your questions on this?

## THE POSSIBILITIES WITHIN YOU

*What if a chain reaction occurs? In other words, one thing happens, which leads to another, which leads to another, and the next thing you know, you are just blasted with things. You can't say no. You love it all. Then you are suffering because there is so much input that you can't choose.*

As you become more aware of consciousness, you become more aware of possibilities. You then need to make choices about the possibilities. When you have something that blasts you and you can't say no, know that it is time for you to become grounded. When you were blasted by that river that was out of control, you became ungrounded. Ground yourself. Imagine yourself setting deep roots. You are now aware of the possibilities. You have the information that is coming into you, and when you have deep roots, the information will not bowl you over. Allow the information to wash over you. Think of a bridge when there is a flood; the water rushes through the bridge. The bridge does not stop the water. It simply allows the water to go through. What might happen is that the water may get to be too high or perhaps it might carry something large, and the bridge is not able to let it go through. Then it may collapse.

As long as you allow the information to come through, then from your groundedness, from your heart and from your third eye, bring the energies together—notice that I'm saying to bring together your first, your fourth and your sixth energy centers. Many of you are now experiencing not having separate chakras; they are all as one. But until that has been fully accomplished, allow the energy of the three to move up and down, bringing them together by imagining them coming to a focus point about two feet in front of your heart. Tap into and work with those energies and evaluate the information coming through you. You can then evaluate the possibilities. Is it this book, or is it that book? Is it this method of healing, or is it that one? Where I am in my life? Is it better for me to stay in this job or to move into this job? Do that by bringing together the energies of your third eye, your heart and your first chakra.

See them come into a focal point about eighteen inches to two feet in front of your heart. What you will discover is that there is a portal there that will allow you to come into the deepness of yourself, who you truly are. You will also be able to communicate with that part of you that is not incarnated. Remember that your entire energy, your entire soul self, your spirit self, is not in this body that you are using right now. There is a part of you that is with me, a part of you that is with all your other friends or companions. Do you realize that some of those you are having the most difficult time with right now are watching you as you are experiencing life and they are laughing? Don't you just hate it on this three-dimensional world when somebody laughs at you? Yes, they laugh, but it is not the laughter of derision and not the laughter of someone making fun of you. It is like the laughter of watching a young one try to walk and then fall down and cry because he or she couldn't make it. There is a part of you that is experiencing this.

## A PORTAL TO THE ONENESS

Now try this, because this is new information. Focus on your first, fourth and sixth energy centers. Bring them together at a point about eighteen to twenty-four inches in front of your heart center. Some of you will simply need to focus on that spot eighteen to tweny-four inches in front of your heart chakra. You will find a portal, an opening, about eighteen inches to two feet in front of you. Just allow your conscious awareness to go through that portal. You will feel the difference. If you can't find it or are wondering if you've found it, try coming at it from above or below. Feel the difference. What did you experience?

*It was almost like a falling . . . I see the portal, the perspective. I'm not through it, but it's there . . . I just went right in it and was aware of being part of it all. It stood still, but everything was moving. It stood still because I was in the space of no time.*

Did you sense the other part of yourself—the part that is not incarnated?

*Yes, it was part of the whole.*

Yes, this will take time to assimilate. This is like the first time you went to a movie where you thought you knew what it was about, but later you found out it was more. Or the first time you were able to examine a painting when it became more the longer you looked at it. So try this exercise and see what your experience is. Who else experienced it? Maybe just a feeling of something? Good, that's the beginning. And you?

*It was wonderful. It looked like gold.*

Anyone else?

*The first time I went high and felt resistance and then I went down. I was trying to make sure I was at the portal. As soon as I went down, it kind of felt like I was falling. I felt very welcomed and I felt larger or bigger.*

Let's just imagine the portal being in front of you and being three or four inches in diameter. Just imagine it that way because there is really no size or shape to it. If you wonder if you've gotten into it, just come out and imagine going above or below it to feel the difference.

*Can it change shape? Is it a star?*

Yes, it can definitely change shape. How many points on the star?

*I'm not sure, but I think it's six.*

Great. So think about sacred geometry and the difference in the energies of a six-pointed star and a five-pointed one. What are the energies they bring in? What are the differences if you came into a triangle or a pyramid or an ellipse or a rectangle? A tetrahedron? There are differences in the energies. What I want to tell those of you who wish to experience this and to investigate it, is to intend for the shape of your portal to be different and to notice the differences in the energies. But do you have to go through it? Ah, isn't that the mystery of it all? Not everybody can do this portal because they are not going to be aware of it. As the awareness of consciousness comes, people will read about this portal right in front of them and more will begin to investigate it.

You can go into the portal with a question. What is your question? It doesn't matter what it is. Go into your heart, go forward, go into the portal and find the answer. Everything is there, because you are entering into the oneness in the pillar of light in front of you. That connection you had is because of this portal within the pillar of light. It is in a special place. And, of course, the paradox is that there is no place. It's there. It is a gateway into the endless.

Some of you have been taught that the area behind you is the time-space continuum. Notice the difference between that and the portal in front of you. You can go deeply into the past through the time-space continuum and deeply into the portal in front of you, which is in the pillar of light. One of the differences in connecting with the pillar of light is that it is no longer in front of you anymore, as you have developed your awareness of consciousness and have chosen to work with spiritual principles, however you have chosen to do so. It is not in front of you because you are now within the pillar of light. There is nothing you have to do now to connect to it. You're in it. It is there. Now that you are in it, what you are doing is simply finding a portal that is within, and there you go into another place, another dimension. Actually, you're going to the total All, to the Oneness.

## ASK TO BE TAKEN TO ANOTHER ENCODEMENT

There are few young adults who would be able to do this right now. But those who are spiritually connected would be able to do so. Those of you feeling overwhelmed with the possibilities right now, do this: Ask your question. Ask, "Which of these possibilities should I choose?" If you go to a buffet and leave with your stomach hurting, you were not able to choose from the buffet the possibilities that suited your physical body best. You had to have everything. Those who have to have everything usually end up with some physical discomfort, that thing you buy those purple pills for. Think of your possibilities as your buffet. You get to select what it is that you want. Perhaps today you would like rare roast beef, perhaps tomorrow you would like lobster and perhaps the next day you would like a simple tofu dish or a green salad. It can vary depending on your energies. There is no judgment; it is just what is best for you.

Enter the portal with the possibilities. Know that it is there until you are able to enter into it. Ask for information and you will be guided through the portal.

As the energy field of young adulthood is stabilizing, it would be wonderful to teach young adults how to access the encodements of the possibilities of profession. When you teach your child how to go within, which can be done at anytime, have your question in mind. Do it now for yourself. Go in through the back of your heart center and ask to be taken to the encodement within your energy field that has to do with profession. In other words, how is it that you want to possibly express your light and love in this lifetime? I've only given you a minute, but did anybody discover anything?

*What I discovered is not what I expected. Painting . . . not painting a house, something artistic. It has been on my mind, but I didn't expect it to be the first thing.*

Okay, that's great. It's something to play with. Remember, it's possibility. Now you know there is an encodement there. It is something you set the possibility for before you incarnated. It is not, as you say, just a wild card. Know that the encodement is there, which means that it was a possibility placed within your energy field before you incarnated.

*Being an editor popped into mine.*

How interesting. That's exactly what you're going to be doing. Do you trust your inner self?

*Yes, I think I will more after this.*

So you can do this exercise and ask to be taken to another encodement, another possibility. This is an interesting way of dealing with these questions, isn't it? Know that the information is there. Those of you who still have young children, teach them how to do this. Please teach them how to do this. You might have to come up with a different word than encodement. It doesn't matter what word you use. You can say circuit, if you wish. You can say computer button. You choose.

## COMMITTED RELATIONSHIPS

Let's say that you are presented with someone who is coming into your life. Here is something that will help those who are presently in a committed relationship and then someone else walks in and they feel physical infatuation. Infatuation is nothing more than a physical reaction. Let us say that you have a strong reaction to this one who has walked into your life, and you are thinking of ending the committed relationship and moving into this other one. Let's examine that. The first thing you must do is remove all judgment from either choice you could make. The second thing that would be very helpful is for you to enter into the back of your heart. Ask to be taken to the encodement that is activated by this person walking into your life, and ask that the purpose of that encodement be revealed to you. There could be several possibilities. One possibility is that you are finished with the committed relationship you are in and you are to join the other one. Believe it or not, that possibility is not the one that is most prevalent for people. It could be, but it's usually not.

Perhaps what you are going to get in touch with is some karmic reason, some unfinished business you need to complete with that person. It has nothing to do with punishment; it's just unfinished business. That means there is learning to do. You could know in the deepest part of yourself that you need to revisit this person, this soul energy. So ask if this is the case or if you are to partner with this new person. Often people come into lives to help you decide commitments. Someone could come into your life whom you have this strong reaction toward, and it's not that you are supposed to be in a committed relationship with this person, but it is time for you to get out of the committed relationship that you are in. You know this is true when you don't feel truly committed to the relationship that you call committed. You know the commitment has ended. It's an interesting way of looking at it, isn't it? I guess your religious leaders would have some difficulty with that perspective.

## KEEP PRACTICING

*I'm wondering how I can go through the portal, find those aspects of myself that are not with me now and get them back through the portal to incorporate them into my present self.*

With the way you have asked your question, realize that you have phrased it in duality. Know that once you connect with those aspects of yourself, you are already bringing that energy back to you. Let me give you an example of something that is being done in science to further explain this. There has now been research on enzymes that come from an individual. They separate the enzymes by miles and miles, and they find that when there is a change in one enzyme, it occurs in the other because it was already connected.

*As a novice, if you can't find the portal, do you just keep practicing?*

Yes. The first thing you must know how to do is connect to the pillar of light. This is very simple. Know that there is a pillar of light that comes through you from the crown. You've possibly heard of that. Then there is actually another pillar of light that is in front of you. Allow your consciousness to move forward until you feel this pillar. Don't try too hard. Relax into it. It's right there. Send a beam of energy from your heart into that pillar. It's just about six or seven inches in front of you—the distance is different depending upon the person.

As you learn to keep your energy connected to the pillar, you will find that you are in the Now. As you live your life connected to the pillar of light, you will be in the Now; you're calmer, you're in your heart and you're also grounded. It's an awareness that is present. It will activate energy within your meridians and your chakras. Work with this connection. As you gain experience with connecting to the pillar, then you can set your consciousness for the portal. Yes, just practice.

## INDIVIDUAL CELLS AND DNA HAVE CONSCIOUSNESS

*I've had the experience in the last couple of days of listening to seminars by great scientists; in fact, a Nobel laureate was one of them. It was about DNA (the fifty-year anniversary of the discovery of the structure of DNA) and about how genes are regulated to lead to the functioning of cells—in particular, programmed cell death, as we call it. As it turns out, what we've learned is that programmed cell death is the normal function that is regulated, as opposed to outside agents coming in and influencing the cell or killing it. We've learned that cell death is a normal function, as are cell differentiation, mitosis and so on. So this regulation process is very interesting, and scientists are starting to learn a little bit about it. There is something about the spirit and the machine, the mechanism of this, that scientists are starting to get a glimpse of, but they're still beating around the bush. I asked questions in the seminar having to do with self-regulation of very small entities, such as genes. How do they regulate themselves? None of that was actually discussed. It was all very linear, the cause-and-effect chain: we go from here to here to here, down the line. I asked, "Is there feedback? Do those individual entities have some knowledge of themselves and what they're doing?" I don't have a direct question, but I wanted to get your impressions about the place of self-knowledge and self-understanding at the level we're talking about—the cellular level, the DNA level.*

You'll find that those scientists will make tremendous strides when they embrace what you call spirituality—when they embrace consciousness, when they embrace the information you'll gain when you go through the portal. One of the difficulties with Western science is the belief (which is starting to change) or lack of awareness that there is consciousness in even a segment, a protein, of the DNA. The consciousness of the cells—of the DNA, of the genes—works in concert with your own awareness, beliefs and value systems, just as in a group. Think of it as group dynamics, if you will. In this small group we're in tonight, if this were a free-flowing interchange where you kept bringing in more of your own information instead of just me bringing in information for you, the group would change according to what is going on with each member of the group. It changes anyway as you each process the information I give you and try to make sense out of it, figure out exactly where this stands, what's going on in your life and how it applies to you.

That same thing happens with the cells, with the genes, with the DNA/RNA within your own system. Scientists say that the human body could really live to be 120 years old. When talking about life, some say they wouldn't want to live that long. What is their belief about what 120 years old looks like? Form your own belief now. Do you see yourself vibrant at 120, or do you see yourself in a nursing home with all your family gone? Do you see yourself just as you are now, or do you see yourself having difficulty walking or not knowing what is going on around you? Those beliefs change the function of your cells. The thoughts that you have—and those you don't know you're having—have an effect upon the community of every cell in your body.

Let's look at your body as a community. Let's look at each cell and each part of each cell—each mitochondrion, each DNA, each protein within the DNA—as a community. You are the one in charge of this community. All individuals within this community have a consciousness. Believe it or not, they don't have will, but they have consciousness. They are responding to your thoughts, your beliefs, your feelings. The whole field that looks at the mind/body connection—of course, it's the mind/body/spirit connection—is actually investigating and working with how the very DNA changes.

There are some scientists who understand what I am saying but are reluctant to speak about it because they do not want to be laughed at. Research shows that when someone is happy and in a place of gratefulness and thankfulness, the double helix relaxes. When a person becomes tense, the helix becomes tense too. When you feel tension in your body, that is communicated to every cell and to every part of every cell. People who have not studied microbiology or cellular biology are not aware of everything that is within the cell, and it has not all been discovered yet. Of course, one of the major parts of the cell will never be discovered under any type of microscope; it's called consciousness. Is that an adequate response, or is there something else you wanted to ask?

## THE EMOTIONAL CONTROLS THE PHYSICAL

*You are alluding to the holistic thing, but I think it goes farther than that, because the implication is that our dualistic structure is profound. Of course, scientists are not thinking that cells, or parts of cells, are conscious. That's one point. But you're also implying that there's something about reductionism. The prevailing attitude in science is that your emotions and your mind are a result of the physical substrate. As I read what you are saying, you're implying that there is something beyond that—that consciousness is supraphysical. That part is the real clunker, if you will, in the duality, with respect to scientists.*

Think of the ego of the human person (I'm speaking of the little ego, not the I Am ego or the I Am presence). Human beings prefer to think that they are able to think and do tremendous things and have awareness and consciousness, and that the chairs they are sitting on or the dog who is here or the cells do not. So part of what has to be blasted through, if you will, is the perception that consciousness is just in a soul that's within a human body. There is work being done on this issue, but not in your traditional, accepted sciences. The physical does not have control over the emotional; it is the emotional that has control over the physical. If your scientists would actually discuss and work with those who are working in the area of consciousness or cosmology—even mental health—they would discover that people who work holistically, as you call it, know that people can have tremendous emotional changes that will change their physical selves. I'm going to say that part of the limitation of the word "holistic" is that people put a limit on it, implying that there is something beyond holism. Those of you who work in this field, you healers and energy workers, know that what's beyond is Oneness, the All.

Some authors—for instance, Carolyn Myss and Norm Shealy—have talked about experiences with patients or clients who have totally and irrevocably forgiven someone in their lives and then cancer, AIDS or arthritis has disappeared instantly or overnight. That kind of information is minimized and not accepted as something to investigate. It is the same when you look into your research on drugs, for instance. One of the biggest research goals is to sift out the placebo effect instead of researching the placebo effect and how you can activate it, which one of your scientists calls remembered wellness. But, of course, there is no money in that. That is where your society is caught.

## AN UNDERSTANDING OF CONSCIOUSNESS IS COMING

*If we will not be able to measure the consciousness at microlevels beyond the faith issue, will we be able to get on the scientists' own turf using consciousness, using logic, using information theory? Even though we don't have the measurements—for example, we can't see an electron—we can measure its effect. Will we be able to turn the tide for them? Can you look into your crystal ball for us?*

What will be occurring is that scientists will begin to shift in their perception of what is measurable. Consciousness is no more measurable than love is, because love and consciousness are the same energy. When I speak of love, I'm not speaking of an emotion. To answer your question, looking into the crystal ball, it is coming. There will be tremendous advances made. Some have already made them. However, the whole of science, the part that's encased in concrete, has not been able to accept it yet. But it is coming. It is coming.

*In utilizing this consciousness for healing and in understanding that if the person to be healed blocks it or is not ready for it, then he or she will not receive it, we know, we have a sense, we've learned that consciousness is a powerful force for healing. Is there some way we can change that spontaneous healing you were talking about before, which occurs probably 1 percent of the time, into something that could be 10 percent or 50 percent of the time? How can we move that probability up with what we do as healing facilitators?*

What needs to be done is actually beginning to happen, and you'll find it occurring even more quickly since the Harmonic Concordance. It is imperative that people become aware of the power of their thoughts and of their words, even very simple things like, "I'll never be able to get well." As the healing facilitator, ask if they could entertain the possibility that they could be well if they could even begin to verbalize, "I hold out the possibility of health," which is different than, "I hold out the possibility of not being sick." Ask them if they could imagine in their mind's eye what they would look like if they were healthy right now. If they are not able to do that, ask them to form a memory of a time when they were healthy. These thoughts would begin acting on the consciousness of the physical. If they are not able to do that, they need to see someone who is trained in the area of helping them get in touch with belief systems and how they work. Remember that not all who have been trained in therapy are able to work in this way. You have to be working with those who are able to bring together the notions of energy and thought and consciousness, along with mental health.

Let us end this session with a special blessing of those who have committed themselves to being with you this lifetime, those whom you call guides. Feel them surrounding you. Feel their love entering into your heart. Absorb it. Know that the reason they are able to love you so much is because they are aspects of you. Good night.

# 16

# The Energy of
# Sexuality and Spirituality

*April 2004*

*G*ood evening. It's so good to be here with all of you. Ah, still tired—still tired, aren't you? Yes, it's going to continue for a time. It will continue, these energies that are coming in. Do you remember some time back when I talked about how you could have new encodements placed within you? I'm going to talk about that. The information I'm going to give you tonight is information you can use in your daily lives, if you choose to do so. It's all a matter of choice, isn't it?

Last month, I talked about how you could go inside and ask to be shown or have revealed to you encodements regarding alternative professions. What I want to show you is how you can call in those who work with encodements, the technicians, and how you can have the encodements adjusted, changed or removed and have new energies placed within you. Know that the encodement technicians (you can call them whatever you wish) have been working mightily over the past few years, because everyone has had new encodements placed within them.

It is true that before you incarnated, the probability was high that this planet would not be inhabited anymore. Earth would cleanse herself, and you all would have instigated that cleansing by annihilating one another. That very high probability was changed. When you incarnated, you knew it was a possibility that you would change the direction from destruction, but it was not a high probability.

What you have done is very momentous. It is true what you hear from other channels: Everyone is watching what is happening on this small planet. A wonderful experiment in consciousness and how consciousness is and can be used is occurring. Remember, you do not develop consciousness, but rather become aware of consciousness.

You will become aware of how you can use these energy circuits I call encodements. They are very powerful energy circuits. All of your life works with these encodements: who you're attracted to, who you're not attracted to, who you are repelled by. Even karmic influences are placed within your encodements: what you are attracted to in regard to profession, what you are avoiding in regard to profession. You outlined all of this according to what you wanted to accomplish in this lifetime. One of the reasons so many of you have done so much in such a short period of time is that you knew the probability of this lifetime being shorter than some other lifetimes you have had.

With the Harmonic Convergence in the late 1980s, the entire flow of energy that began in the 1940s was changed. When your world allowed the energy of those whom you know as Hitler, Stalin and Mussolini to coalesce on your planet, this resulted in the extreme probability of there not being inhabitants upon this planet by the year 2000. The energy for this destructive outcome was formed and put into an almost solid form. You were heading in the direction of annihilation.

## THE SIXTIES ALTERED THE ENERGY OF ANNIHILATION

Those of you who were children of the 1960s—who grew up in the 1960s— began the awakening of your consciousness that life could be different. True, that generation did it through drugs and exploring sexuality in a very public manner. Drugs allowed people to realize that they could enter into different aspects of consciousness. Before that time, the only ones who knew there were different aspects of consciousness were monks, those in the East who did the meditating, the contemplating. Then transcendental meditation was brought to this country of the United States, and people became aware of a whole different aspect of consciousness. Awareness of consciousness began to increase. As people experimented with psychedelic drugs, they found they could be taken into other areas of consciousness. Drugs took them quickly into altered states, but the journey was uncontrolled and unstructured.

When an individual uses chemicals to open up consciousness, those chemicals prevent the individual from having control. You need a companion who can guide you if you venture into areas for which you are unprepared. When you open awareness of consciousness through meditation or contemplation, you have greater control over where you are going, because you are not chemically bound.

When these events began in the sixties, you had chemical awakening or awareness of consciousness, plus those exploring various types of meditation. Notice that at that same time, you had the chemical that you know as the pill, which changed the way women felt about how they could interact as sexual beings. There was greater freedom for women to explore sexual energy. An explosion of investigation into sexuality began and when the energy of sexuality is aligned with the awareness of consciousness, spirituality expands dramatically.

## SPIRITUALITY AND SEXUALITY ARE THE SAME

The kundalini, tantra, is spirituality. Though it is not yet in the mass consciousness, people are hopefully learning how to use the tremendous power of sexual energy for the continued awareness and awakening of consciousness. Remember when we went from the heart through a portal into another dimension? You are aware of the opening through the heart, and when you combine the power of sexual energy with a definite spiritual practice involving this knowledge of the heart—well, you've never had an orgasm like that! Tantra works with this in using all of the chakras and meridians. You would be absolutely amazed at what can happen, what clears when you learn how to harness and manage sexual energy. It's a very powerful energy. Spirituality also accesses the same very powerful energy. So the two—sexuality and spirituality— are one. They are not different.

Let's look at what people like to form in their lives. People generally like to live in peace and harmony. Isn't that what people would say if you asked them? They would like to feel safe; they would like to have peace. Unfortunately, the mass consciousness believes that peace and safety are gained through weapons and war. And of course, that is not how it happens, as you know. In your society, you have separated sexuality and spirituality into light and dark. That is why so many of you have negative and inhibited views of sex and sexuality. All of you are at least familiar with the terms white magic and black magic. Look at sexuality in that way. You can use it for what some would call white, or light; or it can be used for black, or dark. It's just a judgment. Society also has a judgment on sexuality and sexual energy. Energy just is; you can use it to manifest peace and to manifest abundance, or you can use it to interfere with peace and abundance. You can use sexual energy in the same way. The key is to learn how to bring the energies of sexuality and spirituality together.

## THE ENCODEMENT TECHNICIANS

How does this relate to encodements? Encodements are simply individual energy circuits that are connected together. It's like a computer motherboard with all its connections; the electrical current just goes through. Those who make circuits know that if you have any static on your hands and touch a circuit, it will short out. Think about static in your life and how you can short out the encodements when you touch the tremendous energies of spirituality and sexuality. Use that analogy, because the encodements, in a sense, can be shorted out. You have created a dichotomy between sexuality and spirituality, which you must fully merge and align. When you have brought them together and have been able to experience the fullness of those energies coursing through you, you will find that your encodements become fully activated.

These two energies—which are actually one energy—are where you need to place your "plug." People keep looking for what they want to do and feel they are not guided. "Where are my guides? What is happening?" Dear ones, they are always there. It's that you're not plugged in. By the way, part of being plugged in is believing that you are plugged in. In other words, if you have a belief system that says that you are not receiving information, then that belief system will block the information. It's not that the information is not coming in. It's that you have formed an energy block constructed by your beliefs, which block incoming information.

We have now established the groundwork. We're going to ask that those whom I call the encodement technicians come in. I'd like you to meet them. Each one of you will have your own; some of you will have two and some will have three who will come.

## A MEDITATION FOR FINDING YOUR ENCODEMENT TECHNICIAN

*Go into your heart right now. Connect with and become aware of the pillar of light that is around you. Remember when I used to ask you to connect with the pillar of light in front of you? None of you has the pillar in front. It is all around you now. Some reading this will have the pillar of light in front of them.*

*From the area of your heart chakra, go forward with your consciousness until you find the portal. Allow yourself to go through the portal, or at least become aware of it. Become aware of beings who are there specifically for you, your individual encodement technicians. Simply feel their energy. You'll become aware of their energy. Ask them to touch an encodement that has to do with a choice of where you could have lived—what country, what state. See if you can feel that energy and get a sense of it. Now ask them to touch or activate momentarily an encodement for a possible profession that is no longer active but that was active when you were an adolescent. Allow yourself to come back to your body.*

I'd like you to share a little bit about this. Were you able to feel that activation or have memories or recognition? What did you experience?

*The state I experienced was Florida and countries were Spain and Greece. A profession I could have had was a teacher, a schoolteacher.*

Was that surprising?

*I don't remember consciously wanting to be a schoolteacher. It's not really surprising, but it's not anything I ever pursued.*

*I also experienced being in Greece. With profession, there was just a white light around my eyes. It was something to do with my eyes and my head, something mental, intellectual, spiritual or intuitive. I don't know exactly what it was, but it was a very powerful light.*

You experienced an energy when that encodement for profession was stimulated. I would like you to share these experiences so that readers will see what others have experienced.

*I was shocked, because I was immediately taken to Sweden, which is not a country I've ever been attracted to. Then I was transported to Minnesota, which is very funny, because I detest cold weather. But when I came back and began analyzing it, it made some sense, because all of my life I've been very attracted to the runes. The profession was a schoolteacher. This was no surprise, because I've always known that I was to be a teacher. I have just preferred to be an informal teacher.*

That was fascinating for you, wasn't it? That was just to give you an idea of the power of the encodements. Now we will work more with those technicians who are with you.

*I would like you to bring to mind something that has been difficult for you. It doesn't matter what; something will probably pop into your mind immediately. Now I want you to communicate with your technicians. You can go through the portal, if you wish, but you don't have to. Communicate with the technicians. Tell them of the difficulty you have been having, whether it is pain, indecision or anything. Ask them, "Is there an encodement that can be adjusted so that I can have (whatever you have in mind)?" Then you must allow them to do the work. Know that changing an encodement will also change other things. Ask them now to complete their work as you come back into your body. They can work without you. Is anybody willing to share an experience of some kind?*

*I gave them permission to do whatever is necessary to help me with my impulsiveness, to be less impulsive, to tone it down. It seemed like I felt something going on, but I don't know for sure. Time will tell.*

*I've always had difficulty being married. I've been married for nineteen years and I love my husband very much, but the problem is commitment, I think. So I asked them to help me to be happier in my marraige, and I also asked for help with weight loss and quitting smoking. I got very emotional with the marriage part. Something is definitely happening. Yes, something is happening.*

*I asked for some peace around my job, and then I just went down and I was very peaceful.*

*I asked for peace around my children fighting and their differences, and my heart and head became really warm.*

Good. Thank you.

## USING ENCODEMENTS TO MOTIVATE YOURSELF

There is another way to work with your encodements. Is there something that you would really like to develop in your life? It could be gardening, hang gliding, a commitment to a particular ideal or path, something that you thought about but had no inner motivation to do.

*Bring something to mind and ask, "Is there an encodement for (whatever you have in mind)?" If the answer is yes—which is likely, as you wouldn't be desiring to develop it if there was not some interest in there—ask them if there can be an adjustment made that increases the energy to that encodement. In other words, ask your technicians for an encodement that would give this a greater attraction path, that would give you a greater desire and motivation to do it. Come back to your body now.*

I'm giving you less time, because it really doesn't take much time. They work very quickly. Is there anything anyone would like to share about their experience?

*When I asked the question, I got an answer even before I finished asking the question.*

Yes, of course, and that is because it works with telepathy. You already have the question; it's the verbalizing of it. Does this give you some idea of how you can use this information? When you think of yourself as energy and realize that there are actual energy circuits, then you can ask that these be changed, because you are the one who asked that they be placed in there to begin with. You are the one who planned how your energy system would be formatted.

Some of you participated in the actual technicalities. Those of you who are technical now were technical on the other side; you helped in the engineering of your encodement template. There are others of you who simply expressed that they wanted to have certain possibilities and to learn about particular issues. You turned that over to the technicians as if they were building you a computer and you were telling them what you wanted your computer to be able to do. The encodement technicians put together the package for you and then received their energy exchange.

The exchange is of creative energy, but that is for another session. The more you want in your computer, the more encodements you want, the greater the energy exchange. The more encodements you have within you, the more energy you need coming into you to activate them.

Every one of you in this room and every one of you reading these words knows that you asked for many, many encodements; you asked for more encodements than you have ever asked for in any of your other incarnations. That is because you knew of the probabilities and the possibilities before you came to this lifetime, to this planet, to this dimension; you placed within you many different probabilities and possibilities of encodements. That is why so many of you have had a difficult time deciding what it is that you want to do, where exactly your is path supposed to be.

I've spoken to you before that there are very few of you—and none in this room—who have had it ordained that they were going to do one thing and only that one thing. In other words, you did not come down here to find a particular path of religion or spirituality. You did not come down here to introduce a particular idea or thought. No, you came down here with a multitude of possibilities of what you could do.

When the energy begins to activate, remember what happens in adolescence. Hormones are activated, which means the energy centers connected to the endocrine system are also activated. When hormones are activated in adolescence, this thing called sexuality really comes to the forefront. The energies of sexuality and spirituality start coming together. Since there is little spirituality in your current religions, many youths turn to the artificial stimulation of drugs. As the energy begins to flow, various encodements are activated, and then there are choices to be made. Interesting, isn't it?

## AN ALTERNATIVE SET OF ENCODEMENTS

*When we came in with our encodements, did we have an alternative set of encodements if we should continue to survive on the planet? Was there a Plan A and Plan B?*

Yes, but Plan B was not fully developed, because the probability that you would need it was so low. You put it in just in case, knowing that you could then put in others. And you have been putting in other encodements in your sleep state and in your meditations. Also, when you drift off and you don't remember anything when you come back and you're not sure what happened, you have done encodement work and had more energy circuits placed within you.

*So am I updating Plan B all the time?*

Yes, you are truly creating Plan B. You are creating what you want to do, because your primary plan was to end a few years ago. You were all going to go out with a bang, all pretty much at the same time. But then things changed and suddenly you had those who decided to still leave and those who decided to stay behind. It wasn't in the original plan that you would be without the other. It hurts, because the encodement attracting you to the one who has left is still active.

*Where is my Plan A?*

Let's take Plan A for a relationship. The original Plan A was that you would all leave together. Then, when one leaves and one stays, the one who stays still has the encodement for that relationship and so the grief of the other leaving is intense, because it doesn't make any sense in Plan A, and Plan B is not that active. What you have is a skeleton of a plan in your Plan B. Now you have to put it into action and fill in the blanks, as it were. It's like when you buy some property in an area that has not been developed. Let's say the first thing you do is put in a dirt road. As it begins to be developed, you put in things such as a sewer system, concrete roads and other substructures that are necessary. But in the beginning, you just have the land and a plan of what you will build. That is the skeleton; it is not in full form.

Now you are putting Plan B into full form. Some of you are more adept at being able to flesh out your skeleton, putting your blueprint into physical form. Some of you are very good at it, and some of you are feeling lost. You can ask these wonderful encodement technicians to come and help you to put Plan B into full development.

*How do I know when it is the right time to let go versus giving up because of fears that I may not be able to succeed?*

One of the simplest things you can do is what we did tonight. You can work with the encodement technicians or you can call in your other guides who work with you, who, by the way, are various aspects of yourself. You can go into the deepness of your heart and ask questions. Sometimes, if you ask, "Is it time for me to leave?" the question is too charged energetically and your brain gets in the way. But if you ask, "Is it time to deactivate this encodement?" the emotional charge is reduced by phrasing it in a more technical way. What you individually have done is set up a success-or-failure judgment within yourself.

The truth is that you have done nothing but succeed. You have not failed, although that is not something you are able to accept at this time. Everything that you—and I am speaking specifically to you, although this applies to everyone—have done is a success, because you established definite lessons to learn and you have learned them. You are one of the ones who stayed when the others left. You are still feeling loss because of the encodement that is attached to your loved one, who truly was part of your soul.

When you are ready, you can ask if that encodement can be adjusted. It is not that you would lose your loved one; it is so that the pain can decrease. You will still have your loved one in another way. Then you will be able to make decisions with more clarity in regard to your profession, house and so on.

You made a decision on the soul level to stay and your loved one said, "No, I'm going, and I will always love you." You are battling with this particular facet of Plans A and B. There are many others reading this who are in this situation. Know that you can ask for help in adjusting those relationship encodements, and by such an adjustment, you will in no way lose your loved one.

## EXPANDING ENCODEMENTS TO THE MACROCOSM

*Understanding that each of us is a microcosm of the macrocosm, do you have any comments to share with us on how we might apply this encodement work in any way to the macrocosm? I do understand that as we work on ourselves we affect the whole, yet I'm wondering if you have any specific guidance as to how we can broaden this to the macrocosm.*

What a wonderful question! Your planet, a living being, has encodements. You can ask to join her and work with her in supporting her change of encodements. You can help her. The encodements are also set by your intention; some call it a morphogenic field. When you create a belief system and it forms a field, that in essence is an encodement that you have created with your own energy.

Let's talk about the encodement of war, which was created many thousands of years ago. As you read your history, it is a recitation of one war after another. Very rarely do historians focus on invention and creativity; they usually focus on destruction. You can work to affect the whole, either alone or in groups. You can work with the energies of the planet where there are "artificial encodements," that is, encodements that were made here on this side of the veil rather than those placed by beings on the other side of the veil. These artificial encodements are just as active. You can work in concert with the spiritual beings on the other side of the veil to alter the encodement of war.

Some time ago, I taught you the use of Archangel Michael's sword. You can use Michael's sword in conjunction with working with the encodements by asking that there be placed within your planetary system—from the core of the Earth to approximately 2.5 miles above the planet—those encodements having to do with harmony, safety and unconditional positive regard—in other words, love. You can ask that those encodements be placed there and that those already there be activated. You can activate them further by sending energy from your heart. The way to do that, though, is not to send it singly from your heart. You know there is more power in a group.

## A MEDITATION TO AMPLIFY THE ENCODEMENT FOR HARMONY

Let's do it right now. *Get in touch with these energetic structures: the Earth star about six inches below your feet; the minor energy centers at your ankles and knees; the base, or root, chakra; the second, or sacral, chakra; the solar plexus chakra; the heart, thymus, or high heart chakra; throat chakra; the third eye; the crown; the soul star above your head. Visualize chakras extending up to the thirty-third level. Activate all these centers and feel the energy flowing through them. See the light traveling up and down the pillar within you. See it being even more fully activated with your intention. Ask that even more energy and light be poured into you. Feel your heart center becoming lighter and more vibrant. Focusing from your heart center, ask that the energy from your heart be directed to an encodement of harmony. You will be assisted; feel it happen. Don't forget to breathe. Good. Now come back into your bodies.*

You have just amplified the energy of an encodement for harmony within your planet. I want you to know that you had others working with you. Some of you were directing energy to an encodement of harmony within the planetary body; others of you were working with encodements within the atmosphere. That is powerful work. It is work that takes a tremendous amount of energy and focus.

Some of you, either hearing or reading this, might feel yourselves called to work in this way with the planetary encodements. It is sacred work. It is demanding work, because you are pulling through you a tremendous amount of energy. For many of you, your bodies are not quite ready. Be sure that you drink plenty of purified, blessed water and be aware of your own body's needs for electrolytes when you do this work. Green food will help give your body support. I hope this helps to answer your question; it is the beginning of an answer.

*When you are pulling the energy into yourself, what are the mechanics of what's happening?*

We are all one; there is only Oneness. At the same time, it is difficult to talk about this in a world of dualism without getting into duality. First, we'll go from the Oneness. You set your intention, which is what activates the energy. You set your intention to bring a focus of energy into your very being so that it activates your spiritual centers and brings everything together in a cohesion. You actually lose the demarcation of specific energy centers, and then you have just one center of energy. In other words, it's one tube, or pillar, of light. As you bring that energy in, you become more of who you actually are, which is your spiritual, nonphysical self, and you use yourself as an amplifier. You amplify the energy by your intention and by bringing it into yourself. Then you send it out, through your heart, to a specific location.

As you work with this, you will find yourself being the activator of a particular area. You are holding the light and anchoring the light in this place where you live. By amplifying the light that comes through you, it actually dispels the chaotic vibrations. You are bringing the vibrations into harmony, which connects with the Earth's encodements. It forms an electrical or energetic charge that then goes through the entire grid.

## ORGASM WITHOUT MANUAL STIMULATION

*Last week I had an experience that was really intense. I felt like I was becoming one with you. It came after a release, or a discharge, of something that propelled me into this experience, which I usually automatically clear sexually. It kind of clears everything negative. It happened and then it was gone, and I'm wondering what it was.*

You had a similar experience just a moment ago . . . your whole body shook for an instant. Did you feel that? That is when the energy is coming through you. When you make a choice to release something that is holding you back, you are releasing the energy from blockage. The energy of past events is trapped within your physical self. When you release energy from the connective tissue where it is held, then your body can respond with contractions known as orgasm or climax, or the tension can build and build and then release with tremendous relief. When you allow that to happen, you are actually clearing from your tissue the memory and energy of the event that occurred. You become clearer.

It is very similar when you practice tantra and you bring together spirituality and sexuality. The energy of the physical climax, known as orgasm, pours through your connective tissue and it burns off what is known as active memory, the emotional charge within your tissue. That is why you will find that those who practice tantric yoga, who bring together the sexual and the spiritual, don't age. They look young, because they release the low-vibration energy of events that others hold on to. The low-vibration charge ages you because there is no free-flowing energy through the DNA. The energy is what tells your DNA to age, that you want out of here, and then you have death.

So you had an energy charge that came through you and it released in sexual energy. You can do this without the act of sexual intercourse or masturbation. You can release by bringing those energies together, the spiritual and the sexual, and it doesn't necessarily mean you have the sex act, which is the way you know how to do it. But you can release by allowing the energy to flow through you. You can then have a natural orgasm rather than one created by any type of manipulation of the sexual organs. When you are in a place of allowing this to happen, orgasm can occur without manual stimulation.

## A CLIENT MUST ACCEPT HEALING ENERGY

*I had a client who went through some serious surgery but who has recovered and is doing well after just one session in which he experienced a very serious pain along with the good effects of the session. I know that a doorway has been opened, a light has been switched on. We have a choice to turn the light off and run or to examine what's in the room. What can we do to get the other person to stay there, to rummage around and ask questions? I'm thinking, how do we maximize this? It seems very similar to what we're talking about. How do we maximize this in others and, of course, in ourselves?*

First of all, it is not your job to get the person to stay there and rummage around and ask questions. Your job is to do what the person who came to you asked you to do. When you do healing with an individual after something like surgery, you are reattaching meridians and other energy structures that were detached. The pain experienced by the individual was due to the energy charge of a memory. This energy charge, or energy cyst, was around an encodement and was still active, and the individual was not willing to release that energy charge yet. This happens on a soul level or on an other-than-conscious level.

You can help people by presenting to them the healing modality that you use. It is their choice as to what to do with the energy. Remember that whenever you are sending love energy, that is healing. Don't worry about permission. You cannot force anyone to accept healing love energy. If they don't want it, they will not take it. You do not have to worry about it being invasive when it comes from the heart. It can be invasive if sent from the ego. The energetics of asking for permission are a reminder to send it from the heart without the ego involved.

Let's take prayer, intercessory prayer. How many of you ask for permission to pray for others? Not many ask, do they? It is a form of healing, dear ones. It is the same when you are doing Reiki, or any other modality. Know that it is healing and noninvasive as long as you send it in the purity of your heart and are not forcing it on another. The other person always has a choice to accept the healing energy or not. Many of you have sent prayer or healing energy to another and have felt it bounce back. Know that you do not have to worry about asking for permission any more than you have to worry about asking for permission to pray for someone.

You give your clients the process they came to you for. You can offer the individual more by presenting him or her with the idea of looking at the situation from another perspective or possibility. If he or she chooses not to look any further, you have done everything you needed to do.

## PREDICTIONS

*Do you have any predictions for 2004?*

Let me talk about what is changing. Have you noticed that your president is doing strange things? Yes, things that are strange even for him! Did you ever think in your wildest dreams that he would want—he won't call it "amnesty" in regard to immigration—to open the country to those who are here without papers? Did you ever think he would do something like that? It's more than a political move. There are changes occurring in the energy of this planet. Do you notice that this announcement was made after the Harmonic Concordance? The energy is changing. Whether he will survive in his own party by bringing this in is another question.

And now he has announced that the U.S. will go forward to Mars. Do you think the people of your country will back him up? Do you think that moving forward to Mars has the same impetus as John Kennedy's announcement that astronauts were going to the Moon? Moving forward to Mars is a bit more devious than immigration; the military can experiment under the guise of going to Mars in a way it could not do without the Mars mission. That announcement has primarily a military aspect. This is not the same as with former president John Kennedy, whose major impetus was to get to the Moon before the Russians.

*I sense that this is going to turn on the president.*

Yes, it will turn on him. Things are happening. Things are changing, and those of you who were involved in the meditations during the Harmonic Concordance helped to bring this about. He has never known who he is and he knows less of who he is now because of the changes that are occurring.

## THE CENTRAL AMERICAN FREE TRADE ACT

*I've heard that the presidents of the Central American countries do not necessarily want the Central American Free Trade Act (CAFTA), as the U.S. is forcing them to accept the act on the United States' terms. It looks like George Bush is aligning himself with Vincente Fox of Mexico in a show of strength. That's what I see. Would you comment on what higher order there might be to that whole scenario?*

The term is, "things are not as they appear." You have, on one level, exactly what you are talking about. But when you take a group of people who have been living in fear that they will be thrown out of the place where they are living (immigrants in the U.S.) and then they are accepted, it changes the energy of the country. These wonderful beings will be bringing in a new culture with greater freedom. There have been amnesty programs before; they have changed the country every time and they will do so again. These changes are not necessarily what the two presidents want.

There are things working underneath, even within President Bush; his heart is changing and he is not sure of who or what he is. Things will be happening with him that are much different than what he expects or what those around him expect. There is no prediction yet of how it will turn out. We shall see. These two announcements in just a short time are showing a definite change in energy.

There will be many in this country who will become excited about the newest exploration. What will happen is exactly what happened when your country went to the Moon: science will explode again. What has been happening, the bringing together of science and spirituality, will increase. When you bring those together and when you allow people to be in a country freely—even though these new people will not have the same rights—it opens up the heart. It will also cause some unrest, because your country is a very racist country. You have pretty well annihilated the natural inhabitants.

## CONSCIOUSNESS IN THE UNITED STATES

*How is the consciousness in the United States moving in regard to homeland security?*

Many people in this nation have become used to the loss of their freedom and many are not even aware of what they have lost. Many of the people who could make them aware of these lost freedoms are in prison. There will come a time, in 2007 approximately, when people in this country will become very aware of what has happened. There will be some changes. You are actually beginning to see this with your Internal Revenue Service. You have probably read about how the IRS is attempting to stop tax dodgers. You have a system based on volunteerism, on voluntarily giving over your money. More and more people are choosing not to do so and finding ways not to do so. This is the beginning of the breakdown. People are going to realize that they do not want their freedoms to be taken away.

*You're talking about a possible revolution?*

At this time, it will not be a revolution with guns. One of the things your country has learned to do well is to have revolutions through elections. Things will change; you will see that occurring. The nature of elections is changing, becoming more immediate to the point where you could possibly vote at home. You'll see that occurring more and more. All of these energies are moving about, and now you know about encodements and how you can work with them on the larger scale, and that will change things.

*Any comments about Osama bin Laden?*

Osama bin Laden is being used to keep the energy of war going. There really is nothing much about him.

*I'd like to broach the subject of Kabbalah and the concepts of the ancient knowledge—like Torah— being the blueprint of creation that preceded creation. Specifically, in looking ahead, how is the ancient knowledge, which is still hidden, going to benefit us in bridging science and spirit?*

Now that you have greater numbers of people not of the Jewish faith studying and working with the Kabbalah, they are beginning to look at how to manage the energy and the power of that system. As more people access this energy—and as scientists such as yourself begin to study it—it will open up even further the whole aspect of your technology being your spirituality.

I wish now to leave each of you with a blessing. Feel my energy in your heart and know that at any time any of you can merge with the feminine aspect of the divine, which is who I am. Remember that you are also I Am.

# 17
# Harmonizing and
# Assessing Encodements

*July 2004*

*W*elcome. I am Amma. I am the divine mother of the divine mothers. It is wonderful to have some here who have never heard or read me. Others have read what this one has brought through. I am delighted to have you here and see your beautiful spirits, the glory who you are. If only you could believe that: the glory who you are. If you could see, feel, sense, know the perfection you are now, you would never look back to the past, at what you were before. The past brought you to where you are now. If you could see that, you would be able to release the past and go on. There is no reason for you to hang on to anything that happened in your lives in the past, be it good or ill. Keep the learning, make it a part of you and let go of any pain and suffering that was there. You do not need it now . . . You do not need it now! It serves you no purpose. Simply let it go.

## ENCODEMENT EXPERIENCES

Now, what I would like to do is ask those of you working with your encodements, what has been your experience? Is there anyone who has anything to share?

*I did some, and then it settled in and I don't remember what it was.*

Several of you have had the same experience of asking for the encodement technicians to change, add or subtract encodements and not remembering what it was you asked. What happened is that the changes became integrated within you and you don't remember what happened. Have you noticed any differences in yourself? No? [Laughter.]

*I think there is a feeling of something unconscious happening. There is a big question mark of what is going on here. I can now see what you are saying; it was doing what it was supposed to be doing, and now it is fine—either that or it is wishful thinking.*

Let's talk more about encodements, since that is the topic. You began your session helping those who had experienced loss of a loved one in some way, who are in grief and need support, so let's talk about how that affects your encodements.

## ENCODEMENTS AND LOSS

You have encodements that help you relate one to another. Correct? Those encodements are activated and stimulated. Remember, "activated" means they are turned on long term; "stimulated" means they are briefly turned on and then go off. Those of you who have been here have experimented with them being stimulated to see what encodements there might be for places you might live or professions you might have. When you were experimenting, you were using a simple stimulation. The activation is when they are on long term. Any energy that comes in, including grief and loss, has a stimulating effect upon an encodement. There is a stimulating effect for a brief period caused by the energy coming in. If the energy persists over time, there can be an activation or an alteration in the encodement by so much energy coming in, and the original purpose of the encodement is modified. Using a metaphor, it could be like a short circuit. This is the situation in which you could ask the encodement technicians to come in and work with you.

We spoke of this several months ago, of re-grading people who are experiencing what is known in psychological terms as complicated grief. What that means is that the grief is overpowering and you have not been able to resolve it. The loss still feels new after some time has passed. When it has been more than eighteen months or two years since the loss and it still feels as if it had happened yesterday, you have an encodement activated.

*You're recoding yourself. It is an artificial encoding.*

Yes, it is similar to the artificial encodements we talked about. You are, in a sense, recoding yourself, but you are using another encodement to do that; you are changing the encodement's actual purpose. The purpose of that encodement, if it was your child, parent or another loved one you lost, was to bring you together, to form an attachment. When that encodement is overstimulated, the attachment is overwhelming—or obsessive, in some cases. What you can do is call in the encodement technicians and ask that these encodements be toned down, turned off, cleansed. Imagine it like your car battery that has rust on the terminals. You would clean them up. We'll have a chance to do some of that tonight so you can experience it. Yes?

*Would it help if you, when your relatives crossed over, were to be decoded? Would it help to change the relationship?*

The natural grieving process does that; it releases the energy that is there. It is a natural releasing of the energy so that the transition is made from the person being physically present to not being physically present. When there continues to be such a yearning for the person to still be present, the encodement is stimulated to such an extent that it feels as if the person was still there. There is no closure. Several months ago, we talked of a yearning still present when someone passes on before they were supposed to. When I say, "supposed to" (knowing everybody passes on at his or her proper time), I mean that the timing is not as it was originally planned. Free will does come in for you or someone else; you can make a choice to leave this life sooner than originally intended. Or, as in the year 2000, there was a decision for the people on this planet to make, and you decided to continue to live as a human race upon this planet.

## FEW WERE ENCODED BEYOND 2000

As a review, none of you here had many encodements placed in you beyond the year 2000. There was the possibility—but not the probability—that you would still be here. When the least probable occurred and you stayed, there were open encodements in regard to relationship; they were not set for closure, since everyone was going to leave at once. Some people in partnerships decided to leave the planet, and some chose to stay. The ones who stayed were left with open encodements and overwhelming grief. You can call the encodement technicians to come in and turn off that encodement. It is as if the circuit had just so much energy built into it. There was a knowing when the encodement was originally placed that there would be an end to the physical relationship and the encodement would work through this process through the natural grief process.

This still leaves the question you asked, which is a very good question. Let me rephrase it, if I may. Is there a way to use encodements to pass through the grief cycle more quickly? The answer is yes. You can ask the encodement technicians to come in and quicken the normal process of the detachment that occurs when the person is no longer in the physical. That can be done. It is, however, difficult for you to do. The encodement technicians can make the changes, but you can continue to re-stimulate the encodements by your desire to not let go of the individual. It is a joint venture. You are cocreating with the encodement technicians. You are asking them to make changes. You must allow that to occur by being willing to let go of the other person.

You humans are not very adept at that. That is not a judgment. It is just how you were made. You were made as very, very strong community people. It is unusual to be able to be a hermit. There are not that many hermits who are emotionally healthy, although they might grow spiritually in a particular way. Did you know that? Because of the way the human is made, you have encodements for community. Those encodements are mutually activated and provide a synergistic effect upon your growth emotionally, spiritually, mentally and physically. Am I making sense for you? That about hermits is just an aside; their relationship encodements are not active and you would find they would not make good partners. Does anybody have questions on that part?

*That procedure would work on all relationships, wouldn't it?*

It would work on all relationships.

*Like for a divorce or separation?*

It works in a divorce or separation. For those of you working with people who are going through a divorce, it is important to recognize this. You can help them go through the process with the encodements. This one is asking me-while I'm talking-if that is what those of you who do Body Talk are doing when you harmonize the energy: Are you changing encodements? Yes, you are. You can make the process more powerful by holding in your mind the idea of encodements in what you call other modalities. Yes?

## HARMONIZING ENCODEMENTS WITH BIRTH ASTROLOGY

*Are encodements only about relationships? Not that relationships are not in everything, but you keep saying it is connected. I'm wondering about life in general being related to encodements. I don't fully understand them.*

There are encodements for every aspect of your life. There are encodements, energy circuits, power points that are present for possibilities for professions; they are for relationships, for where you might want to live. What is interesting is when you combine the astrological influences upon your life with the encodements, you will have an even greater understanding of their power. Your encodements were placed within you based upon where you were going to be born in regard to astrological significance, and they would be activated and stimulated by the astrological energies. This is why there can be great difficulty with people who were born by induced births.

Think about that. When you decided to come into the body, you decided when you would want to be born and what the astrological conditions would be. Before you entered your body, you were much more aware of the influences of the entire universal energies upon you than you are now. Those of you whose children were induced—your children knew those were possibilities. You would find, however, that a child who was not induced but was born at his or her own choice, has encodements and astrological energies at the time of his or her birth that meld together easily; the energies that stimulate and activate the encodements are stronger than they would be of persons born at a different astrological time.

*For the baby who was induced, does that make it harder for him to follow his path of life?*

It makes it a little more difficult to follow the energies his encodements were set for. It is not just about the spiritual path. You might find that some people who were induced might be rather obstinate, because someone told them when they were to come and overrode their choices. They will subconsciously resist people who want to prevent their own free choices. See how that works? That doesn't mean, as I'm sitting here with mothers whose children were induced, that your babies are lost. They are not. There are changes that can be made.

Now that you know about encodements, you can make a very simple change. If you yourself were induced, you can ask the encodement technicians to harmonize your encodements in conjunction with the astrological energies at the time of your birth. They will make minor shifts. It will take some time for the effects to occur, because they have to adjust all of your encodements—and you have approximately 1,538,000 encodements. Approximately . . .

*Are you speaking of asking on behalf of our children or for ourselves? Another question I have: Can the technicians help us have an encodement assessment?*

First I want to answer the question about asking on behalf of your children. Most people in here cannot ask on behalf of their children, because their children are older. Those with children under five years of age can ask on behalf of their children. You can ask for your young children; however, you must connect on the soul level for your child and ask if that is okay. Some of the children might enjoy the change in the energy, especially the more adventurous children. Let them know that there is a time they can ask for encodement adjustments. Most children will not be interested in working with encodements when they are adolescents. You will probably have to wait until they are past their mid-twenties.

## Assessing Encodements

The other question you asked is an excellent question. You can ask for an assessment. Would you like to do that now?

I would first suggest that you ask for an assessment of your encodements in a particular area of your life. Remember that every area of your life has encodements. You won't go wrong in asking for an assessment in any area. We will then ask for a general assessment, and you will see why I suggested we ask for an assessment in a particular area.

First choose the area for which you would like an encodement assessment. It could be job, relationship, spirituality, location of where you live, lifestyle, abundance. Are you ready? Since there is one who has not been introduced to encodements, let me go through the steps.

*First you want to center and ground. Enter your heart chakra from behind. From the back of your heart, enter that place where you will feel the infinite space that is there. As you travel, you will find your altar. Your altar is in the very center, in the sacred place of yourself. Do whatever you wish at your altar. There may be paper and pen there. Some of you have a quill. Whatever you wish to have at your altar will be there. Now proceed forward and know that you are in the pillar of light. Ask to be taken through the portal. As you go through the portal, you will feel even more limitless. If you cannot feel it, know that it is happening.*

*Call upon the encodement technicians in whatever way you wish. Ask them to be with you. You may find they take you somewhere. Your intention is to ask for an assessment of your encodements. Again, please do this for a particular area. I'm going to give you a couple of minutes . . . Ask for a report if you have not already received one . . .*

*Ask to be taken back through the portal. Go back through your heart chakra. Feel yourself settling into your body. When you are ready, come back into this room.*

Not too many want to come back to this room. What did you discover, those who wish to share your report? You do not have to share.

*One overloaded and two broken. This was in the relationship with my husband.*

*(Another person) Amma, I asked about abundance. I found myself in a whole village with the mountains surrounding me, all the people surrounding me. That was the abundance: the community. It was overflowing.*

*(Another person) Earlier I had asked to have an encodement activated; it was a relationship question. I was taken to this person's house. I was standing outside the house, saying it was not time to enter; these things don't happen overnight. Certain other people's encodements are affected by mine being reset, turned on or tuned. Other people are affected beside just me and the other person.*

## A CHANGE IN YOU AFFECTS OTHERS

What you found in your encodements is very important. We had been talking about encodements as if they were in isolation to an individual. What you have introduced and demonstrated is that no encodement is in isolation. As I stated earlier, you are people who want to be in community. This means your encodements are connected, because you are one. Therefore, you will have those connections that occur.

When you change an encodement in yourself, think about the possibilities of what could happen. It could have what you call a domino effect. You might not like how the dominos fall. It might also bring changes in regard to other people, because your energy is now different. It does not change the encodements of the other person. The change in your encodements will alter your energy. Others will perceive your energy differently, although not necessarily on a conscious level.

*Can you have the encodements within you changed by hypnosis? If you were hypnotized to build your self-confidence, would that change your encodements?*

What that does is add another energy that could actively stimulate those encodements. The difficulty with hypnosis, why it doesn't always work, is that some have encodements that do not allow anyone but themselves to facilitate change within them. In other words, when you are in a state of hypnosis, you have someone else facilitating change within you by suggestion. You could do self-hypnosis, which is simply a state of deep relaxation and can be safely done following the process of going into your heart, going to your altar and so on.

*Is the encodement process hypnosis?*

What you are doing with the encodement technicians is that you are stip-
ulating what you wish to happen. You do not have to do the ritual we just
did to change your encodements. Simply go into your heart in whichever
way you choose. You need to be centered and grounded. I was working to
have you centered and grounded. You do not have to go through the portal.
That was simply an example of what you could do. You only need some quiet,
and then ask the encodement technicians to make the adjustments for the
changes you desire.

What happens with hypnosis is that you enter a state of relaxation, have a
focused intent and someone else brings an energy into you through his or her
words. There are some people who are encoded so that would not happen. That
is why some do not do well with hypnosis. Does that answer your question?

## A FULL ENCODEMENT ASSESSMENT

To show you why we did a limited assessment, we will now do a full assessment. Are you ready? You do not have to do this if you do not want to. We
will not go through the portal this time.

*Simply be centered within yourself and grounded. Ask for the encodement techni-
cians to come. Ask them for a full assessment of your encodements within the first
eight layers of your energy field. Ask for a simplified report. After you have received
your report, come back into your body.*

Was this more difficult? This is why you focus on one area for an assessment.
Does anyone wish to share the experience?

*I kind of could see them in relationship to where my physical body is. Two of them were just blowing
energy like roman candles. I asked that those be torqued down a bit and they did. There were eight
that were leaking energy, twelve that were misfiring and, I believe, they said, eight or ten that were not
connecting up at all. I don't know what that means.*

And that is the simplified report! Anybody else?

*I saw flashes of color of orange, blue and yellow.*

Did you get a sense of what they represented?

*Too much orange, and they were trying to balance with other colors.*

Anybody else?

*I've been working with encodements for a couple of years now. There were four encodements
pointed out. I asked if they were in the wrong place. The technicians laughed and said, "There is
no such thing as wrong encodements. They are just encodements and they were placed as you
asked." It was quite plain. The technicians were very proper. They took their job very seriously.*

Interesting, is it not? You saw the energy blasting out of some of the encodements and asked that they be repaired. Have you noticed a difference in these
few moments since the encodement technicians did the work?

*Now that you mention it, I noticed that as they worked with the encodements, there seemed to be some sort of line connecting the two that were blown out, almost like a grid. Now I seem to be more awake.*

Good. As you pay attention, you will discover that other things will happen. There are other modalities you use, so the changes will not all come from this. See how it all fits in together? Anyone else?

*The first time, I saw blue, and it was a definite blue. I don't know what it meant. It was just all over. The second time, things were dark.*

## ASK FOR MEANING

We've done this very quickly. What you would do, and I suggest you do this at some point in your meditation, is ask for an assessment and ask for what it means—what do all the colors mean? For instance, you found out the colors were about balancing. You don't have to know. But some people do need to know. They can get caught in their heads and have to know. Their curiosity is part of who they are. All of you are curious people. You might ask, "What is that encodement about?" referring to the two that were blown open or those that were leaking. You could ask about the cause. I must warn you that you might receive the answer to what caused it and it will not make any sense to you. They do, in fact, speak a different language—"in-code," if you will.

It is much easier if you would ask to do an assessment of your encodements for a particular area. You could do health. Divide it up. You could do the systems of your body. "What are the encodements for my immune system? Please show me what needs to be brought into balance. What do the encodements mean?" Ask about the particular encodement that seems to be dark. What does it mean that it is dark? Listen or see or hear, depending upon the higher-sense perception you use, what that means for you. Then ask, "What will happen if I make this change? What will happen?"

I can tell you that if you have an encodement that was, as you described it, losing a tremendous amount of energy, that would be like a mechanic saying there is oil gushing out of your car. It doesn't really matter what is happening. They just want to plug the leak. They know it is not for the best of the engine. You knew intuitively that energy rushing out was not appropriate, was not healthy. You don't want leaking encodements any more than you want a battery that leaks. You don't want things leaking.

Some may be what you call misfiring because you have set them to misfire. In other words, they are putting out a little bit of energy at a time, not a consistent amount of energy. Before you have that adjusted, ask, "What is this about? What does it relate to? What would be the change if I had it firing continuously?"

Because relationships are so dramatic, let me use this as an example. If you have an encodement that has to do with a relationship—it could be a friendship, a close relationship, a relationship with an animal—if the encodement is misfiring, you might want to ask, "What does this do to the relationship? If I have you set the encodement differently, to where there is a continuous state of energy, what would that do?" Each of you would receive a different answer. Take that information and decide if you really want that encodement changed.

We have been playing with the encodements the past few months. This is actually serious business. In a way, you are changing the fabric of your life. The changes in your encodements can change your DNA. That is how powerful this process is.

## WHERE ARE THE ENCODEMENTS?

*Where are these encodements located? A minute ago, you said, "the first eight layers." Where are they?*

They extend way beyond your eight layers. I just wanted to put a limit on the assessment, or you would have been overwhelmed with the information. The encodements are located throughout your physical body and your energy body. Your energy body extends beyond what people call your aura. The aura is simply the part those who see, can see—about eight layers. Your aura extends even farther than that, otherwise, you would not all be one, would you? It is the interconnection that occurs; the part of the oneness that is differentiated into you becomes denser.

Encodements actually go out everywhere. You have encodements related to your culture. You have encodements related to your chosen religion, your chosen spiritual path. Some of you raised in a particular religion who have moved away from that religion and feel a tremendous shift, a change to where you are not really connected to that religion, have had a change in encodements. This occurred on a soul level; you can do this work on a soul level, usually when your conscious mind is turned off while you're sleeping.

*Do I carry over the same encodements from past lives?*

There are some you would carry over. There are others you would not carry over.

*In what important ways do encodements relate to the DNA and to the strand we don't see?*

The encodements provide an energy that can activate different areas of the DNA. The DNA is most completely activated when you are in your heart all the time. Is anyone here in his or her heart all the time? Of course not. You have a tendency to go up and down from the head, the heart, the gut. When you are in your heart, the energy for the DNA is most active. When all your DNA is active, that is when what you call marvelous, miraculous things can be done. They really aren't miraculous. Miraculous means "out of nature," does it not? The encodements are an energy that can support the DNA; they work in tandem with each other. Encodements are the energetic level; DNA is the physiologic level.

The ten strands of the DNA you do not see in the makeup of the twelve strands are more directly related and connected to the encodements. The unseen strands feed into the physical ones you can see with a microscope. In other words, the other ten strands of the DNA—those that you do not see—are like the energy field, if you will, of the DNA structure. The encodements support and work with the DNA. There are encodements within the DNA.

It all works together. You are wondrously made—wondrously made. I know many of you have looked at the physical body and have heard how much can go wrong with that physical body. You even wonder how miraculous it is that not more people have such tremendous things going wrong. You are wondrously made.

*Is it through encodements or is there another way to approach speaking to yourself on a cellular level to make specific change?*

You can do both. I would begin by first speaking to your cells on a cellular level. That is your physical consciousness connecting on the cellular level to the cells' physical consciousness level. You want to bring the cellular level into alignment with what you consciously want. Your encodements can work on a subconscious level.

## TV, RADIO CAN PROGRAM
### ARTIFICIAL ENCODEMENTS

Many of your natural encodements were damaged by artificial encodements, by what has been programmed into you by other sources, such as television and radio. Do you realize that television and radio are hypnotic? There are not that many people who have encodements to not allow themselves to be hypnotically programmed. If you are programmable, then you have to be very careful. You have many, I think you would call them "zombies," walking around due to damaged encodements resulting from outside programming. Do not believe, dear ones, that the programs are just what you think you hear. There are subliminal messages occurring, especially on your television. There are subliminal messages coming through your radio. Ah, they will tell you it is not so, but it is so. It is so.

Begin first to speak consciously to your cells. The reason I say this is that when you are working with your cells, you are asking them to come to the remembrance of the perfect way of functioning. When that occurs, it is in alignment with how you were originally made. The change would not have as strong a domino effect as changing encodements would.

When you change an encodement within yourself, it will affect all those around you. The cellular level does not directly affect those around you, except for when there is a strong change in your energy field. The change can cause changes in relationship with others around you. The encodements would have a direct energetic change, and the change in relationship will be much faster if that relationship is affected. Any other questions?

## FEMININE AND MASCULINE ENERGY

*What is your definition of the feminine energy and of the masculine energy?*

Ah, the feminine energy and the masculine energy . . . The feminine and the masculine energies are defined only in worlds of duality. In worlds not of duality, there is only one energy. What has happened on this planet is that the energies were caused to separate. In other words, they were almost torn apart from each other so there could be a feminine and a masculine. The decision was to have the feminine be the softer of the energy, the gentler of the energy and the finer of the energy. It is actually of a higher vibration. That is not a judgment as to what is better. The feminine energy is just of a higher vibration.

The masculine energy was decided to be stronger; it would be harder and the vibration would be denser. That is interesting, isn't it, when people talk about being grounded into the Earth and that vibration being lower. You might expect the opposite. Now some of the masculine and feminine energies come together. The original separation was similar to taking a ball of energy and ripping it apart in the middle to separate it. It really is all one energy. Does this answer your question somewhat?

*We hear a lot about the feminine energy coming, which is why I was asking.*

You have energy that is of a softer and gentler nature when it comes in. When demonstrated in the physical, it is more of the heart energy coming in. The masculine energy is more the power of the thought or the mind. The feminine energy is more the power of the heart. In worlds not of duality, the energies are harmonized and come together as one, and you have the perfect interaction of what you call masculine and feminine, of the heart and the mind.

Those of you working at developing integration of the heart and the mind will see that within your brain, as the right and left sides come together and merge, you discover how your senses are of a higher level. In other words, you will be able to see frequencies others cannot see, such as those who see auras. You will be able to hear frequencies others do not hear.

*So if you have a lot of masculine energy and then you start incorporating more feminine energy, that means it will change your thinking and everything. You won't be able to think like you used to think.*

No, you will not be able to think as you used to think. Have you noticed how the pictures of some of the great saints such as Babaji, Jesus or Sananda have a feminine quality to them that is not in other men? That is because they have harmonized their energy. Other questions? No? Then, to finish, let's do some more with encodements.

I would like you to select an area of your life in which you seem to be having a difficult time getting the results you want. Everybody have one in mind? You have two? Choose one; it doesn't matter which. You can do this with the other one later. When we go into this, you might be told to do the other one first. Just listen. Ask which one is the most important to do first.

Go into your heart. You can choose to go into your heart from the front or the back. I can tell you, for this work, it is easier if you enter your heart from the back.

Now simply call the encodement technicians. They've been waiting to do this part tonight. Tell them the result that you want. What is it that you want to see happen in your life? See yourself in that place you want to be. Ask the encodement technicians to make the changes necessary to facilitate that result. If they seem reluctant to make some changes, ask if there will be some repercussions to the changes that you need to become aware of. When you hear the repercussions, you can make your decision as to whether you want them to make the changes or not.

Now, dear ones, acknowledge what you have received by blessing yourselves. See the energy of the blessing surround your energy field. I leave you with my blessing to each one of you.

# 18

# Healing the Past, Living in the Present

*August 2004*

*What can the average human being do on a daily basis to change the present circumstances of his or her life? Is it by changing the past or is it by holding the vision of the future he or she would like to have?*

*D*ear one, as is so often the case, the answer is in the question—with a small addition. One must change the energy of the past, live fully in the present and send creative energy to the future. Now let me expand, because this initial answer, which might appear simplistic, can be complex in the actual doing.

Regarding the past: One simply needs to release the energy of the past. The low-vibration energy attached to a situation is there only because of your interpretation of the events of the past. Even the most horrendous experiences—the loss of a child, rape, murder, torture—result in tremendous pain simply due to the interpretation of the events.

For instance, in the loss of a child, a parent's worst nightmare, the interpretation is that the child should never have passed on, the child should always be with the parent, no parent should have to bury a child and other such beliefs. As long as the individual holds on to these beliefs, the pain of the past will be increasing in the present and will continue to increase in the future. The entire body/mind will be affected in an adverse manner.

The answer is to live fully in the present, to accept what is as it is. Mourn for the loss of the child in this lifetime. Allow the body/mind to release this precious soul to his or her continuing journey. One can seek assistance in this process by calling in the encodement technicians and ask that the attachment to this soul be ended. Most parents would be reluctant to ask this. They believe that it would not be right to release this soul and the feelings they have toward the child. They believe, in error, that it would nullify the love they have for their blessed child.

## MOVING ON, WITH LESSONS LEARNED

Dear ones, the life you are living is transitory. It is only a play, and you will enter into another play at another time. When a person leaves, for whatever reason, that person will review this play, plan for another and then begin anew. As long as you remain attached in pain to the one who has left, you are not allowing yourself to move on with your play.

Look for the positives, the lessons in whatever happened in the past. How you interpret a past event—as a betrayal, a failure—does not matter. It just was. Look for what you learned. Focus on what you learned and bring that forward. Bring the core of the learning into your present. If you do not do this, then all that occurred was for naught in your present. When you finish this life, you will take the learning from what happened. You can do it sooner and have a happier and easier time.

For any event in the past, ask if any encodements were damaged by what happened. If they were, ask what would happen if they were repaired. If you want the result shown to you to occur, ask that they be repaired. If you choose not to have the result, simply tell them you wish to leave them as they are.

You can also ask to be healed of what happened in the past. There are many ways to do this; choose what appeals to you. Know, however, that you must want to release the wounds of this past event. You must be willing to totally release all pain, all hostility, all animosity, all wishing for it to be different. What you have left is the learning. Ask for the energy of the learning to be fully assimilated into your bodymind.

The key is to stay in the present. If you are remembering something in the past, the event is not happening in the very moment you are in. However, you are keeping the past continually with you if your mind stays in the past and not in the present. Stay totally in the present, with absolutely no interpretations about what is happening. The present just is. If you are alone, notice your aloneness. Notice the space around you. Notice your feelings. Focus on the energy of your feelings. They are simply energy packets. You place the interpretation on them. If you simply watch them, focus on them and notice them in a detached manner, they will dissolve. "Oh, there is the feeling of anger. Look how it is getting bigger. Look how my stomach is tightening up. Look how the energy is moving." Continue these observations as you are focusing on the energy. Soon the energy, like a soap bubble, will become thin and dissolve. You can do this if you wish.

## THE MOVIE OF YOUR FUTURE

When you are in the present, you can dip into the future. How do you desire your future to be? Imagine your future as a movie you are in. You can see, hear, touch, taste and smell the events. Play this movie over in your mind. If thoughts and feelings come up that deny the movie, ask the encodement technicians to come. Ask if any encodements have been damaged that need to be repaired for your "movie" to manifest in the future. You can then ask that those changes be made, but do so only after asking for information on the results of those changes. If you agree to the result, ask that the changes be made. If there are no encodements for your movie, ask to be shown the encodements you originally set in place for this life. Specify the area you would like to be shown. Ask about damage to encodements. Ask to be shown the results with the damage and the results if you did not have such damage. My blessings upon you and upon those you love.

# 19

# Polarity and Poverty

*October 2004*

*What can a lightworker do to mitigate the effects of the strong polarity happening in our world?*

*Y*ou have asked about the increased polarity between human beings during this time. Your tender heart is wounded when you see how human beings hurt one another, even kill one another, for minor infractions. I want to address this issue with you as well as another one that weighs on your heart—the issue of those in deep poverty. I am addressing both of these now because the issue of deep poverty also concerns the polarization of people.

Know that polarity occurs when you are at the brink of deep change. Those who fear change—which happens to be much of the population—do all they can to hold on to the old way of being. This includes old or comfortable beliefs, habits, thoughts and feelings. I am now going to address several aspects of what is occurring. Although I will be speaking of them one at a time, they all interact with one another. The interaction has a synergistic effect—an exponential effect rather than a simple multiplicative effect.

## HUMANS RESPOND TO FEAR WITH WITHDRAWAL AND ANGER

Many people have a great fear of change. They know what life is like now in their particular situation, but they do not know what life will be like if they change. There is an expression, "The devil you know is better than the devil you do not know." In this expression, note the focus on the concept of "devil," which, as you are aware, is simply an energy constructed by humans to explain away destructive impulses. They would rather make someone else responsible for these events than accept their own part in manifesting their own reality.

Humans have a tendency to respond to fear in one of two ways. The first is to withdraw from engaging in life. Some call this denial of what is happening. The second is to respond with violence in thought, word or action. This anger is a masking of the fear. Anger is an energy that has force, has drive. Fear resulting in withdrawal has almost no energy, resulting in great passivity and victim consciousness.

The changes that are in process in the consciousnesses of many are going to result in the changing of the power structure of your governments in individual countries, and therefore on the planet. Those presently in power sense this to the depths of their being. They sense that they will be losing power. They have been enjoying this power over people, dictating what is and what is not to be. Their lives thrive on this power. This is why so many politicians and corporate executives become ill when they are no longer in a position of power over people. They fear this loss of power because they know on an other-than-conscious level that their very lives might end.

Those who thrive on having power over people have little understanding of the personal power that resides within. They are not aware of the great power contained within, in the aspect of the self—that is, who they truly are, their spiritual essence. Those who thrive on having power over people are not able to comprehend the tremendous power that comes from working with and helping people to discover their own power.

Power comes from the very source of All That Is, from the great I Am. Power is the creative force. Power created the planet you are on. Power created humans as they are now. The highest forms of power come from pure love energy. Other forms of power are a distortion of this energy, resulting in the anger, hatred, fear and violence you are experiencing on this planet.

## YOU ARE AFFECTED BY CHEMICALS AND SPIRITUAL ENERGIES

The chemicals that are now in the human brain are exponentially increasing the acting out of polarity through violence. The pesticides and petroleum products in your food, air and water block the pure, healthy action of neurotransmitters in the body. Note that neurotransmitters are not simply in the brain; all neural tissues that extend throughout the body, in the connective tissue and even in the heart, are affected by these products.

The food that the Western world eats, which is now spreading throughout the planet, also interferes with the functioning of the brain. The chemicals in the brain are altered from their healthy functioning. The neurotransmitters are again prevented from responding as they were created to respond. There is hyperactivity in the brain, which results in people acting upon feelings that do not go through the heart center. The result is that people are able to kill people for any reason whatsoever.

The other factor affecting the planet is the spiritual energies that are coming to the planet. Your very DNA is changing. Long dormant DNA, both in the two 3D strands and in the ten multidimensional strands, is becoming activated. Those who are working to integrate their newly activated DNA through spiritual practice are finding that they are becoming observers of what is happening on the planet. In other words, you and others like you are watching what is happening to those who are not tapping into their spiritual natures.

The violence you see as polarity, dear one, is not between opposite poles. The violence you see is often—not always, but often—among those who are holding tightly to their fear of change and fear of their spiritual nature. You, precious one, are at one of the poles. You watch what is happening to the others with a heavy heart because you do not see them as "other"—you see them as your brothers and sisters. The ones who are not aware of the Oneness have established the polarity from their fear. They have placed you and others like you at the other pole. As you well know, there are no poles. There is only the Oneness.

## STRATEGIES FOR COUNTERACTING POLARITY

And now for the strategies you can use:

- Stay in your heart. There is no way I can emphasize this enough. Just as a master musician always practices scales, you must always practice being in your heart. Practice until you have left your body. If you enter into fear or into anger, go into your heart.
- Bless those who hate you. Send to them the highest vibration of love and light that you are able. Bless those who have been harmed. Send healing love to them. Bless yourself. Ask for the highest vibration of love possible to cover you and fill you.
- Where there is great discord—whether it be in a country, a workplace, a street or a home—send loving energy from your heart to cover that area. Focus the energy with your intention to surround and transmute the anger, fear and hatred present.
- Join with others to surround anger, fear and hatred with loving energy.
- Forgive. Forgive yourself. Forgive others.
- Eat healthy food. Drink pure water. Keep as many chemicals as possible out of your body and out of your brain. As much as possible, avoid taking chemicals manufactured by pharmaceutical companies into your body.
- Love yourself first. If you do not love yourself and hold yourself in the highest possible regard, you will not be able to do so for others.
- Accept that people have chosen their lives as they are. Yes, offer them a new possibility, but do not force it upon them. Their lives are their choice.

## HELP OTHERS TO RISE ABOVE FEAR

Now, dear one, about those in extreme poverty: You cannot know the purpose of those who have chosen this life. Some have chosen this life so that they might help others learn compassion. Some have chosen this life to experience poverty. Still others have chosen this life to learn how to change what they have created. You can simply offer possibilities. Once you have done so, then it is up to the others to decide whether to make the necessary changes. Remember that not everyone is able to rise above fear. There are even times when you get caught up in fear.

I hope this helps you, dear one. You are a bright, shining light. Others are attracted to that light. Others fear that light. Remember always that you are love; thus, you will always manifest that love. My blessings to you.

# 20

# Your Diet, Your Health, Your DNA and Your Politics

*November 2004*

*G*ood evening, dear ones. Look at your bright light, all of you. Some of you have been having a tough time. Energies are different, aren't they? They really are. They are coming in faster. They are coming in stronger. You are getting new vibrations that you could relate to color. New colors are coming in, and the cells are adjusting to these vibrations.

## HEALTH AND DIET

Your bodies were not originally made for these vibrations. The new children coming in have bodies that are made for these vibrations. Their bodies have been made in such a way that they will adjust as the vibrations increase.

We can do a bit of work today on encodements to help your body adjust to these vibrations. What is happening is that your body was made to be, let's say, more rigid. We are talking about rigid in regard to cellular structure. The children coming now have bodies that are more fluid in regard to cellular structure.

You are going to get tired; you are going to feel discombobulated. You are going to wonder if you are even going to stay on the planet for very long. You will wonder if you are getting ill, or if there is something you really need to attend to. So let me give you a few tricks in dealing with this energy.

There is no way I can emphasize enough how important your diet is. When I talk about diet, I am not talking about dieting to lose weight. I am talking about diet as in a food plan. Every one of you here knows what you are to eat. Every one of you here knows that you are not doing it. So I want you to know that your choice is to have things happen to your body in a more drastic manner because of your choice of food. Know that I am also speaking to the one I am coming through.

*But Amma, Oreos are good for the soul!*

They might be good because they feed the inner child. They are not good for the assimilation of this energy. Know that those wonderful, tasty things you eat, whether they are Oreos or ice cream or cookies or fried foods, all of those things work well in a body of low vibration because they are low-vibration foods. As you raise the vibration of your body and the vibration of your very self, you need higher-vibration foods.

You are sitting here saying, "I am doing all that, so how come I am still having these things?" That is what you are wondering, is it not? That's right. We'll talk about that in a little bit. Just let me put this in now. You think you are having a hard time. Imagine the time you would be having if you weren't doing that.

## INSTRUCT YOUR BODY TO ASSIMILATE ONLY THE GOOD

Eat live foods. You know what live foods are, do you not? As you eat live foods, they will nourish your cellular structure. It is crucial for each one of you, before you put anything in your mouth, be it a live food or a dead food, that you ask a blessing upon it. Ask specifically that as much as is possible the energies of the food be adjusted to be more easily assimilated by your body. Ask that the parts that cannot be assimilated pass out of your body easily. Many of you were taught, in the particular religions that you were brought up in, about blessing.

Many of you now send energy to your food, whether it is Reiki or another form of energy. However, there are some of you who are sending the energy and not including the words of blessing. You need both the energy and the blessing. They go hand in hand. That is very important. Now I want to give you a couple of ways to send energy to your food.

For those of you who are Reiki attuned, that is a wonderful way of sending energy. These other ways are not better than that. Know that. What would be best for all of you is to include words of blessing and thanksgiving.

What you are eating gave its life for you, be it animal, vegetable or mineral. It gave its life for you. Some of you say, "Mineral? I don't eat minerals." Remember what salt is. Think of all the salts you eat, the minerals within your food. Before you eat, before you drink, take a moment and thank it for the gift of its life. The energy you eat will be transformed and will recycle, just as you will recycle into a different body when you leave this body. You thank the food and drink and ask specifically for your body to be aware of and to recognize the energy that is coming in.

Let this food or drink that you are getting ready to put in your mouth know that it is coming into your body. Ask that what you take in by mouth work in union with your body. Such words will facilitate the energies melding as much as possible, giving your body strength and sustenance. That which is not needed—which, dear ones, includes pesticides, other chemicals, hormones and all of those types of things—ask that the body simply release. What is now happening is that your body is holding that which you do not need in your cellular tissue. Ask the body to release it. It is that easy.

## EAT MORE LIVE FOODS AND FEWER DEAD ONES

Your body was given a message by you and the collective of humanity that anything put into its mouth was to be for its sustenance and was, therefore, to be digested and assimilated by it. Well, that doesn't work well, because you have chemicals, pesticides, hormones, antibiotics and genetically modified foods that are not healthy for the body. You need to instruct the body to assimilate those things that you want in it and then to release the other things and not store them. Makes perfect sense, doesn't it?

Remember that what you are eating is conscious. Even the cells of dead food have consciousness. What is dead food? It is food that has been cooked, food that has been separated from its life force. Dead food includes raw fish and raw meat, because these have been separated from their life force. You have your live foods, which are your vegetables, but know that the longer a vegetable is separated from its life force—from the time it is picked until the time it is cooked—the more it loses its life force. It will then become dead. You usually call this "spoiled," right?

*How about freezing?*

The very high temperatures of flash-freezing will preserve half the life essence. Most people are not able to do flash-freezing in their homes. Your frozen foods have more life within them than your canned foods do. When you are sending energy to your food, ask that the cells accept as much energy as possible so that they can be as vibrant and alive as possible.

There are times in your own daily life when you feel very vibrant and alive, and you have other times when you have difficulty getting out of bed in the morning—or sometimes in the afternoon! When more energy is being brought into you, you feel more vibrant and alive.

## VERBALLY BLESS YOUR FOOD AND ATTUNE IT TO YOUR ENERGY

*Does a verbal blessing have more power than a mental blessing?*

Yes, a verbal blessing has more power than a mental blessing. And you know exactly why, don't you? It is in the power of the spoken word and the vibration that comes from the spoken word. I would suggest that each of you sit down and write your own blessing so that it becomes easier for you. Some of you have blessings from the particular religious tradition you practice. The important thing is to say these words of blessing with meaning, to say them consciously.

Do not speak unconsciously. When you give a verbal blessing, you do not need to proclaim it loudly. You simply need to proclaim it out loud, and this proclamation can be simply made to your food.

There is more power where two or more or gathered, as you have heard. There is a synergy as the two or more energies come together. The result is more than one plus one equals two. It is more than exponential.

A verbal blessing will enable the food to be assimilated more easily into your own body. This means, by the way, that when in a group where one person is leading the blessing, that person is blessing the food to his or her energy. It is to that person's vibration that the food is being blessed and is being assimilated; it is changing into that person's energies. You want your food to be blessed to assimilate to your energy. Correct? So it is still important, when you are in a group and someone has led a blessing, that you yourself speak to your own food. A blessing in which a group is gathered—let's say a family meal or a bigger gathering—where you have a buffet and one person leads a blessing, brings a group energy where everybody is consciously in tune to the food. Still, when you sit down to your individual plate, you must connect with your food to give your blessing, your thanks and your energy, and to ask that it be assimilated in accordance to your energies. Does that make sense?

## THE MORE A FOOD IS REFINED, THE LESS BENEFICIAL ENERGY IT CONTAINS

Live foods, as you know, are vegetables, fruits and sprouted grains before they are cooked. When you feel the need to cook foods, cook them as little as possible so that the natural enzymes still live. These are all things you read in your nutrition books. They are things your friend Edgar Cayce has spoken of. The enzymes keep the balance, the pH balance, exactly where it needs to be.

The other thing is to drink mainly water. You could add some fruits or citrus juices to your water. Many of you enjoy caffeine, which is fine, but also know that a little imbalance within your body can be caused by caffeine. Again, to lessen the imbalance, it is important to bless and speak to your food, asking it to be assimilated in accordance with your energy.

Certain sugars are very detrimental to the physical structure as it changes with the new energies. I want to separate the health perspective from what you are hearing from the medical community regarding the effect of sugars upon the body. One of the reasons that so many people are having weight problems is not due to the sugar that is eaten by your population right now. The difficulty is that people have developed a thought form, a matrix, that says, "If you eat this particular food, then you will enlarge." If you have developed this belief, you will get larger if you eat certain foods.

Imagine if you were trained and raised to believe that if you ate this particular food, say ice cream or cake or candy, you would get very, very thin, that you would lose a tremendous amount of weight. If you believed this to be true, then that is what would happen to your body. You realize that, don't you? So those of you who are having difficulties with the amount of weight upon your body are having these difficulties because you have connected to the energy of what certain groups of people believe to be true. Have you noticed that the more your country has put an emphasis on obesity, the greater the number of obese people?

*Can we decode our emphasis on obesity?*

You can alter the encodements that connect you to the energy of what one of your scientists calls the morphogenic field. You can separate yourself from the morphogenic field of the current belief about nutrition. I am hoping that most of you here know that the food pyramid put out by your government some years ago is not correct and healthy for your body. All those carbohydrates will not help your body to shift as it needs to shift, because they keep your body in a rigid structure. When you take in live foods, because they are alive and shifting, your cellular structure is able to shift.

When you refine, you actually take out what is left of the life essence. When you remove the enzymes, you are taking out what is left of the life essence. That's what refinement does. So eat your whole-grain foods when you take the carbohydrates. Eat your brown rice. Get to know all these other grains that are now coming into your country. There are many people who will say that wheat is bad for you because your body has eaten so much wheat that it has started to form an allergic reaction. If you eat the sprouted wheat, your body can assimilate that more easily.

As with any allergy, there is an emotional anchor tying the allergy to your body, and you can eliminate that anchor. Know that you can change these things. For those of you who have been concerned about your weight, I would suggest that you not be concerned with it anymore. There is no reason to be concerned about it.

## PAY CONSCIOUS ATTENTION TO EVERYTHING YOU PUT IN YOUR BODY

*What about refined sugars?*

You will find that the more a natural substance is refined, the less life essence it has in it and the more it will keep your body in a rigid structure. You will find that pure cane sugar is actually healthier for you than corn syrup. You will find that such things as stevia (*Stevia rebaudiana*, a natural sweetener) are healthier for you than refined sugar. Molasses is healthier for you than refined sugar. It is the same with honey.

The more something is refined, the more of its life essence has been taken away. Remember, substances we find in their natural state still have consciousness, life force. When you acknowledge the natural substance, what is left of the ability and strength of its life force elevates to its fullest potential. You acknowledge the substance through blessing it and communicating with it. When you wish to have your Oreo, instead of feeling shame at eating an Oreo and satisfying your inner child, welcome the Oreo. Look at it. Thank it. Tell the Oreo about how much fun it was to eat it when you were a child, whether you tore it apart and ate it or dunked it in milk and enjoyed the flavor of it. Let your body celebrate the coming of the Oreo. Then you will eat one Oreo and not twelve.

When people are in an unconscious place regarding their food, an element of shame enters in because they feel they shouldn't be eating unconsciously. Instead, if you consciously eat your ice cream or drink your glass of wine or your soft drink, you will have great enjoyment. Such enjoyment brings positive effects, not negative ones, upon your body. You will choose to have less because you will be satisfied. You will be paying attention to your body. When you eat unconsciously, you are not paying attention to anything.

## THE PACKAGING OF FOOD ALSO INFLUENCES ITS ENERGY
*What about teas?*

Here is the problem with teas. I am talking about herbal teas. If you can find a source of herbal tea raised organically and packaged without chemicals, that would be healthier for you. Some of the packaging itself has chemicals. You are aware that there are some coffee companies that are now packaging their coffee in plastic containers. If you are going to drink coffee, drink it from cans or from paper, from packages that are not plastic, because the chemicals that are in the plastic seep into the coffee.

If you want to lower the amount of caffeine you take in, you find decaffeinated drinks. Correct? Know that "decaffeinated" means that there is less caffeine, not that there is no caffeine. Be sure and drink things that were decaffeinated in a natural manner, as with water, not with chemicals. You might ask: "How am I to know this when I'm at a party?" You simply bless. You thank. You communicate with the substance that you are getting ready to put into your body. You have your body meet that substance. You ask that your body assimilate whatever it needs within the substance and release the rest. There is no reason to be worried. I am telling you what will make things easier for your body. Have no fear of the food. When you become afraid of it, the food becomes your enemy because the food becomes afraid of you. A battle within your body follows. These are guidelines. These are not rules.

## THE ORIGIN AND HEALING OF THE CRAVING FOR SUGAR
*How do I handle my craving for sugar?*

Intense craving for sugar is an allergic reaction to sugar. One thing to do is to release the allergic reaction that is present. Another thing is to talk to the craving and find out what other emotional components are present. Many, if not most, intense cravings for sugar have to do with a yeast infection that has invaded the body. Think also of a yeast infection being a "leavening" agent involving thoughts, feelings and beliefs—by this I mean thought forms and beliefs that act as yeast and elevate the emotional components.

Physical craving results from an influx of insulin lowering the blood sugar. An overrelease of insulin is three-pronged. First, it is a reaction to the mental state of the individual who has a belief system that either this food will release insulin, or that he or she should not have this food because it will change his or her insulin production. These beliefs do not have to be conscious. The individual simply needs to be tapped into the morphogenic field.

There is also a chemical reaction to the food in which the body misidentifies the chemical. There is a worrying located in the pancreas that the body is not in balance. The pancreas overreacts, just as you might overreact to an event. Remember that your pancreas is a living being contained within your body. Those of you who have studied Oriental medicine know that the pancreas is a worrywart. In addition, what does stress do to your body? Those of you who have been studying the effects of stress have discovered that one of the things that happens is the overproduction of insulin.

What is stress? Is stress not worry? What else is stress? Stress is not living in the present. Those of you who feel stress right now—what is it you are stressed about? Is it about what I am saying? Are you stressed about sitting in the chair or on the floor? Are you stressed about anything happening at this very moment, even if it is the information coming in? Is it not that your stress comes from the future or goes to the past? Stress comes from moving outside of the present. If you would live in the Now, there would be no stress.

## DNA Activation

Here are other things you can do to help your body assimilate this energy. Talk to your cells. Let your cells know that there are new energies coming in and that you know that they were not constructed for this energy. Just because they were not constructed for this energy does not mean the cells cannot change. How many of you have heard it said, or perhaps you might even have said, "This is the way I am. I can't change." You know that is false, don't you? You can change. The same is true for your cells. Your cells can change. Tell them how to do it.

There is new DNA. Actually, it isn't new DNA—it is just that the DNA already there is becoming active. Both the physical DNA and the spiritual DNA are becoming active. You can talk to your cells and let them know about the increased activation of the DNA. Sit in meditation, or if you do not like the word meditation, sit quietly and have a conversation with the cells of your body. Tell the cells about the new energy coming in. Tell them there is a new vibration, even a different color, and it resonates differently within the body than the old energy. Let your cells know that they have permission to change however they need to in order to accept this energy.

When you do this, you will be facilitating the change in your DNA. You will be changing the structure of your DNA, because you are asking the cells to do major structural changes. For those of you who have remodeled a house, does not your house look different after the work than before? You have changed the structure of your house. When you change the DNA, you are doing the same thing.

## STAYING IN YOUR HEART CENTER FACILITATES THE ENERGY

Another thing that will help you to assimilate the energy is to stay in your heart center. Do this by entering the back of your heart center. The front of your heart center keeps you present in this three-dimensional world—four-dimensional, if you include time. The front of the heart center is where you are in this incarnation. When you go into your heart center from the rear, you are entering into the time of no-time and the space of no-space. You can travel interdimensionally. You can travel into the spiritual essence of your DNA. From the back of your heart center, you can contact the other ten strands of your DNA that exist on a spiritual level. Since the other ten strands of your DNA are multidimensional, not four-dimensional, they are not in the physical.

Focus on the front of your body, and then focus on the back. Notice how you feel differently in your back than in the front. Do you notice that? Notice the space you feel from the back. The front of you is more solid. The back is more amorphous. From the back, you are entering what is known as the time-space continuum. You can travel from the time-space continuum. The front of you is located in this physical world. Spend some time at your altar. Go into your heart through the back of your heart center and find your altar. Speak to your DNA, the other ten strands, as they are becoming more and more apparent.

You actually have an infinite number of strands of DNA. You have individual strands connected to you in this incarnation and in this world. You have other strands connected to your multidimensional self. The planet herself has DNA that is also multidimensional. Right now, you work with 12 strands. You will then find, after the 12 strands, that you will work with 33 strands. Yes, those who actually have the 24 are moving out to the next layer, if you would call it a layer, to 33 strands. Then you will go to 133 strands. So the DNA increases geometrically until you can become aware of the fullness that is your connection to All That Is. The infinite number of strands is the result of holographic structure.

## STRING THEORY AND DNA PARTICLES

*How does this relate to string theory?*

In string theory, there are little particles. These particles come together in an organized structure. When you have just the simple particles, you have chaos. As the particles form DNA, you have organization within the chaos. Know, however, that there is organization even within chaos.

**Can the pineal gland connect to the master cell within the body and help with the replication of your own personal DNA?**

Yes, it can do that. A nuance is that the master cell is not actually physical. It is an energy concept. The master cell is a type of encodement. You can enter into its energy and reconnect its energy with other cells who have "forgotten" who and what they are. Would you like a demonstration?

*First of all, think of something that you would like to change. Begin by picking something minor. Of course, nothing is ever minor. Choose whatever you wish that you would like to change on the physical [laughs]. Let's stay with the physical, so you can see it.*

*Go into the back of your heart center. Feel the difference in entering into your heart center from the back. If some of you are having a difficult time getting into the back of your heart center, raise your entry point about an inch and a half and enter through there. There you go. Now metaphorically move forward into your heart center until you come to your altar. From your altar, send a beam of energy to your pineal gland. It is in the center of your brain. If you don't know exactly where, don't worry. Just intend for the energy to enter your pineal gland. Feel that activation. Know that your pineal gland contains its physical element and its spiritual element, its multidimensional element, just as your DNA does. That is why you activate the master cell with your pineal gland.*

*You are now in your multidimensional heart center. You are connecting to your multidimensional pineal gland. Now intend to connect with what is being called the master cell. In other modalities, it can be called the original eight cells or the original matrix or blueprint, but for our purposes, master cell is a nice, compact concept. You might feel the energy of the master cell in one of several places. Most of you will feel it at the base of your spine.*

*Simply intend for the connection between your pineal gland and your master cell to be made. You will note that you are then connected from the crown area into your heart and the base of your spine. You will be centered and grounded. Now send the message to your master cell about what it is that you want changed in your physical body. Once you have relayed the information, ask that the master cell connect with all the cells and realign the instructions of the functioning of the cells to the perfection originally intended.*

*Breathe into the energy of the connection. Intend, see, feel the connection becoming stronger. As the master cell sends out its communication waves to the cells you are speaking to, the information is transmitted. The clearer, the purer—and when I say purer, I mean devoid of emotion, not devoid of energy—the purer you can make your communication, the more powerfully this works. Now know that the communication has occurred and come back.*

Being new at this, most of you have a little doubt as to whether this works, so you might need to repeat this process until you feel yourself more centered and devoid of doubt and emotion—not devoid of energy, but devoid of labels.

## BREATHE OUT DISCORDANCE

Something else to help you assimilate these energies: Know that your relationships with others and how you manage the energy of those relationships have much to do with assimilating the new energies. Stay in your heart center. It does not matter in this case whether you come into the heart center from behind or from the front. When you stay in this place in your heart center and relate to the heart center of each person, you will better assimilate the new energies. Your heart-center energy is the highest vibration energy you have.

When you have an altercation with someone, a discordant interaction, your energies are not in sync with each other. Take some time to breathe the discordance from your body; go into your heart and acknowledge, at least mentally (if you cannot do this with the wholeness of your soul, of your self), that the person is an aspect of the One, an aspect of the God, an aspect of the Christ. Acknowledge that the person is on his or her perfect path. Acknowledge that you yourself are an aspect of the One, an aspect of the God, an aspect of the Christ and are on your perfect path. In other words, you are removing judgment. Except for the work with the master cell and the DNA, most of this information you have heard before, and it is simply being put into a different package. How you assimilate the energy is up to you, up to your choice.

## IMMUNITY FROM THE FLU EPIDEMIC

*I sat through a lecture this past evening on a subject a little more earthly, regarding a phenomenon that has occurred in the past five years: chemtrails. They are essentially a release of raw jet fuel and ethylene bromide, which has now been included in the jet fuel, over populated areas. The effect of this is to lower the immunity of the population. This is happening more frequently in populated parts of industrialized countries. Ken Welch, who gave the speech, was demonstrating reverse speech. He had cause to believe that this phenomenon was due to forces within the government that are planning to release a deadly flu virus, like the Spanish flu of the 1900s. This would be around Christmastime, when kids are out of school, so that the older population would be primarily affected. Its purpose is to save the country from the demands of Social Security. What I want to know is if there is any validity to these concerns, or are we just making a mistake by including impurities in the jet fuel?*

The difficulty with what Ken Welch is bringing out is not the information itself but how you receive the information. It is simply information to become aware of and then use to counteract the effects of what is happening. Yes, there are forces within the government concerned about not only the demise of Social Security but of many other pension funds all over the world. Unfortunately, there are not just forces within the government; there are forces outside of the government as well that control the government. I do not wish to promote fear, so when I say this I hope that you will listen from your heart center and know that it just is.

This is something that has been written. You can find information on this, if you wish. There is something that some call the sinister secret government (SSG). These are the forces that actually control the governmental structures. If you want to call it a conspiracy theory, you can call it a conspiracy theory. These are the forces that you as lightworkers are actually fighting against, but you are not using weapons of fear and you are not using weapons of destruction. You are using the energy of the heart and you are using light.

## EARTH CHANGES, THE COMING FLU
## EPIDEMIC AND THE CHEMTRAILS

There are Earth changes occurring right now. These Earth changes do not have as much to do with changes in the Earth as they have to do with changes in the population of Earth. There will be changes within the Earth. Those of you who have read other channels will have read of these things and how you can send energy to offset these effects. Know that the chemtrails and what they can do to the population are real. It does not matter whether it is maliciously intended or not. Chemtrails do lower the immune system. You will find people who are very aware of chemtrails and notice that their children become ill when the chemtrails are present. Yes, there is the fear of what will happen with the older population. One of the reasons for the plan to send out these chemtrails when children are not in school is so that the children will not pass the infection to one another.

The important thing for you to do is to build your own immune system. What we have talked about will help you to build your immune system: Stay in the heart, talk to your body and talk to your cells. Talk to the air you breathe. There will be a grave illness over the next year. Actually, it will extend for about eighteen months. It very well could end the conflict in Iraq, just as World War I ended because there were not enough people left to fight. Yes, people were sick in 1918. People had transitioned. Millions. More people died from that flu than died in the two wars combined.

Now, that is the information. Are you going to live with it in fear? If you do, if anyone reading this information chooses to live with it in fear, what is the first thing that happens? Your immune system becomes compromised. I have used this example before. When you get in your car and you put on your seat belt, do you do it in fear? You have gotten used to it, right? It is a protection. You realize that it is a safety mechanism. Do you put it on in fear? No. You attract nothing to you that is negative when you put on the seat belt.

This information about chemtrails is valid. There are some malicious bodies who are having this occur, but it is not actually as widespread as some would like to believe it is. For instance, your present president is rather clueless about it. But he is also rather clueless about these other governmental structures that are working.

*When you start to talk about this flu and fear stuff, sometimes I wonder what I am doing here. I just want to run away from here. But at the same time, I feel like maybe I have to balance . . . but balance what? I need some guidance, because I am completely lost.*

First, I want to contradict you. You are not completely lost. You are simply confused. You are here to balance staying in that place in your heart. You are here to stay in your integrity so that others can see you and know that there is another way to be. That is why all of you are here. You are meant to be here. You will not escape being near this flu, no matter where you go. It will be world-wide. There is no reason to be in fear about it; it just is.

Do what has been suggested and work with your children also. They have a greater protection than you do. Most of you here are not the actual targets. There are a few of you here who are the targets, three of you especially, who are targets of the flu. Anyone over the age of sixty is a target. Does that help bring you a little bit of peace, even though there might not be understanding?

## MISSIONARIES TO AMERICA

*Yes, but at the same time, I have a very strange feeling. When I go back to the place I was born, it is beautiful. I feel like I want to be there. But at the same time, I think no, you do not have to be here. Go away. And I think it is dangerous for me there. But at the same time, I want to go there, because I am tired of being a foreigner in this place.*

You are right that there is a danger for you to be there. And the danger is spiritual. The danger is that you will feel so protected, so at home, that you will not grow. You are very perceptive. You have a great deal of insight. Know first of all that it just is. The problem is your resistance to what is. And you are homesick. It is very difficult to be a stranger in a strange land with different cultures, different values and different ways of thinking. And yet you are very important to this country. You are a light for this country, and so are all of the other immigrants who are coming in with their different ways of thinking and their different cultures. It is difficult for you and it is a job that you accepted.

In essence, you are like missionaries. You are missionaries to this country, as are all the others who come, whether they have documents or not. It is a way of helping these people who live here and are having a difficult time opening themselves to others. It is a blasting open of themselves to a different kind of life. Those of us on this side of the veil are here to support you in what you are doing, and we recognize how difficult it is for you.

You are lightworkers. You have chosen to be a lightworker in another culture. Everyone else here is a lightworker who has chosen to be a lightworker within his or her own culture. The two people here who might be most able to under-stand that concept are actually two lesbian women, because they are also of a different culture. They feel like aliens in their own country. You are aliens in a different country. Know that you are doing exactly what is needed. You have no idea what you are contributing to the growth of this country and this culture. You will not know until you leave—not leave this country, but leave this life.

## Build Up Your Body to Fight the Flu Epidemic: Herbs
*Are there certain herbs that could help in a flu epidemic?*

Build yourself up with any of the immunity-building herbs. Echinacea is one of the best. This is the time to do a cleansing of your body. Do your liver cleanse. Do your bowel cleanse. Do your kidney cleanses. Do cellular cleanses. The more you release the toxins from your body, the stronger your immune system will be. Do emotional cleanses. By emotional cleanses, I do not mean scream and holler and hit things; I mean release fears.

You have information that the flu epidemic is going to come. It will be here. The flu shot, by the way, will not help in this flu epidemic and, in fact, I want you to know that the flu shot will compromise your immune system.

*Ken Welch did say that the flu shot that the children would probably get, although not protection against the virus itself, is close enough that it will give the children some protection, even if it is a different type of flu vaccine than what is given to adults.*

And, in addition to that, children do not get caught up in the fear that adults get caught up in. That is extra protection for them. Yes, it is a different flu vaccine that will be given to them. There will be some adults who will receive a flu vaccine that will provide them with some protection. But most adults will not receive that.

There is a vaccine that only the elite will receive, but it will backfire on them. They will not be in a place of love in their hearts. Some of them might survive this flu, but their bodies are going to be compromised in other ways. You, however, do your cleansing now. Cleanse now.

## Build Up Your Body to Fight the Flu Epidemic: Colonics
*What about colonics?*

Colonics are helpful for some people and they will help undo the sludge caught in the colon. Be selective about the person who does it. If colonics were not helpful, your government would not be trying to stop them. An intestinal cleanse will be, over time, as good as colonics for most people. There will be some people who will need colonics, because they are dealing with a greater influx of parasites in which the material gets stuck. There are some good intestinal herbs that will get the peristalsis going, and that will work just as well.

Another technique that works well is drinking a quart of warm water with a few teaspoons of salt mixed in. You take it in the morning. It will assimilate and pass through your body. You will not throw it up. You drink it very quickly, by the way, although it is a lot of water to do that with. It will actually start to cleanse your body and your whole intestinal tract, whereas a colonic cannot get into the small intestines. Your body will begin releasing the salt water in about an hour. Do this and stay at home until you have finished releasing the water.

## BUILD UP YOUR BODY TO FIGHT THE FLU EPIDEMIC: JUICES AND CHARRED OAK KEG

*I ran into a product the other day composed primarily of mangosteen juice. I understand that it has been used in Southeast Asia for many hundreds of years, and it is supposedly the greatest thing ever to come along for rebuilding the immune system. It seems to be very effective in treating a lot of things. I just wondered if you had any spiritual insight on this.*

It is a juice that could help. Another juice that could help would be your noni (the Indian mulberry, *Morinda citrifolia*) juice. There are other, similar juices out there. The greatest thing that can help your immune system is the cleansing we have already discussed, and that doesn't add any extra expense.

*Is the charred oak keg a valuable tool to have around in case of flu?*

The charred oak keg and brandy that you mentioned will aid against flu. That is why I instructed this one [the channel] to get it. The keg is sitting outside the door right here for her to start using it.

*I have recently had a very violent throat infection. I have never had anything like it before. I am wondering if it had any special significance.*

The throat infection was caused by several things. One of them was that you are struggling with speaking your truth. The other is that the throat infection is actually going to build your immune system against what is going to happen in the future. You need to be particularly careful to protect yourself from the air inside airplanes. I am going to suggest that you get some good sprays that are citrus based. You can spray something citrus based into a handkerchief, something cotton, and keep it in the cabin. Every once in a while, breathe in the scent from your handkerchief.

It is important for you to use the Edgar Cayce modality known as the "charred oak keg" when you are at home. It will strengthen your lungs and it will kill infection for you. You need to use it every time you get back home. It will strengthen your lungs. You, more than anyone else here, will have a greater exposure to this flu, because your work requires that you go on long trips by plane.

## POLITICS IN AMERICA

*Ken Welch did pick up something through reverse speech technique: that the president was aware of some of the things that have been going on.*

Let me put it this way. He is aware of them just as any soldier is aware of a general outline of the plan but not the exact strategies. Does that make sense? The president, the current Mr. Bush, is not as aware as his father was or as aware as the president who preceded him.

*I read on the net that George W. Bush is a clone.*

Actually, he is not a clone. It makes a very good story, but actually he is not a clone. Many people are concerned about him, but your president is actually acting within the integrity that he possesses. And he acts in the way that he believes things need to happen. It is another war that is occurring. Your president is not a very complex individual. He is a rather—and I do not mean this in a derogatory manner—he is a rather simple individual. If you want to know complexity, get to know his father.

*Could he be called a young soul?*

He is a young soul. Yes, he is a young soul.

## DIFFERENCES BETWEEN BUSH AND KERRY

If Kerry had been elected, the complexity story might have changed, but the whole way in which your government is going would not change. If you look closely at Kerry, there are a couple of differences between him and your present President Bush. Kerry has a greater ability to think in complexities. He is more versed. For instance, he would be more aware of what you are talking about than your present President Bush would be. However, the only difference between Kerry and his beliefs and the war you are now in is that Kerry is a Democrat and your present president is a Republican.

If Kerry had been president at the time of 9/11, he would have done similar things, just not as quickly. He has a greater ability to manipulate people, and he would have been able to manipulate other governments to join him in what is happening in Iraq. So what would have happened if Kerry had been president during 9/11, or if it had been President Gore (who, as you know, did win the election)? If it had been either of them, the same thing would have happened, because that is what the controlling government actually wanted to happen. It would have happened at a different pace. It is the difference between someone who plows through your football line with sheer force and another who finesses his way to the goal line. Your country would not have been as isolated as it is now.

*You say that Kerry or Gore would have taken the slow approach and marshalled the other nations. Wouldn't the world be totally different?*

Would the world be totally different? The totally different part would be that the United States would not be isolated. There would still be the war, but the United States would not be isolated. They would have the support of more people, more countries. You travel to France or Italy or any of your eastern countries right now, and they don't think very highly of the United States, and they would not think very highly of you. That would not be happening if either Gore or Kerry had been in power. They are not bulls in china shops, and that would have made a difference in the way the United States is viewed. At the same time, the terrorist influence would still be present.

The problem that you have right now is not necessarily the country of Iraq. It is the factions that are present in Iraq. The United States and Great Britain and other countries are trying to relate to Iraq as if it is a country. It is not a united country. It is tribal. Kerry would have entered the war in a more tactical manner. Kerry would have listened to his military officers. Gore would have listened to his military officers, but not as much as Kerry would have. Problems occurred because Bush did not listen to his military officers. He listened to his vice president. Kerry and Gore are stronger personalities and would not have been as influenced by a vice president as the current president is.

*I have two questions. I noticed on the Internet the other day that there was an individual known as John Joseph Kennedy who has declared himself to be a write-in candidate. Do you have anything to say about him?*

He is symbolic of the next line of politicians who will be coming in after the next election. No, it is not his time yet, but he is preparing for the next time. And he is preparing your country for the next time. Things need to progress, and they are now doing so.

## A FEW QUESTIONS ON RELIGION AND PURPOSE

*I have a personal and practical question. How do I teach my kids in some religion? I am afraid to move from my religion, but I am having a really hard time reconciling the things I don't like from the Catholic Church with the things I like. How can I teach them to believe in Jesus Christ and also many other things I don't believe, for example, that you have to give your money or you have to be afraid of the devil and things like that? At the same time, I want to go to another church.*

First, know that your children don't need a religion like you did. You want them to know their spiritual selves, to come to know the God within themselves. There is no need for fear. There is no devil except the one who is manufactured. So what you want to do is to teach them to connect with their own angels and guides and the spiritual resources within them. They need to learn how to work from their hearts, the things that we are teaching here. They don't need religion, but if they would like to participate in one, they can. They are very different than you are.

You might find that they want to be at church occasionally, whereas at other times they rebel against it. They will feel the discordance that is there. Simply teach them to connect with God through their hearts, to learn how to talk to God in their hearts and stand in integrity. That is what they need. They don't need the structure that is called church.

*Do you have any kind of guidance for me? I don't know what I want.*

To find out what it is you want is to find out what it is you want. To find out what to do is to find out what it is you want. Start paying attention to the things that give you joy. What brings you peace? Discover how you can use those things that give you joy and peace in doing your next work. Does that help at all?

*Not really.*

I would suggest that you find someone who can act as a coach for you, and there are many. Not a therapist, but a coach. He or she will help you take some forms of testing to help you identify what it is you would enjoy. You have lived for so long in a way where you could not express yourself or come to know your gifts and talents. A coach would help you come to know your gifts and talents.

Now, dear ones, let us end with a blessing. Join your hearts together. I will join mine with you. Feel the oneness that you are. Release the belief that you are separate. My love is with you always. I am Amma, the divine mother of the divine mothers.

# 21

# Believe That You Are Love Incarnate and Ease the Effects of Earth Changes

*January 2005*

ood evening, dear ones. It is so wonderful to have all of you here. Let me tell you about channeling, for those of you who have never been to a channeling before. Very simply, this one [the channel] allows my energy to come into her. She translates the energy into her own language and then expresses it. The clarity of my message depends upon how clear she is. I must admit that sometimes she stands there on the side and makes comments about things or wants me to interject things. We, she and I, can be having an interesting discussion behind the scenes at the same time as she is relating information to you. That is, as simply as possible, what channeling is.

All of you have channeled at some point. Remember those moments of inspiration when you later wondered, "Where did those words come from?" That was when you had opened yourself to the divine energy so that it could flow through you. Those of you who are from the Judeo-Christian tradition have read much channeled material. You call it your Bible. That was channeled information that you learned was the inspired word of God. Correct? The Bible and all spiritual materials were inspired and could be called channeled.

## AMMA IS THE FEMININE ASPECT OF THE I AM

So, who is Amma? Who am I? Well, I am the divine mother of the divine mothers. I am the divine mother of everyone. Many people have heard of Mother Mary, of Quan Yin, of White Buffalo Calf Woman. Some of you have even heard of Athena, who many of you thought was myth only. People think of them as divine mothers. Well, I am their divine mother. Who or what am I?

I am from the oneness of the God essence, which is neither masculine nor feminine. I am from the fullness of love, a love no one here on Earth understands or knows in its fullness.

Most people think of love as an emotion. Love as I am speaking of it has no emotion. It simply is. Love is the creative energy. Each one of you is a demonstration of love's creative energy. You were created from love. Because you are in a world of duality, there needs to be a masculine and a feminine essence of the God energy. In a world of duality, you have good and evil, black and white, up and down, right and left, male and female. Something is or it isn't. That is duality.

Most of you grew up knowing of God, the Father. Only in the past two decades have you heard about the feminine aspect of God in your Christian tradition. In your eastern traditions, there has always been a feminine aspect of God. I, Amma, am the fullness of the feminine aspect of God. The masculine aspect of God, using the masculine complement to my name, is Abba. You have Amma and Abba. Those of you who have studied the Jewish Kabbalah know of Kether, the crown, the undivided energy you call God. This energy then divides into Binah, where I am, and Chokmah, where Abba is. I hope this gives you some understanding.

The only thing you need to know is that I am love. I love you and loved you into being. You are of my energy. I am with each one of you, day by day, minute by minute and second by second. If I withdrew from you, you no longer would be. And you would not even know that you weren't any more. You just would not be. The same also is true of Abba. If Abba withdrew, the masculine God essence, you would no longer be. For those of you who feel so alone, thinking that no one is there and no one cares, Amma and Abba are always there.

## ONLY YOU CAN DEFINE YOURSELF AS LOVE INCARNATE

Of course you say, "But I want someone I can touch," and I understand that. The experience of separation is part of what you came to learn in the human condition. You knew only oneness. You came to experience separation so that you would come to know who you are. You experience who you are not so that you can come to know who you are. You do not need anyone outside of yourself to tell you who you are. Yet all of you here, including this one I am speaking through, identify yourselves by what others have said about you. This usually starts at a very, very young age. If a parent said to you at one time, "You are stupid," and perhaps it was said to you more than once, what is it you believe? You believe and remember that you are stupid. How many times do you remember the depth of love someone has shown to you?

So often humans hold on to the negative that is presented and ignore the positive. Many cannot even see or hear the positive when it is present. Some of you grew up in homes where there was more anger and hostility than there were demonstrations of love and peace. Some of you grew up in homes in which there were more demonstrations of berating than there were of uplifting. Some of you grew up in those homes because that is what parents thought they were supposed to do. Some parents did this from ignorance, some from their own woundedness, and some from a belief system that their words and actions would keep you in line and toughen you up.

## RAISE THESE NEW CHILDREN AS YOU WOULD WISH TO HAVE BEEN RAISED

There has been much discussion of late about the new children who are coming into the world. They have been coming for a while. Perhaps you have heard of them. The Indigos, the Crystals, the Rainbows and now those of the platinum ray are coming in. People are saying that you need to treat them differently. Well, dear ones, it isn't that they need to be treated differently than how you were treated. The fact is, you need to treat them in the same the way that you wanted to be treated. You wanted to be treated with love, with respect, with honor, did you not? That is how you need to treat these little ones. When you were in school, did you not want to learn in the way that was most exciting to you? To have your mind stimulated? Did you know that even little babies are excited about newness?

So it is not that these new children coming into the world need a different type of education than you had. They need to be given the type of education that you needed. Every way to treat and to raise the children who are coming in is exactly the way that you wanted to be treated, to be raised and to be loved. Correct? Wouldn't you rather have been told, "Honey, if you do it this way, you will be more successful" instead of "You're so stupid; you will never understand how to do anything"? And yet how many of you were told in this second way? So the way to raise your children is simply to raise them in the way that you would have wanted to be raised and to speak to them in the way that you would have wanted to be spoken to.

It has been said that children should be seen and not heard. Every human, no matter how young, desires to be recognized, to be validated. That desire comes from the yearning for community, for oneness that is innate in each of you. Children who are not recognized will learn either to make themselves known in some way or to retreat within their woundedness and attempt to disappear. If the child attempts to make him- or herself known, it will be through achievement or by making trouble. Correct? The authorities call the phenomenon of becoming known by making trouble "acting out," but you should know that attempting to become known by achievement is also acting out. Acting out is an attempt to get love, and if not love, then attention. In either case, the individual is acting a part, not being the love he or she is. Another person might attempt to hide him- or herself. By hiding, the precious one attempts to be like vapor drifting into the atmosphere, thus becoming one with the atmosphere.

The hiding of the self is an attempt to not be different, to be one. Unfortunately, the desire to experience oneness cannot be achieved by either means.

All of you fit into one of these categories or somewhere in the middle, don't you? Your job, dear ones, is simply to recognize that you are love. You are love and you are beloved. You will not be able to find love from somewhere outside yourself. Even the one who you believed loved you the most let you down at some point. Most people, most human beings, have such a fragile hold upon themselves that if someone who loves them dearly lets them down once, they begin to doubt that they themselves are love or are deserving of love.

This being human is a difficult road, is it not? It is much more difficult to be human than it is to be a star brightly shining in the sky. It is much more difficult to be human than it is to be a tree. You have many choices before you. I can give you some simple rules of how to be human easily.

## TWO RULES FOR EASILY BEING HUMAN

The very first one is: Learn to live in your heart. Learn to live in your heart. Think of what would happen if you were driving down the wonderful freeways here, or even a side street, and while you are in your heart, somebody suddenly speeds past you and cuts you off. How differently you might respond in thought and action if you are in your heart rather than in your head or your gut. You might say, if you are in your heart, "Oh, I hope nothing is wrong." If you are not in your heart, you might give them a signal with your hand. You humans do interesting things with your fingers! [Laughter.] How do you know when you are in your heart? When you are in fear, you are not in your heart. When you are anxious, you are not in your heart. These are very simple feelings to recognize. So the first rule is to practice being in your heart.

The second rule is to realize that you and only you can determine who you are. There is just you. It is not your mother or your father or your husband or your wife or your partner or your best friend or the person down the street or the priest or the rabbi. It is you. You have an amazing responsibility, do you not? Do you realize that all the doubts you have about yourself come from yourself? It does not matter, my dear ones, what anyone else thinks of you. It matters only what you think of yourself. If you are affected by what someone thinks about you, it is only because your greatest fear is that that person is right. I can tell you that the only time someone else is right about you is when he or she looks into your eyes and into your heart and tells you, "You are love incarnate." Then that person is right. You are the embodiment of love.

Think for just a moment of how you would act and be if you were the embodiment of love. If you truly believed that you are the embodiment of love, would you be different? Would you respond to events differently? Maybe you would have a smile as big as mine if you truly believed that you are love incarnate. Your task while you are here in this incarnation is to remember that you are the embodiment of love. If you tell someone that you are love incarnate, he or she will probably exclaim, "What hubris! What pride! What arrogance!" Someone might even say, "Blasphemy!" And you know what? That person would be wrong. And if you could giggle about such misperception, I would giggle with you.

Think of what you do when a little child makes a very innocent mistake in language. This one is remembering when she was living with her cousins in college, and they were getting new ductwork for the air-conditioning system. Her four-year-old cousin wanted to know if there would be feathers. Don't you just laugh at those things? When people tell you negative things, they are no different than that little one who got ducts mixed up with ducks. When you know firmly who you are and you know it so firmly that it isn't a belief, that it is a beingness, then all you do is smile and go on. Your anger and your fear would disappear, because you would not be worried if these people were correct. When you live in your heart, you shower love upon those who do not know the truth. Perhaps your heart might grieve a bit because they are not aware of who it is they are. It is that simple.

## TRULY BELIEVE THAT YOU ARE LOVE INCARNATE

You are in a world where your newspapers and your televisions and your radios are filled with information about people who do not know who they are. They do not know that they are love incarnate. They do not know that they carry within them the God essence. Dear ones, if each one of you chose to leave your bodies this instant, would the God essence within you be gone? Of course not. The God essence is what left your body. Right? And all you have is the shell, these clothes, these physical clothes that you call bone and skin and blood. They are nothing more than clothes. It does not matter what this bone and skin and blood looks like. It is the knowledge of what is within. That is what is crucial. These are words that you have heard before, perhaps in a different way. To know and remember who you are—that is my challenge to you.

We are going to do some work tonight, since I have all of you gathered here together. It is time to do some work. For those of you who might be in fear of what it is that is happening to this planet, I am going to show you some actions that you can take to help while you are here. You wonder how it is that you can help the world situation. Be in your heart, know that you are love incarnate and know, dear ones, that so is everyone else. Would you make those gestures to others with your hands and fingers if you truly believed that the one who was passing by you was love incarnate? I don't think so.

You help the planet and everyone on it by changing your beliefs, by changing the misperceptions that run your life. This change could happen with the snap of a finger or the blink of an eye. You could change your entire life in an instant, this instant, if you chose to believe that you and every person you see are love incarnate. Think of what it would be like if you drove your car today and saw another car coming toward you and you said, "There goes love incarnate. There is another one, another love incarnate." What would that do to your doubts about whether you are alone or not? Each one of you is love incarnate.

## THE SWORD OF ARCHANGEL MICHAEL

The work we are going to do tonight is to work with those who do not realize that they are love incarnate and who don't have anybody to tell them that they are love incarnate. Would you like to do some of that work? Would you be willing? If you feel uncomfortable doing this work, you can sit, listen and be supportive. Some of you do not know how to go into your heart center from the back. You know that your heart center is in the center of your chest. When most people tell you to focus on your heart center, they are talking about focusing on the center of your chest.

*Enter your heart center through the back. Bring your attention to the center of your upper back and enter your heart center from there. Feel the space that is there through the back of your heart center.*

*You have entered into a place of infinity. Imagine yourself moving forward in that space. You will come to an altar, your sacred space, the sacredness of yourself. Notice your altar, what it looks like. Some of you have ornate altars. Some have a little table. Some have a cloth on the ground. This altar is simply a placeholder for you, a sacred spot that you can come to. You can write things upon it. Some of you have a pen and a notepad, some have a computer terminal, and some of you have quill and paper. You can come to your altar to talk. You can come to talk to me. That is how I come to this one, at her altar.*

*You are now going to use your intention. Invite a beam of energy to come down into your head as you are there at your altar. The beam will go straight through your spine, anchoring into the center of the Earth. Feel the energy and the power. All of you here have heard of the one known as Michael, the Archangel Mich-a-el, el meaning "of God." He carries a sword in his hand, and he will give you his sword. Hold out your dominant hand, and he will place his sword in your hand. Grasp that sword. Feel the hilt of that sword in your hand and hold it in front of your heart. Feel even more strongly the love energy in your heart. Ask that more and more love energy come into your heart. As the energy expands your heart, send some of that energy down your arm and into the sword. Feel and see the sword, how it becomes brighter and stronger.*

## A MEDITATION TO REDUCE THE POWER OF THE FLORIDA STORMS

*We are going to do some work to lessen the ferocity of the storm that is coming to your United States coast again. I want you to feel yourselves as part of a huge circle. Notice that each one of you is as big as a space shuttle or larger. Now, if you wish, if you are holding the sword up with your physical hand, see your spiri-*

*tual self holding the sword and relax your physical hand. Still see yourself standing there with the sword. Now send a beam of energy from your heart into the heart of every person. Feel how you are now connected. Feel how you are connected to one another and to the Earth through the beam of energy that goes into every person's heart center.*

*Now, dear ones, see yourselves in a huge circle with the storm in the middle. The wind and the rain do not affect you. You might sense them, but since you are in your heart, you are not affected. What is holding the storm together is its center. Isn't it interesting? In its center is calm. It is the outside that rages. You are going to relieve some pressure from the center of this storm. Take your sword and pierce the sides of the center of the storm. It would be as if you had a huge inflatable raft or balloon and you pricked it with a pin to slowly let the air out to relieve the pressure. Allow this tremendous pent-up energy to go into the atmosphere. This will also relieve pressure from Mother Earth, because the storm itself relieves pressure from Mother Earth. You might even feel a little difference in the pressure.*

*This is a sword of love, not of destruction. Know that. Now, dear ones, feel yourselves coming back. Feel yourselves in your bodies. Wiggle your toes, take a deep breath and open your eyes.*

The process you did is very simple. It has more power when it is done in a group, because you remember your oneness when you are in a group. The ordinary human forgets about oneness when he or she is separate. The ordinary human believes that the skin identifies the boundaries, but the skin does not identify the boundaries. You continue to be one.

You can do this process on the San Andreas Fault, on any storm, on a volcano. This process helps relieve the pressure. Remember that your planet is a living being. Pressures build up just as they do in you. Some of these pressures do not come simply from what is happening beneath her skin, her mantle. Some of these pressures build up because of what is happening to the beings who are living on her skin. When you stay in your heart, when you remember that you are love incarnate, some of the pressure is relieved. When you send love energy from your heart to the heart of anybody who is with you or near you or on the other side of the planet from you, you are doing something to relieve the pressure on the planet. Are there any questions?

## SOME HUMANS ARE MANIPULATING ENERGY

*What about all the hurricanes that are hitting Florida? Spiritually, what is creating that problem in Florida?*

Ah, the questions. So much occurs on this planet that most people are not aware of. It is not just spiritual forces that come from what some would call divine energies. There are those who are masters at manipulating energy. An example of those who are masters at manipulating energy are those who do advertising. When was the last time you found yourself buying something and then realized that you did not really need it? Whoever developed that ad is a master at manipulating your energy. Does that make sense?

You have probably read in what some call science-fiction books about people who can manipulate the weather. Have you read about that in your science fiction? Are you aware that that can happen now? It very much can happen that the weather can be manipulated. Now, what would be the advantage of having this state called Florida in chaos in November? If they are in survival mode, they cannot be worried about the government. There are also energies that bring other energies. There has been chaos in that state, has there not? A state that has produced chaos has attracted more chaos to it.

But back to the forces that are manipulating the storms coming into that state. This is a pivotal state. You know that this past election was not the first election that was manipulated, stolen from someone. There are some of you here who will remember the election between Kennedy and Nixon. Kennedy did not win that election. Did you know that? No, that was another one that was "stolen," as you might say. Very interesting. So it is not the first time that this has happened. And it will not be the last. So does that answer your question?

## THE EARTH NEEDS CLEANSING AND IS CLEANSING HERSELF
*Yes, I just thought that maybe Florida needed a cleansing.*

It does need a cleansing. This whole country needs a cleansing. This whole planet needs a cleansing, does it not? Do you realize that there are very few places on this planet that do not need a cleansing? Think about what has happened in this young country. It is a very young country, is it not? Not the youngest in the world, but it is a very young country.

Several hundred years ago, it was not very populated. There were those who came across this land with great animosity and hostility and a belief that they were the only ones who deserved the land. There was much killing. This is all being cleansed. How you respond to these cleansing events will determine what else happens. Can you stay in your heart through all this? There is unrest, is there not, in your country? There is unrest in many places, all over the planet. How are you going to respond? Unrest occurs when changes are coming. There is no reason for unrest if there is not going to be a change. When you are lying in bed, when do you move your body? When you are going to change, turn over or get out of the bed! So that is what is happening. Change is coming. Any other questions?

## HUMANS MUST MESH SEXUALITY AND SPIRITUALITY FROM A YOUNG AGE
*I am concerned about the Earth changes, but I am more concerned about the way human beings are expressing their sexuality. The media is pushing kids, younger and younger, to have an active sexual life. They treat sexuality like it's just a hobby and has no importance. I believe that you have to respect your body as well as respect your spirituality and your mind. You say many changes are coming. Is the way sexuality is viewed being affected by the changes?*

There is a tremendous amount of misunderstanding about sexuality, the sexual act and the energies contained within that act. People want to experience power, do they not? The sexual energies are spiritual energies, and the spiritual energies are sexual energies. What has happened in your world is that the two have been separated, torn from each other to the point that you have no longer an understanding of the power of sexuality and spirituality when they are combined together.

One of the most tragic things is that young ones are being trained to use the powerful sexual part of themselves without the complement of the spiritual part of themselves. They see no connection between the sexual and the spiritual. This began centuries ago, millennia ago, when there was a separation of the physical and the spiritual in ancient Greece. It occurred even more strongly in your Christian tradition. It came to be seen that using sexual energy, even between two people who loved each other within a marriage, was at least a little sinful. Many people are not aware that this happened.

Children and adults are both being given extremely conflicting messages through the media. They are told by certain institutions that it is evil to use their bodies in a sexual manner, yet advertising demonstrates sexual energies being used for ulterior purposes. Most people do not know what is happening. People need to go within themselves to learn how to use this power, this energy. It would be much easier if young ones were taught from the beginning the power of physical sexual energy with the power of spiritual energy.

All of you have had experiences of the words that come from the mouths of the little ones. Don't they say the most amazing things? You wonder where these small beings acquired such wisdom. They have not lost their spiritual connection. If the spiritual connection is nurtured, then they will not lose it, and they will come to know the power of it.

## THE BACKLASH AGAINST SEXUALITY WITHOUT SPIRITUALITY

How old are most children when they begin exploring their bodies? Any mother who has changed a diaper can tell you that. And yet in this country and some other countries, children are taught very quickly not to touch themselves in certain places, correct? The children need to be taught how to channel the powerful sexual energies until their minds are mature enough to learn to manage the energy. Most teenagers in this country do not have the maturity to know how to use this energy, this power.

What is going to happen? You are going to find that a backlash is going to occur. Just as a rubber band will snap back, so will the use and knowledge of the sexual and spiritual energies. More people are now studying the kundalini energies, which are sexual, physical energies. They are able to connect the sexual energies with the spiritual energies. You are going to see great power unleashed. You are going to find more people looking for meaning in sexual union. More people are learning that they can do something different with their bodies to control the physical energies, the sexual energies, and discover, when they open their hearts, what happens to the power contained within their bodies.

If each of you learned how to use your sexual energies and join them with your spiritual energies, you would be amazed at the power you could harness. Once you are able to do this, you could release all the pressure from the storm known as Ivan. The kundalini energy is tremendous. It is amazing. The sexualization of young ones without the knowledge of spirituality results in people not knowing who they are. They will not know how to use the energy that is within them. They will need to learn. There will be teachers who can teach them.

## RELEASING THE CREATIVE ENERGY INTO MANIFESTATION

*I have read that if you enter a state of meditation and essentially focus on an item that you would like and go deeply enough into it, you can create a mental orgasm, like a sexual orgasm that you can manifest. Can you describe how to proceed in that way and also bring in the spiritual energies in order to accomplish such a manifestation?*

Orgasm is the creative force unleashed. There are those who are able to bring themselves to physical orgasm by meditation. It is simply the manipulation—and I do not use "manipulation" in a negative way here but in a positive way—of the energies.

*Just as we began when we were working with the storm, go into your heart center through the back, as that is the entryway to infinity. There is no duality in this sacred space within you. You have to describe it in dualistic terms because that is the language you have, but there isn't duality in that space. Have the beam of energy come straight through you to ground you into the Earth. Think of the creative force within your planet. Do you realize that your planet could cleanse itself completely of everyone with a few little hiccups? Some might call them earthquakes, a little belching. Tap into that energy to ground yourself. Being a human, you need to be grounded.*

*Breathe deeply with your entire body. As you breathe in and out, feel the energy coming from above as well as from the center of the Earth running up and down through you. Feel yourself expanding. Feel your heart center beginning to expand. Be fully conscious of the energies and release attachment to the physical body. Now that the movement is active, bring to mind what you wish to manifest. Could it be a ring that you lost? You could focus upon the ring you lost and your intention of bringing it to you. As the energy reaches its peak, you could bring the ring to you or manifest a ring you would like to have.*

Some people, when they first learn to manifest in this manner, might experience it as a physical orgasm. You can manifest such things without the physical sounds and experiences that go with the orgasm. For instance, you could do it in public without calling attention to yourself. Those who do manifest things are fully aware of the energies within them and transmute the energies into what they wish to create. The Master Jesus was able to do this.

**A critical mass?**

It is not a critical mass in the sense of physicality. It is within the energy. It is learning how to use, to manipulate, to bring together the energies of what is called love. That is how you were created. Does that answer your question?

## RELIEVING DEPRESSION AND PRESSURE

*How can we relieve depression from our lives? I still have a feeling about the storm in my life. How can I touch my life and relieve the pressure?*

Can you think of one thing in your life that would relieve the pressure? Not even one thing? What could be a nonmaterial way to relieve the pressure? The pressure you are feeling is self-imposed pressure. You relieve the pressure by changing your belief system. What happens is that people believe they need to perform or be a certain way or they will lose their houses, jobs, spouses or whatever. Everything outside of yourself has to do with how you identify yourself.

If you and your husband were able to change your beliefs and realize that events happening in the world, your job and your family just are, then the pressure would be relieved. Do not put a value judgment on what happens, whether it is good or bad. Without the judgments, the pressure is relieved. You might say, "But there is so much to do. What would happen if I don't do it?" Well, there you have another value judgment. What will happen if you do not do it? Sometimes things just don't get done. You might discover that your world does not fall apart. Pressure comes from the way you look at things. By changing your perspective, you can change your beliefs. Pressure comes from your mental and emotional responses to what is occurring.

## CHANGE YOUR JUDGMENTS ON SITUATIONS

How many of you are in absolute turmoil about what is happening in your country in regard to its policies in Iraq? How many of you are aware of what is happening and have some concern but are not in emotional turmoil? Now, how many of you know people who are in extreme emotional turmoil about what is happening?

You can turn on your radios or televisions and hear the turmoil. Who do you think is more peaceful within themselves about what is happening in Iraq? Them or you? Do you see what I am saying? Now, if you had the same emotional responses of turmoil, you would be putting tremendous pressure on yourself. That does not mean that you would not weep if someone you knew was killed or someone you knew lost a loved one. I do not mean that. This is an exercise in being in the world and not of the world. Do what it is that you need to do, but do not accept the judgment of the world about what is happening.

Even if someone here lost someone very precious due to physical death, it is the belief that that person is lost that causes the pain and anguish. What if you changed that belief to one that many of you think you believe—that there is no loss of them? You could communicate with them on the other side. Perhaps you might miss the skin contact. But it would change that feeling of grief. Isn't that correct? So it is about how you view things and how you understand things. Change your judgments, and the pressure will change.

## NEW INFORMATION ABOUT ENCODEMENTS

*Can we talk about encoding?*

Those of you who have done encodement work before, what is it you would like to learn today? I will do some beginnings and also build upon what we have done before.

*When you last talked about encoding, I described that I had a pain in my foot. We went through the encoding, and I had a problem with bringing the energies up; there was a restriction. I haven't had that problem since, but the pain has moved over into my head. Can you tell me what went on?*

Okay, we need to not just remove one energy blockage without removing all of the other energy blockages. Do you think that is what it is? We will do a little bit of that. Does anyone else have something that they would like to ask about encodements?

*How do I know if I am really doing this correctly?*

First of all, there is no way you can do it incorrectly. Does that relieve any pressure? You are not the one who does the work. The encodement technicians do the work. You are the one who does the asking. You cannot incorrectly place encodements within yourself, because you are not the one who places them. There are artificial encodements that you do place within yourself by your thoughts and feelings and your acceptance of the thoughts and feelings of others.

## NATURAL ENCODEMENTS AND ENERGY ENCODEMENTS

Let's begin with the very basic information. Natural encodements are energy circuits that the encodement technicians have placed within you. You have many encodements that were placed within you before you incarnated. You met with your council, decided what things you were going to learn in your life and who was going to be in your life. You decided what you were going to take from other lifetimes and explore in another way. You picked from your soul groups the people who were going to incarnate with you and play different roles. In other words, you decided upon the script and the actors in your play. The script is in outline form for the more experienced souls. For all of you, it was in outline form.

Now what you need are the directions for the play. Those are the energy encodements. Those of you who have been born here in the United States of America have encodements to help you fit into this culture. Those of you born in other countries who are working to fit into this culture have encodements for the country you were from, and because you were going to experience this country, you have some encodements here also.

We have done a bit of work on having your encodements fit in with this culture. Those are natural encodements. You can have other natural encodements placed within you when you sleep. When you sleep, you also work on the inner plane. You can also work with your encodement technicians to further develop the energies for what you now wish to do. At night this work occurs on an other-than-conscious level. The work that we are going to do is on a conscious level.

## ARTIFICIAL ENCODEMENTS

Then there are artificial encodements. Those are encodements not placed by the encodement technicians. They are energy circuits similar to thought forms. Fear can produce an artificial encodement; jealousy can bring about artificial encodements. Basically, you would do better if you did not have artificial encodements. You would like them to be gone.

*Do we need to know what they are?*

No, you don't, not the particular parts of them. This is the simple part. You simply need to know what questions to ask the encodement technicians. Simply put, if you can imagine it, it can be done. If you can conceive it, it can be done. First go into your heart center through the back. Go to your altar. Now, some people like to stand at their altar, and some people like to have a chair that they sit in. Do whichever you prefer. Call in the encodement technicians. Simply say, "Encodement technicians, please come." You might feel something. Some of you will see the technicians. Usually there are three, occasionally there are two and occasionally four. Rarely are there more than four or less than two, but it does happen.

## USING ENCODEMENTS TO IMPROVE YOUR PHYSICAL HEALTH

*For those of you who have not done this work before, ask to be shown your encodements for physical health. The technicians will simply stimulate them for a brief time. Now think of a health problem that you have. It could be a pain in the hip, any health problem. Ask if you have any natural encodements that have been placed within you that have to do with this health issue. If the answer is no, we will do another step in a moment. If the answer is yes, ask them what the purpose is of these natural encodements in regard to this health issue. Are these natural encodements bringing about the health issue? In other words, did you have them placed in you because of something you wanted to learn? Ask, if there was something you wanted to learn, whether you have already learned it. Ask if it is possible to change the health encodement to one that would match the health that you would prefer to have.*

*If you get answers that lead you to believe that it is possible to change these encodements, that you could have a different type of health than you have now, you* can ask the encodement technicians to please change the encodements so that the body will show this new health. Know that the encodement technicians will not go against a soul reason for the encodements. In other words, your other-than-conscious self, the deepest part of yourself, the highest essence of yourself, will overrule your conscious self.

Now ask if there are any artificial encodements leading to this health problem. Ask what would happen if these artificial encodements were removed. Once you know what would happen if these artificial encodements were removed, you can decide whether or not you want them removed. If you want them removed, ask the encodement technicians to remove them. There are times when there are so many artificial encodements the technicians will remove them in stages.

Now we are going to use a question we have not used before. Ask if there are any artificial encodements blocking the free flow of energy within your physical, mental, emotional and spiritual body. Just for fun, ask the technicians to highlight them. You will see them like little lights. Ask what would happen if these artificial encodements were removed. You might ask that all artificial encodements relating to energy flow be removed right now. You could have a physical reaction; you might become very tired from the removal of these encodements. If you think that the result of removing all of them at once would be a little more than you want right now, you could ask them to remove maybe 50 or 25 percent of them. For those of you who sometimes have pain that moves, simply ask if there is another blockage preventing the flow of energy that is causing that pain.

## USING ENCODEMENTS TO REDUCE NEGATIVE EMOTIONS AND PROBLEM SOLVE

Choose an emotion that you have that you would rather not have—perhaps anger, fear or jealousy. Ask the encodement technicians if there are any artificial encodements amplifying these emotions within you. Ask what would happen if these artificial encodements were removed. Depending upon what their answer is, you can ask them to remove the artificial encodements or ask if it is safe to remove all of them. They might ask you to define what "safe" means to you. Then ask the technicians to remove the encodements, if you so desire.

Those of you who are in a particular field of work—whether that work is in the medical field, the mental-health field, being a mom, being a dad, being a grandparent—you can ask if there are any artificial encodements preventing you from doing your very best and working to your fullest potential. You can ask that these encodements be removed. Ask what the result of removing them would be so that you can make an informed decision. You can also ask if there are any natural encodements already placed within you to assist you in your field that are not yet turned on or that could be amplified. Then ask what would be the result. If you like that result, you can ask the technicians to make the adjustments.

If you find yourself in a situation that befuddles you by or that you find yourself unable to handle, you can ask the technicians if there are any encodements within you *that would help you to handle this situation. If they say yes, then ask if they are turned on. If they say no, ask the technicians to please turn them on. You might want to know the result of what would happen if they were turned on. If they say no, there are no natural encodements within you and there are no artificial encodements preventing this from happening, ask if they could add natural encodements that would assist you. Remember, you can go back at any time and fine-tune your encodements. You can always change what is done. You cannot change what has already happened due to the changes. In other words, you cannot change the consequences that have already occurred.*

And now, dear ones, as you are in this special place already, I am calling around you all of your angels and guides. I ask them to hold you in their arms and surround you with love. I suggest that you ask them to help you learn how to stay in your heart. Ask them to help you remember that you are love incarnate. You agreed to work with them. They agreed to work with you. Use them. Use them. And, dear ones, I send each one of you love from my heart to your heart as I am Amma, the divine mother of the divine mothers. I am your mother. My blessings to you.

# 22

# A Daily, Weekly and Monthly Practice

March 2005

*Amma is asking that you go into your heart. Most of you are familiar with going into your heart from the back of the chakra, as she has been teaching. She wants you to go into the back of your heart chakra and also to feel yourself going into the front as well. In essence, you are bi-locating in your same body. Simply ask to be open to what you need to hear tonight and there might be something that pops into your head.*

*G*ood evening, dear ones. I want each one of you to experience what it is like from the beginning to listen with your heart. I have been talking about listening with your heart. I have talked about the importance of watching your thoughts and your feelings and of controlling them. We have talked about encodements. I want to continue in that vein.

## THE GREATEST FORCE IN THE WORLD

The greatest force in the world is what you are made of, and that is love. I say something almost every time about love, don't I? Isn't it appropriate that you always keep in mind that of which you are made?

Living in a world, a society, where the word love has been perverted so much, it is very difficult for people to come to realize that love is what they are made of. Remember that I told you to look at one another and at yourself as love incarnate. You are love incarnate. You are love in a body. That is what you are, and each person whom you meet is love incarnate. Whenever you say anything or think anything derogatory about another person, and that means yourself as well, you have just negated love incarnate.

You have just negated the essence of who you are, and the essence of who the other person is.

I want to talk seriously, maybe I should say intensely, and really impress upon you the absolute necessity, priority, imperative—what other word can I use?— that you need to learn to stay in your heart and monitor your thoughts. Those of you who have been reading my words or have been listening to me know that I am not a being who likes to talk about things that are difficult and negative in the world. I usually only say those things when someone asks, and even then I am very careful about what it is that I say.

## CHALLENGES TO LOVE

However, dear ones, it is important for you to know that difficult times are coming. Decisions have been made. Before, those decisions had not yet been made. Plans had been made, but decisions were not made. Decisions have now been made and things are going to get very difficult for those of you who call yourselves lightworkers or those of you who call yourselves spiritual people. This is a direct result of the election that you just had [the U.S. elections].

Certain people are using the election results as a mandate to hold a particular religion up as being the only true religion. We are talking about the religion you know as Christianity. And I want you to be aware that anytime anyone holds up a particular ideology as being better than another and then denigrates anyone who does not follow it, that is not love.

Please know that when I talk about these things, I am not saying that there is anything wrong with Christianity. Some of you may have heard the comment that the one known as Gandhi once made years ago. He said, "I like your Christ. I just don't like your Christians." And, of course, he was commenting on how Christianity was being practiced and portrayed. If you read not only what is called the canonical scriptures of the Christian faith, but also some of the apocryphal scriptures of the Christian faith, you will find that much love is in there. I wish to challenge each of you who has been raised in a Christian tradition to read what is known as your gospels of Matthew, Mark, Luke and John. Read those and see what is in there. Focus on the core of the message. The message is love. If you wish to read any of the other Christian scriptures, I suggest the epistles of John, because you will find that everywhere in those three epistles, he talks about love.

I want you to know that it is not in the way of love to make fun of anyone or to criticize people for their judgments. It is certainly not in the way of love to deny anyone his or rights or livelihood or life because of belief. It is perfectly appropriate for you to set boundaries for people with whom you do not agree, who are negative or who are filled with hatred. However, dear ones, it is imperative that you do this with love.

## BOOT CAMP OF LOVE

Feel my intensity coming through this one who is talking. You are now entering into the time for which you have been trained. Your boot camp, as it were, was to learn how to be in a place within your heart, to be steadfastly in a place of love. I have emphasized—and many of your most marvelous teachers of all different faiths and religions have emphasized—the importance of love. They say it in different ways. They might talk about detachment. They might talk about not getting caught up in the cares of the world. They might talk about harming no one. It is all the same message. And now, dear ones, if you want to help hold or anchor the energy of love onto this planet, you must do what you have spoken about, what you have heard and what you have been trained for.

There are some of you here who are going to experience great difficulty with people who act toward you in a way that is not loving. There will be criticism because of your spiritual beliefs, your spiritual practices or, in many cases, your lack of religious practice. I want you to be aware of these things and to know that you are going to be refined in fire. You will see how strong you have become. It is going to be a difficult few years. Did you notice I said years? I didn't say weeks, and I didn't say months. So let's talk about how to handle these things. Of course, the first thing is to stay in your heart. I am going to give you a daily, a weekly and a monthly routine. I am going to be very direct about this because it is that important.

## A DAILY ROUTINE
### ~ Breathe from the Heart ~

When you get up in the morning, as soon as you become aware that you are awake, immediately connect with your heart center and breathe in and out of your heart center gently and easily. Within your heart center resides the essence of your soul, the essence of who you are. Breathe in and out for a few moments so you can come back to yourself, become aware of yourself and become fortified for the day. That is the first thing. You must start your day in that way, breathing in and out, saying whatever prayer or invocation that you have. If you do not have one, get one. It can be a prayer that you learned from your childhood. It does not matter. It can be spiritual affirmations that you have decided to write out for yourself. Begin your day in this way. Then you may get up.

If you are one of those who needs to go to the bathroom right away, have your prayer or invocation written right there so you can read it as you are finishing that part of your morning. When you begin your day this way, you will be able to connect with the energy of love—which is myself, the God, the Ain Soph, whatever you wish to call us. It would help if you consciously saw yourself as connected while you breathe in and out of your heart-self. See yourself connected to that energy of love, and bring that love energy into yourself. Then say your affirmation or invocation.

## ~ Ask for a Word or an Image to Hold in Your Heart ~

Sometime before you begin your day, ask for a word, a sentence, an image, that you need to hold in your mind and your heart for that day. It could be about someone whom you are seeing that day, or something you are not aware of that is going to happen. Whatever it is, hold it in your mind.

## ~ See Your Day Happening Exactly as You Wish ~

See your day happening. If you are ruled by your calendar, sit with your calendar and see your day happening in the way that you wish it to happen. If you drive to work, see yourself driving to work exactly as you'd like to. If you are taking the children to school, see yourself taking the children to school exactly the way you'd want it to happen—smoothly and easily. See yourself being able to slip in and out of traffic with no problems. You are preparing the energy of your day. If you are someone who has a number of appointments every day, sit there with your calendar and see yourself with each person, whether it is the doctor, a personal appointment, a cashier at the grocery store or a loved one; see yourself there. Open and fill yourself with the feeling of love from that other person or persons.

## ~ See All People as Love Incarnate ~

For each person you see, say in your heart and your mind, "Ah, love incarnate. There is love incarnate." When you see yourself in the mirror, say "Ah, there is love incarnate." This is a "busy list," isn't it? It's nothing you haven't heard before. The difference is putting this down in practice.

## ~ Have Mindfulness ~

Learn how to be conscious. Be aware. Some people call it mindfulness—be that way. If you are gathering the children together and putting clothes on the children, be aware of what is happening and where they are. There might be times when you are ushering them to school, and you become aware that maybe this isn't the day for them to go to school. That thought might enter your mind; follow that thought.

## ~ Bless Your Food ~

Bless your food and drink before you place them in your mouth. And if you forget, be sure to bless that which you have already placed in your mouth. Thank the essence of that food for giving its life for you, whether it is animal, vegetable or mineral. And again I wish to say, dear ones, that it does not matter what it is that you put in your mouth; all of it is life and has consciousness. Thank it for giving its life for you, for giving its essence for you. You learned that at your parents' knee, most of you, to give a blessing before meals.

## ~ Heal All Difficulty ~

Whenever you are having a difficult time with an individual—and many times it is hard to be conscious when you are in a difficult situation—as soon as you can become conscious, as soon as you can become aware, ask for healing for yourself and the other person involved in the situation. It does not matter how you ask for healing; just be sure to ask for it. If you find that you have some animosity toward that individual, then it is imperative that as soon as possible you disconnect yourself from that animosity and simply look at the other person and say, "Here is love incarnate who has come to teach me something," and then look for the lesson. Look at what it is you are meant to learn. Realize that sometimes, you are the one who is the teacher.

## ~ Give Thanks for Life ~

At the end of your day, go over in your mind all of the things that you need to give thanks for-things such as getting up out of bed in the morning; having clothes to wear; having food to eat; having a place to sleep, even if it is under a bridge, even if it is over a grate. Give thanks and be filled with gratitude for each thing that has happened in your life that day, even if it was an automobile accident or losing a loved one or dealing with great trauma or crisis. It is time to fully recognize and realize that everything that happens is there for you to learn from. It is a gift. Even the most horrible thing that you can think of is a gift. You have to be able to open the package, though. You have to be able to look within that situation and find the gift that is there.

## ~ Bless the People around You ~

Then, if you are living with someone, as you end your day, ask for blessings upon that someone. Those of you who have children, place your hands upon your children and ask that they be filled with love. Ask that they be filled with all the love they needed but didn't receive that day. Ask that your spouse or partner or roommate be filled with all the love that he or she needed that day but didn't receive. And then, precious one, ask that you be filled with all the love that you needed that day and didn't receive.

## ~ Ask That You Sleep Wrapped in Love ~

The last thing to do before you close your eyes for sleep is to ask to be wrapped in love throughout that night. I would suggest that you carry these steps with you until you learn them.

## A WEEKLY ROUTINE

It is crucial that you have special time for yourself to commune with Spirit on a weekly basis. Now, notice that I didn't say that on a daily basis you needed to meditate for an hour a day. If you do the ten things that I have suggested to you, you will find that your entire day will become a meditation. I highly recommend that you spend time—some time on the weekend, whatever you consider to be your weekend—with your spiritual connection, whatever you call it, whether it is with me, Amma, or with Jesus or Mary or God the Father, the Holy Spirit or Allah. Whatever your spiritual connection is, spend a minimum of about an hour focusing on it. It can be in the community. Those of you who have a church or synagogue, please feel free to go there. Feel your spiritual connection with consciousness and awareness. If you do not have a faith community that you share with in this way, then sit quietly or walk quietly somewhere where you can feel the connection. There is no need for words. It is simply to connect.

I also suggest during this time that you review what has happened during the week and identify places you believe you could improve upon. There is no failure or what you call sin. Everything is simply an opportunity to learn. One of the best ways to learn from these things is to see a situation where you were not happy with how it occurred, and then discover or imagine one, two or three other ways you could have handled it. There are always options as to how you handle situations. It may or may not have changed the other person if you had handled it differently, but it will certainly change you. So it's a learning experience.

## A MONTHLY ROUTINE

You have a daily practice and a weekly practice. Your monthly practice is to arrange to take off one full day each month just for you. Incorporate in that day that which gives you joy and life, that which helps you to be most connected to joy and life. It could be anything. For some of you, it could be going to a ball game; for others, it could be going to a symphony or to the beach. Even a good movie will do. For some, it might be writing quietly in your journal or playing with your children or grandchildren or great grandchildren. It doesn't matter what you do. It's important to take that one day a month to just do.

If you do these things and you begin doing them immediately, then what you will find is that when the difficulties come—as they will come—you will handle them with greater ease, and you will not be caught up in the drama of them. You might have to face people saying that you don't care about things, because you are not caught up in the drama, but that is their issue, not yours. It becomes your issue when you react to their words. What I have said here is crucial for this time.

## THESE ROUTINES ACTIVATE ENCODEMENTS

I have spent a lot of time talking about encodements. What these practices do for your encodements is to activate them. Encodements get fully activated by love. These routines are love in practice. I know it will take some time to make all this a practice, a habit. Those of you who have children know how difficult it is to make it a habit for them to brush their teeth or take a bath. But then, when it happens, you don't have to say another word. It just happens. How often as adults do you forget to brush your teeth? It happens occasionally, but it's not often that you forget. And sometimes you might forget that you have already brushed your teeth, because it has become such a habit, and maybe it is only when you pick up your toothbrush and it is wet that you realize you've already brushed.

I want you to have these ten things—the daily routine—be like that. Let them become a habit, but not such a habit that you will have to remember if you did it or not. You will then be so connected and so conscious of who you are and what you are that you will be able to handle whatever comes to you. This does not mean that you will not have emotion. This does not mean you will not have anger. This does not mean you will not have grief or joy. What it means is that you will be able to handle whatever happens, and you will remember who you are and be conscious of who you are.

So as you do this, your encodements will become activated—those that are not already. And raising yourself to a high vibration will help dissolve and change artificial encodements. It will also help bring into alignment encodements that have been damaged or thrown out of alignment. It will be as if you had a kink in the water hose and you were able to put a great rush of water through the hose, so much that the kink straightened out. By doing what I have suggested and outlined for you, you will be connecting yourself to the biggest water hose you have ever known.

You will find wondrous things happening to you. You will find that as you plan your day in the way I have suggested, it will be almost as if the freeways part in front of you, and you are the only car there. You will be delighted and surprised at how easily things can be manifested when you are connected to this energy source. You might even wonder why those around you are not handling things as easily as you are. And when they are talking about the great difficulties occurring or the great fear or anger they are feeling, you might be confused, because you are not feeling that and things seem to be going pretty well for you.

Who is most able to move the boulder? Is it the one who has exercised, or the one who has not? These are exercises. And they are very important if you wish to be able to handle the things that are coming with joy and ease. Because, dear ones, it is not that you have been appointed to be anchors of light. You have not been appointed to be anchors of light. You volunteered to be anchors of light. Yet you think, "Wait a minute; I have never been to a channeling before. I have never been here before. I have never volunteered." Yes, you have, or you would not be here. You are here and it is time.

I wish to leave you with this. I wish to leave you with the knowledge that there is only love, and that no matter what happens, that is all there is. That sounds like a song, doesn't it? If you follow what I have suggested, you will find that your life will change for the better, and it can change dramatically for those of you who feel like you need a dramatic change. For those of you who have already been working in this area, life will just feel more centered and more in line with where you have been going.

Now I wish to gift you, each one of you listening and each one of you reading right now—if you agree, for I cannot do anything without your agreement. I ask the encodement technicians to give to you the highest vibration and level of encodements that will fit in with your energy and with your soul path. This will open you to the highest essence of yourself. Just feel that happening now. My blessings to you, dear ones. It has been delightful to be here with you. Know that I am Amma, the divine mother of the divine mothers, and I am your mother.

# 23

# Encodements and the Tsunami

## March 2005

*G*ood evening, dear ones. How wonderful to see so many new faces this evening! Thank you for coming. I'm sure you have many questions about the tsunami. May I make a few comments?

First, many of you have heard comments about this being a disaster formed by human beings. I want you to know that this was not a conscious and deliberate human-made disaster. The Earth needed to shift and stretch. She did so. Although she is concerned about you humans, her first priority is taking care of herself. This shift of her surface was delayed as long as possible.

You, as humans, have great emotion about what you see as tremendous loss of life. Dear ones, there are thousands more who left the planet in those few minutes than the 150,000 that you know about. The loss of life was closer to 250,000. There were many whose bodies will never be found, and even more who had never been counted before. There was a tremendous shift in the energy of the planet. Those of you left behind are filled with grief or filled with fear. Those who lost loved ones wonder how they will live their lives without them. Others wonder how they can begin their lives anew. You here in this country, so few touched by the death on the other side of the world, are in fear as to whether something could happen to you.

### THOSE WHO LEFT THE PLANET DURING THE TSUNAMI AND WHAT YOU CAN DO

Let me first address the loss of life. Even though you know on an intellectual level that there is no true death, you still fear what you call death. Dear ones, how can I emphasize to you that the leaving of this body of yours is not really different than your choice of the clothes you wear to cover your body? One body is simply exchanged for another, just as you exchange one shirt for another. This body of yours is a simple vehicle to house your spirit, enabling you to learn the lessons you chose to learn for this lifetime.

You fear death. You fear a great tsunami engulfing you. I can tell you, dear ones, that drowning is not a difficult way to leave this particular lifetime. It is over very quickly. The ones who suffer the most are the ones who have been left. The greatest terror for those who did leave was the realization that they were in danger. They are now crossing over. Do not hold them back. Allow them to leave. Many will be quickly returning.

Now I wish to give you some more information. I want you to hear this from your heart. My purpose here is not to produce fear and panic. My purpose is to give you information so that you will be prepared. Hear these words from the place of your heart. Hear these words and prepare with the same dispassion you have when you buckle your seat belt. You do not go into fear and imagine horrible wrecks when you put on your seat belt. You simply put it on. That is how I want you to listen to what I am now going to say. This is simply information so that you will be prepared.

I want you to know how important it is for you to build up your immune system. There will be much more loss of life due to the disease brought about by the rotting bodies. There will be an illness, a disease, that will spread through those who are left. This disease will come to this country from those who return from assisting those who have lost so much. They will carry this disease with them. This disease has not been known before. There will be a commingling of what you call germs with the energy of fear. The very DNA of these germs will be changed. The fear will cause a tremendous discordance in the DNA and alter it. That is why you must build up your immune system.

## STAY OUT OF FEAR

You know what it is you should do. Eat foods that nourish the body. Bless your food and drink. Exercise will build up your immune system. And, most importantly, stay in your heart. Stay out of fear. If you could only see what happens to your immune system when you move into fear—it weakens considerably. You can control that. Simply stay in your heart. Yes, dear ones, the Earth changes you have heard about have begun. They have been occurring. There will be more natural disasters. There will be earthquakes. There will be floods. You have unusual weather in various parts of these United States right now. There is loss of life. The complexion of the land is changing. This change is natural. You wouldn't even notice it unless you were sitting on the place where the changes are occurring.

## THERE ARE THOSE WHO KNOW THE RHYTHMS OF THE EARTH

Some have asked if there will be super tsunamis. There have been stories on your televisions about these super tsunamis. You wonder if an island will crash into the ocean and send great tsunamis to the East Coast of the United States. You wonder if that will happen in your Gulf Coast area and California. I can tell you that there is always a chance of such movements of the Earth. The probability of that happening is not large. Right now changes are more likely to happen to California and Japan than to the East Coast of the United States or to the Gulf Coast area. If you have contracted to leave the planet at that time, then you will go. Listen to your inner knowing. Listen to your dreams. If your dreams are insisting that you leave, then I suggest you do so.

There are tribes in the area where the tsunami hit who did not lose their lives. The people of these tribes live in tune with nature. They know her rhythms. They knew the signs to go to higher ground. They did not need any technical "early warning" system. If you learn to do the same, you too will know what is happening with Mother Earth before the early warning signs given by technology.

The general outpouring of funds from those here in the United States was a surprise to your government. Your president believed that he was demonstrating compassion by initially designating 35 million dollars to assist those devastated by the water and its aftermath. You, as a people, taught him differently. Many were willing to give from their funds to help those so devastated by this event. Your willingness to give demonstrates that your compassion is very close to the surface. When you are aware of tragedy, your heart is moved and you act.

Any energy you give from your heart, whether it is in the form of currency, objects or time has a multiplying effect. The energy of fear, anger and misused power is lessened by all that is given from the heart. The gifts you are giving from your heart have a greater positive effect upon the energies of the planet than the money given from any of the governments. The vibration of that given by governments or institutions is affected by the energy of the giver. Governments who give because they want to "prove" something to the world community do not have the same high vibration as those who give from their hearts, from compassion. Governments or institutions that give from compassion manifest a higher vibration energy. Those who distribute goods from their hearts, no matter who the goods were given by, increase the vibration of that which was given.

## YOUR PERSONAL POWER TO SHIFT THE EARTH

Some of you have asked if there is anything you can do to change the shifting of the Earth. Of course, dear ones. Consider your own bodies. Just because the doctor has told you that you are very ill and will soon leave the physical body does not mean that has to happen, unless, of course, it is how you have decided to go. If your leaving is simply a possibility, you can change what happens in your body. You change it through what you put into your mouth, your ears and your eyes. You change it by what you entertain in your mind. Any low-vibration energy you allow into you and that you keep in your being has a discordant effect upon your body. Change that, and you will change when you leave your body.

This is also true for this wondrous planet you live on. She is a host to you. Your energies do affect her. If you wish to change what is happening within her, change what is happening within you. That would be the first step. If you wish to go further, use the tools you have to balance the energies within her. You can send love to her from your heart. You can go to an area of unbalance and balance the energy. Yes, you can assist in changing what is happening within her, just as you can assist what is happening within you.

## CHANGING THE DIRECTION OF YOUR LIFE

Now, dear ones, let us continue with the discussion of encodements. As many of you are calling upon the encodement technicians, you are having many questions. Lately, the questions have revolved around how you can change the total direction of your life. That is what I want to discuss with you this evening.

For those of you not familiar with encodements, encodements are energy circuits similar to a computer operating system. Before you incarnated, you decided what it was you wanted to learn in this life and how you wanted to learn it. You then worked with the encodement technicians to develop the encodement structure that would bring about your plan. The encodements that the technicians put in for you are what I'm referring to as "natural encodements." Energies placed within the structure by feelings and emotions are "artificial encodements."

Remember that you are a whole. Any decision you make to change one thing in your life affects every other thing. It is impossible to make an isolated decision that goes no further than that one decision. Those of you who have been experimenting with encodements have probably already found this out. There are unintended consequences to every action. Some are wonderful surprises, some are horrid and others are neutral, and, of course, they can fall anywhere in between those extremes.

## MAKING AN EFFECTIVE LIFE PLAN

If you wish to make a new life, you must remember two things. One, change is very much possible. Two, you cannot go against what you want on a soul level. For instance, if you make a plan to win the lottery in your conscious life, the soul-level aspect of yourself might choose to hold fast to your learning about abundance or poverty in a different manner. In other words, the highest aspect of yourself must agree with your plan. Some guidelines for developing a new life plan are as follows:

- Know what it is that you wish to learn. This is similar to having goals. At this stage, you do not write out how you want to learn it. Simply finalize what it is that you want to learn.
- When setting up the "how tos," be as broad as possible. These are the objectives. If you wish to travel the world, simply state your intention. Do not state exactly how you want it to be done. You will want to state what you would like to experience: excitement, wonder, fun and so on.
- Set up your plan for each of your bodies—physical, mental, emotional and spiritual. Bring in all aspects of your life, and do this on each level. In other words, you will want to express what you wish to learn about relationships in regard to your physical, mental, emotional and spiritual bodies.
- Be aware of how one choice will affect every other choice. Making a choice about what you wish to experience in regard to relationships with others might be a choice not to experience something else. Be aware of such conflicts.
- You will set up conflicts and paradoxes. That is part of life. Your choice to make is deciding which conflicts and paradoxes you wish to have. That is true even now.
- Very few people will set aside the time and energy to do a thorough job of this process. That just seems to be a peculiarity of human nature. Those of you who are architects, computer programmers or engineers might have greater awareness than others about how one decision can affect the whole. This is truly an exercise in working through the details while keeping your vision on the big picture. Ask the encodement technicians for help in this area.

## WORKING WITH THE ENCODEMENT TECHNICIANS

Once you have identified your master plan, it is time to call in the encodement technicians. For those who haven't used the encodement technicians before, enter your heart center from the back. Go into the sacredness of yourself, to your altar. Call the encodement technicians. You will then ask them to assist you in implementing your new encodement structure.

Go over your plan with them. Ask them if there is anything that you left out. Jot down whatever comes to your mind. Ask them what changes will occur if this plan is implemented. What would be the unintended consequences? Are those consequences acceptable to you? If they are not, ask the encodement technicians what else could be done to achieve something similar without that particular consequence. Continue the process until you are ready to have the technicians either continue or you decide not to proceed. This is not a process to be done in one night. Take your time.

When you are satisfied, ask the technicians what artificial encodements must be removed before the new structure is put into place. Before you ask them to remove the artificial encodements, ask them what will happen if they are removed. You then decide, based upon their answer, whether you want to proceed or not. There might be too many artificial encodements to remove at one time. Ask them to remove a percentage of the artificial encodements. Before having them do the removal, be sure and ask what the consequences will be.

Once you have finished with the artificial encodements, ask if there are any natural encodements that have been damaged that need to be repaired before the new encodement structure is put into place. Again, ask for consequences. If the consequences are acceptable, ask them to proceed. Once the damaged encodements are repaired, ask if there are any natural encodements that need to be activated before the new encodement system is put into place. Again, ask for consequences. You might want to activate a few at a time so that your energy has time to adjust. There is no deadline for this process. Take your time.

If there are any consequences that occur that you do not like, you can go back and have the technicians reverse the changes. The changes can be reversed, but the actual consequences of the changes cannot be.

If you are ready to proceed with the placement and activation of the new encodement structure, ask the encodement technicians where to start. Follow your inner knowing, your intuition. Make changes one system at a time. For example, take one lesson you wish to implement. Begin with that lesson and implement it one body at a time. The technicians will work with the etheric bodies first.

Dear ones, this process is for those who would like to rework their entire lives. If you wish to rework just one area of your life, begin with that area. Work with the encodement technicians, first asking about artificial encodements, then damaged encodements, then inactive encodements. You might attain the changes you wish from this process alone. Remember, any change you make will affect all areas of your life.

Now, dear ones, know that you are dearly loved. You are loved now, with your lives exactly as they are. You will be loved no matter how you change your lives. There is nothing, and I do mean nothing, that you can do that will lessen how much I love you. All I can do is love. I express that love to you every day.

Go into your hearts now, dear ones. Feel my love for you. I am at this very moment, no matter when you are reading this information, pouring my love into you. You are dearly beloved. And I am Amma, the divine mother of the divine mothers. I am your mother. You grew in my womb. My blessings are upon you.

# 24

# Encodements to Alter Your Belief System

*April 2005*

ood evening, dear ones! How wonderful to see all of you gathered here together. It's time for more and more people to experience the love that I am and the love that you are. I'm aware that many of you have not read the messages that I have given before, so I will give a very brief introduction about what I will talk about tonight. We're going to talk more and more about encodements.

## ENCODEMENTS ARE LIKE YOUR OPERATING SYSTEM

Now let's talk about encodements. Many of you have not heard about encodements. They are energy structures like your computer program or your operating system. Some of you who know more about encodements might think they are just as difficult as the Windows operating system. Sometimes they malfunction too, but I can tell you that they are much easier to fix. Encodements are energy circuits that are the foundation of your energy field and your physical body.

Very briefly, before you incarnated, you mapped out what you wanted to accomplish in this lifetime and what you wanted to do. You worked with technicians—we call them encodement technicians—to map out your energy field so that you would be attracted to what you wanted to be attracted to, neutralized against what you had no interest in, and repelled from that which didn't want at all.

There are encodements for every aspect of your life—physical, emotional, mental and spiritual. They come from the deep area of beingness. They call you onto a particular religious path or spiritual path. Remember that religion and spirituality do not always go together, although it is much easier when they do. This path could be as mundane as being called to live in a particular place, city or country. Those of you who have a desire to travel have an encodement for that.

Encodements correspond with your astrology, because it all works together. This was a marvelous plan that you put together. It was not as easy as saying, "Oh, I think I'll be incarnated." It took much "time"—a metaphor on the physical level—to plan exactly how this was going to work and exactly when you would come into the planet so that your astrology and your encodements would be right. The encodements were easier to work with and to develop because sometimes there are those on this planet who "fool" with the astrology. This is what happens when there is induced labor, such as when the doctor decides that you should come earlier so he can go fishing. For example, you might have planned to come in January 18 and here you are on January 10. This doesn't quite correspond with what you had set up.

That's what encodements are. You can work with your encodements and strengthen them. That is what we have been talking about for a year. I'm not going into it any more than that basic explanation.

## MAP OUT A PLAN FOR YOUR LIFE USING ENCODEMENTS

We're going to go to an advanced level of working with the encodements. I'm going to tell you how you can map out a plan of how you want your life to go and how to work on it with the encodement technicians. Interesting concept to think about, is it not? I'm going to give you the bare bones, as it were.

First, know that all of this has to be done in conjunction with the great I Am at your soul level. The encodement technicians will not do anything that is contrary to what you wish to do on that level. The ego level, the little I am, often does not want to pay attention to what is going on with the big I Am. The little ego might want to win the lottery and the big I Am says, "Oh no. That's not in your plan. That's not what you're going to learn in this life." So know that by doing this work, you cannot go against your soul path.

Know also, however, that all of you, unless you were born after 1987, were born with most encodements ending at about the year 2000. Your plan for this life ended at about the year 2000. You knew when you incarnated that the probability was that there would be no more human life on this planet and that you would self-destruct. That changed in 1987 with the Harmonic Convergence. That was the big shift when everything changed. That is when a critical mass of humans said they were going to shift this planet, and everything shifted.

You might wonder how it can be that the Earth was shifted when there is still so much war. I can tell you, dear ones, that it did shift, because you are still here. What is happening now is what many of you call a healing crisis. Healing crises are difficult. Many of you know this because you have gone through one. Some wish that they could leave their bodies rather than go through a healing crisis. And some think that even now. This healing crisis will continue for a few years.

For those of you who feel rather directionless or rudderless, who do not know which way you are going, it is because you do not have encodements set up about how to move your life in a new direction. You knew that there was a possibility you would still be here after 2000, so you had a few encodements for that, but you believed it was a higher probability that you'd be watching the big ending bang, not the big beginning bang. You wanted to see what would happen. Things changed, and now you're here.

## DISCOVERING YOUR LIFE PLAN

Let's talk about how to work with your encodement technicians so you can map out what you want to do with your life. It is a simple yet complex process. It's a paradox. The complexity is that you, in your society of faxes and microwaves, would like it to happen in an instant. It takes some planning. You have an opportunity right now to make a decision as to how you want your life to go. You know the exercise where they tell you that if money were no object, and there were no other objects, how would you like your life to be? Well, that's what we're going to do.

Sit down and think, "Okay, if I were changing my life now, how would I create it?" Then look at every level of your life—physical, emotional, mental and spiritual. Look at the most mundane things, even those you hardly think about. Some of you might think about where you would like to live. Look at what type of thoughts you would like to have, what kind of emotions you would like to feel, what types of people you would like to be attracted to, what you want to experience physically. Consider these deeper questions, not just the superficial ones. You want to understand what you wish to experience on the deepest level.

You might wish, for instance, to experience on the deepest level what love truly is, not from the place of human emotion, but from the energy of creation. You were all created from love, the essence and substance of the creative force. I am love and you are love. You don't believe it; however, I happen to know it. What if you chose to map out your life so that you knew in every atom, electron and quark of your being that you were love? What change do you think that would cause in you? These are the kinds of things you can do.

Architects have many pages of blueprints for their buildings. Seeing the building façade, we think, "There it is." But do you not need the electrical, the plumbing, the foundation and the structure? There are many pages of planning. When you are working on developing yourself, you need many pages or layers of planning for what it is that you want to do.

Those of you who play computer games where you can, for instance, build a city, can see how the interactions of a change made at one level affect the others. If a choice is made to change the electrical or the plumbing, it might change the entire structure of the building. How are you going to make the foundation? What will you use for the structure? Will you use wood or steel? In this same way, if you want to develop exactly how you want your life to go, you have to look at every level.

How do you want your abundance to manifest? People always say they want lots of abundance. In what areas of your life do you want the abundance? Is it just physical abundance you desire, or is it also emotional, mental and spiritual abundance?

What do you want to be attracted to in your life? Maybe this is the time to study painting, something you've always wanted to do. Think about what that would mean. Choosing to do something in one area might mean that you can't do something in another. You cannot paint and write at the same time, for instance. Both could be done in the same lifetime, but they must be done at separate times within one life. You cannot be an architect and a mayor at the same time. You can have both of these energies within you, but you are still one or the other. So any choice you make precludes other things.

Once you make your plan in the multiple layers of your life, you can then work with the encodement technicians to put that plan into effect. You might think this is overwhelming. It is, and that is why most people don't do the serious personal work of changing themselves. It seems too overwhelming.

Every person here, and all of the people who read this, could develop themselves to the point of doing miracles with a snap of the fingers. You could reach into your pocket and pull out a thousand-dollar bill just like that. You could pull out ten, twenty or a hundred of them. It is even within your potential to develop yourself to such a place that you could expand this room until it could fit twenty or thirty more people. Are you aware that you could develop yourself to that point? It would take time, energy and discipline. Why do so few people do it? Because very few want to take the time, energy and discipline.

## AS A BEING OF LOVE, MANIFEST WHAT YOU WISH

I can tell you that you are love. As a being of love, you can manifest anything that you wish. You can get excited about that. You have probably heard it said that if you have the faith of a mustard seed, you can move a mountain. Does what you manifest demonstrate that you have faith even the size of a mustard seed? You have to know in the deepest part of yourself who you are. You are love. When you know that, then you will be that. Then you can manifest whatever you want.

You could decide to manifest a body that would be twenty pounds lighter or heavier when you woke up. Are you aware that there are those who have actually done that? There was one from a culture that considered you more prosperous if you were heavier, so he woke up heavier the next morning. He knew who he was.

If you wish to really and truly change your life, the first thing you must do is have the intent to do it and know what it is that you intend to do. If you wish to act as a being of pure love and that is your intent, yet you continue to hold thoughts of fear, anger or jealousy, then you are not following your intent. When you choose how you want your life to be, there are certain things you also choose not to do.

The simplicity is that you have the opportunity to choose. You can alter things in layers. How do you want to be in the physical? How do you want to do relationships? How do you want your mental and spiritual lives to be? Do you want to learn to teleport or bilocate? Would you like to be so much a being of love that a snarling wild animal could come to you and be tamed in an instant because all you did was pour out love? That could happen. You might recognize in your own life the things you say and do that are totally contrary to what you say you intend your life to be. That is because you have to change your basic belief systems.

No one hearing this message was raised with the belief that you are a being of love. I'm sure you remember many negative comments indicating you were stupid, selfish, prideful or no good. All of you have been told something like that at one time or another. And that's what you've chosen to believe. What would happen if you chose in this instant to believe that you were a being of total love? You have no idea how much your life would change, in an instant, if you believed that. If you choose to change your life, then sit down and map out how you want your life to be, being very aware that making choices for certain things precludes choices for others. It's just that you can't learn two contrary lessons at one time on this planet.

Once you have that done, sit down and talk to the encodement technicians. Ask them to help you manifest your life in this way. They can then work with your encodements and make changes. Some of you have felt your pain disappear by working with the encodement technicians. Some of you have lost weight as you've worked with them. Others have increased the information coming to them by making certain choices. That all can happen. The only thing you have to do is decide to do it. That is the biggest thing in this human life, isn't it? Decide to do it.

*Can the encodement technicians help us change our beliefs?*

That's a very good question. Beliefs in and of themselves can form artificial encodements. Let's take a belief that's very common in humans—the belief that you're not lovable. If you have that belief, it doesn't matter how it came to you. It forms artificial encodements that are very strong. What happens is that the artificial encodement has a reaction with other encodements. For the sake of metaphor, you have an encodement in the center of you that says, "You are not lovable." The energy from that encodement deactivates other encodements that say, "You are lovable," and this can distort other encodements. So it is a chain reaction.

## A MEDITATION TO CHANGE YOUR BELIEFS

*The first thing I would suggest you do if you have a belief you would like to change is to go into your heart center from the back. Try that now. There is a front to your heart center and there is a back. The heart center goes front to back. The front of the heart center is in this three-dimensional physical world. Go into the back of your heart center. Feel the difference. Now go into that space of no-space, that time of no-time. You are now in interdimensionality. Go to that sacred space within yourself—I call it the altar within yourself. Some people call it the threefold flame. It does not matter what you call it. It is the sacred space within yourself.*

*This is the simple part: Just ask the encodement technicians to come. Most of you will experience three energies coming. Some will have four. A few will have five. What is the belief that you would like to change? Bring that belief to mind. Ask the encodement technicians if there are any artificial encodements holding that belief in place. If you receive a "Yes" answer, ask, "What would be the result if these encodements were removed?" If the result is okay with you, then ask the encodement technicians to remove the artificial encodements that are holding the belief in place. Some of you might experience your energy shifting as this is happening.*

*Now ask if there are any natural encodements that were distorted, damaged or deactivated due to the artificial encodements. [Channel's Note: Natural encodements are those put into place by the encodement technicians. Artificial encodements come from other sources.]*

*If you receive a yes, and most of you will, ask what the result would be if these encodements were put back into the form they originally had. If that is okay with you, you can then ask that it be done. They might tell you they do not wish to do it all at once. I would suggest that you listen to them. Have them do only as many as are safe for you to have done at one time. The shifting can cause tremendous changes.*

You have just changed a belief system. In order to keep it changed, you have to act upon your new system. You must go through the process of determining what you want as a new belief system. This is necessary because if you don't, out of habit you will act out of your old belief system. It's important that you become aware when you are acting from the old belief system and stop it. There is such a thing as habit. These are patterns in your brain that you must change.

*Do thoughts directly affect the encodements or do the encodements directly affect thoughts?*

The short answer is that it works both ways. You can change encodements and it will affect thoughts, while thoughts can also affect the encodements. It's not a simple process; rather, it's a complex, dynamic system. That is why you must watch your thoughts. Thoughts can produce artificial encodements or deactivate natural ones. Energies from others can do this too. That is why it is imperative for you to stay in your heart, especially when there is so much fear and anguish going around the planet right now. There has been much fear and anguish for a long time.

## HOLD TO YOUR FAITH LIFE

So dear ones, with that, I would imagine that there are some questions.

*You said in a previous channeling that decisions have been made. What were these decisions?*

There are several decisions that have been made. First there are decisions, since your [U.S.] election turned out the way it did, that it was a mandate and that people believe in a certain way in regard to their faith life. If you don't respond in the way that these folks believe you should respond, they are going to say that you do not have a faith life. It is happening in spite of the fact that this country was established in order to not have this very thing happen. Your country was founded on freedom of belief. The other thing that is going to happen is that a very large group of people are going to feel disenfranchised. And there will be some violence. So that is going to happen. You will find that the war you are having in the Middle East is going to escalate and will spread to some other countries.

*Thank you. This is a relief. I am so happy hearing your words about the daily practice of where and how to start. I am so happy with that. I am realizing that my job, my work in this life, is about being a lightworker, or more specifically, not to be a cleric or a teacher in school, but to learn to connect myself with God and maybe to open some people's eyes about that. Is there anything specific that I can start with? I know I need a little push to keep going in that direction.*

If you find that you are having a difficult time following the ten steps that I outlined for you, go into your heart from the back and talk to the encodement technicians. Ask them if any artificial encodements are preventing you from getting started on this program and staying with it. The energies of fear and violence form artificial encodements that surround people and prevent them from being connected to their love. When individuals cannot be connected to their love, they cannot be connected to the essence of who they are and they cannot discover joy.

The words that I say to you are not meant to put fear into you. I hope that what it does do is give you a resolve to do something and to realize that you can do positive things. Those ten things that I outlined to you—all of those things, including the weekly and monthly steps—are all positive things. They are all things you can do to bring yourself to an awareness of who you are and to stay in that place.

## A MEDITATION TO SPEAK WITH THE ENCODEMENT TECHNICIANS

Let's do a little exercise with this. For those not familiar with the process, I will give you some instructions. You have your heart center in the front. Your heart center is positioned front to back.

*Imagine that you are actually entering your heart through your back. For people who are not used to that terminology, place your hand on your heart. Bring your attention to your hand, bring your attention to what is underneath your hand and then feel yourself going even deeper into your chest, almost to the point where you see/feel your heart beating. Now do that from your back. Imagine that you are going in through the back, from the center of your back, into the center of yourself. And if you are in the correct space, what you will feel is limitlessness. It is almost like entering another world, another dimension, a time of no-time and a space of no-space. As you move deeper into your heart center, you will find your altar. Some altars look like a little table. There are some that have a waterfall. It doesn't matter. It is representative of the sacred space within yourself—the center of your sacredness.*

*While you are there, ask for your encodement technicians. Simply say, "Encodement technicians, please come." Most of you will become aware of another presence. There are usually about three. Some people have four or five beings, energies or essences. Even if you do not feel them, know they are there. And now ask if there are any artificial encodements in place within you or around you that are interfering with your ability to complete the steps that Amma just outlined. If you get a yes, and I think you will find that all of you got a yes, then ask that they please remove them.*

*Now ask, "Are there any natural encodements that have been damaged or altered that would interfere with my ability to complete the steps that Amma has outlined?" If the answer is yes, ask that these encodements be repaired and put in proper alignment. Now ask if there are any natural encodements that need to be activated so that you can easily participate in the twelve steps that Amma has outlined. Now thank the technicians. Become aware of yourself now and come back to this room.*

## THE WORD OF GOD AND RELEASING PAIN

*During our most recent session, you mentioned the power of words and the power of thought. In the Gospel of John, we are told, "In the beginning, the word was God and the word was with God." Can you tell us what this word is?*

The word is actually the creative force of God. Although the word is spoken of in the Christian tradition as being the Christ, know that it is actually the creative force of God. So the word is actually that which resides within that which, when spoken, brings manifestation. The actual word for the word of God is Aum.

*I have a pain, and I have not been able to relax here. What is going on?*

You have an energy blockage in your hip. You are holding your knee, but the blockage is actually in your hip. Your hip is also out of alignment. In fact, your pelvis is out of alignment. You would benefit from a chiropractor. You would also benefit from your own decision to move forward with whatever it is that you are afraid of moving forward in. Or you might benefit by finding someone who could help you to come to a place where you can release the emotional blocks that keep you in fear about moving forward in your life.

You have some encodements that are out of place from your accident, and there are artificial encodements that were put in. Be with your friend. She can take you through the process of helping to get those to work through the encodement technicians. She will show you how to do that. It is a very simple process. Do that first. Are you seeing a chiropractor? You need to see one again, because your pelvis is out of alignment. Think of the pelvic girdle as being foundational. You have had your foundation shaken. There is a lot of encodement work that can be done and a lot of energy work that could help you out.

It is going to be very difficult for you on the plane tomorrow. If you decide to go on the plane tomorrow, you need to be up a lot. In other words, you need to get up every ten minutes or so to keep moving. You have some physical things that are occurring, but the fear is eating you alive and shaking your foundation. So work with your friend. She does good energy work, and she knows how to work with the encodements. She can lead you through this.

## LOVE AND SPIRIT: A DISCUSSION

*You have mentioned that we are love incarnate. Can you distinguish between love and spirit? Because I know that we are also spirit. Which came first, love or spirit?*

In one way there is no difference between the two. It is just that spirit has more definition to it; love is an energy. It is an essence. It is the creative force. It is what creation comes from. Spirit is what is created out of love. Love came first; then spirit came. You have the godhead or the wholeness. Then there was the division into duality of the male energy of God and the female energy of God. It is still God, but it is a division. The spirit of that which you are comes from that. The spirit is more individual. Love is oneness. But the spirit is created of love. It is like the vine and the branches and the grapes.

In the way I am speaking of spirit, your spirit is the manifestation of the creative force of love. There are also those who speak of spirit as in the Holy Spirit, which is actually the love energy. It is the force. It is another way to discuss the creative force of God. When you read in your Hebrew scriptures that the Spirit moved upon the land, that is the creative energy of the love essence that went forth. The word was spoken, and you talk about that as being the Christ, but there are three in your Christian tradition. You have the Father, the Son and the Spirit. It is really the God essence. The Father, the Spirit, they are all actually one energy. They are just different ways of looking at that one energy.

It is a very complex theological aspect to grasp. You have the Christ essence itself, which is the essence that came down to be incarnated, and you have the personification of the Christ essence, which we say that each one of you have. That is what has come down and what resides within you and you can fully activate it. The Holy Spirit is that creative force that moves within you, and it is all love. It is simply three different ways of speaking of the same energy, as in ways of doing things. If you use yourself as a metaphor, we could say that you are a father, you are a grandfather, you were an employee at one time, you are an astrologer, you are a student of Cayce—all are the same energy of you, but in different times and different manifestations of that energy.

*Are love and consciousness the same thing?*

Yes.

*Is there any color that we should use to visualize love coming down? Would any particular color help?*

If you ask for a color for yourself or for another person, you will find that the color is that of the vibration most needed by you or the other person, and at that time it will come down.

*You have indicated that we need to raise our vibration. One of the difficulties that we get into is with the cells of our body when they are raised in vibration. It can create an unhealthy situation if the cells are not able to accept the higher vibration. What is the best way to go about altering the cells of the body to accept the higher vibration?*

That is a very good question. We have talked before about how the strands of the DNA are changing; the spiritual strands are becoming active now. As the spiritual strands become active, then the physical cellular structure also changes. One of the things you can do—and you could add this to your schedule in your morning meditation if you wish—is that you can talk to the cells of your body and ask them to stretch open just a little bit more each time to accept a little more light. Then you can also call down light energy of the color that would help those cells the most. Most people will find that the color is going to range in the light purple area, the blue adding a little more red to it until you get to the light purple that will cleanse the cells. Those of you who are familiar with the work of one who is known as St. Germaine know that they talk about his violet flame. You can use that.

## WATCH YOUR REFINED SUGAR INTAKE

The other thing is to watch what you put into your mouth—that is, your food. Your cells are actually held in a rigid form by sugar. I am speaking of refined sugar. If you went out and chewed on a sugar cane, it would not have the same effect upon your cells as it would if you put in two tablespoons of sugar or drank a soda. I think I have mentioned before that your corn syrup is one of the worst sugars for your body. If you absolutely have to have a sugar, it is much better to have regular granulated sugar than it is to have corn syrup, which is what you will find in most of your sodas here in the United States. You have to have true sweetness in your life; when you have true sweetness in your life, the desire for sugar goes away. That desire actually comes from the fact that you are not able to derive sweetness from your life in other ways. So you have to feed yourself with sweetness. Interesting, isn't it?

When you are able to connect to the sweetness of life—and the process I have given you is going to help you to do that—what will happen is that you will not need the extra sweetness. You will actually find that not only is it too much, but it can almost be nauseating in a way. Part of what happened to you is that you got reconnected to the sweetness in your life in a different way, so you felt full, and you didn't need the other [speaking to the one who talked about weight changes that she has experienced]. So what you eat can change. Artificial sweeteners can have a very negative effect upon your physical and cellular structure, and you need to be aware of that. The things that are best are the ones that are as little refined as possible.

**Is stevia all right?**

Stevia is okay, but realize that what you are actually getting from stevia is a refinement of stevia, whether you use the liquid or the powder. If you could get stevia leaves as you get mint leaves, you could sweeten your tea by putting a stevia leaf in it, and that is different because it is a more natural form. Anything that is changed from its natural form is changed in its molecular structure in some way. There really is no artificial sweetener that is healthy for the body.

## HONEY AND MAPLE SYRUP ARE BENEFICIAL NATURAL SWEETENERS

One person asked about honey and another asked about pure maple syrup. You are getting these things in their full essence, and what you are getting from both of those is that they still have tremendous amounts of life force in them, both the honey and the pure maple syrup. You would want to have the grade B pure maple syrup because it is not as refined—they don't filter it as much, and it has many more minerals in it. It looks darker, it's heavier and it works just as well. At times there are some problems with honey in the changing of the structure when you cook with it. It is just something that is in the quality of the honey itself. Maple syrup would actually work better, but, of course, it doesn't work in recipes in holding breads and cookies and cakes together. So when you have a sweetener that is in as pure a natural form as possible—like honey and maple syrup—it is actually better for you.

Honey will work better in colder things than in warmer things. You could use the pure maple syrup in either. When anything is altered, you are changing part of how it is structured. And in your body, everything was made to fit together. Your body acclimated thousands of years ago to the molecular and cellular structure of the plant and animal kingdoms at that time. What has happened now—and I am not talking about the actual genetic mutations but about your genetically modified foods—is that in those foods that have been modified artificially, where they actually pluck part of the cellular structure out to put another part in, that is much different than the natural change and division in the mutations of cells. There is a change in the life essence that they have not discovered yet, and that is because most of your scientists who are working in this area do not understand or believe in consciousness.

*Would Splenda be less harmful than the refined sugar or artificial sweeteners?*

For some people, yes, and for other people, no. It depends on how each body handles it. It is supposed to be less harmful, but it is not really, because it still causes a change. It actually has a large sugar molecule that they have altered. It is having an effect upon the pancreas that the scientists are actually not aware of yet. So it is not the best thing. But it is better than NutraSweet or aspartame, and it is better than saccharin. The best choice would be to find the sweetness in your life. And then you will find that you do not need any of those. It doesn't mean that you can't have them, but the craving would be gone. You would be satisfied with a piece, a half piece, a square of chocolate, or one muffin instead of twelve, for instance.

## THE COMING CHANGES

*I have two questions. The first is for those of us who are just getting into this. Where can we go to read and get caught up on this? The other question is, are you talking about reconnection, changing the DNA in each of us, going back further in time and also adding extra strings to our bodies?*

Let me answer your first question of where to get other background information on this. You can go to the website www.lighttechnology.com, or the *Sedona Journal of Emergence!* You might find that there is a way to do a search to see which issues have Amma's information in them. It would be during this past year. You can also ask around and see if anybody has them.

When you said reconnection, are you talking about the Reconnection? The Reconnection can help with the cellular changes as you are reconnected to everything. It is a technique from Eric Pearl that he was gifted with. However, know that the strands are already there; everybody has them. The Reconnection helps to connect those strands together. There are also some things, such as holographic healing and others, that do the same type of work. There are a number of things out there. That is what's so wonderful about this time you are living in. Even with this work in encodements, there are other things out there that are similar. This is fairly new information, and it is not coming out in as many ways yet. The Reconnection and holographic healing—and there are even others—are coming about so that different peoples are being affected in different ways. You can actually become reconnected if all you did was follow the twelve steps that I just outlined—really followed them.

*Can you tell us what is going to happen in the year 2012 on December 22?*

It will actually not be much different than what you have experienced in your Harmonic Concordances and Convergence and the other alignments that are occurring, except that those of you who are more aware will actually feel the shift in the energies, and you will feel more transparent. There is not going to be a tremendous cataclysm associated with December of 2012, but there will be a very definite shift in the energy that some of you—all of you here and some others on the planet—will feel. There are different cataclysms that are building up simply because things are shifting, and the discordance that is growing in the planet is actually going to assist that in occurring. You are going to hear of more volcanoes. You are going to hear of more earthquakes. You are going to hear of more flooding. You are going to be surprised that you are going to have an unusual winter here in Houston. It is going to get pretty cold here at some time. There are some other areas that are going to feel warmer. There is going to be more cold than there has been for a little while.

*Will we need to abandon Houston?*

No, you will not need to abandon Houston. Some parts will be affected, like the really low-lying areas around the Texas City area, but not even all of that will be affected. Galveston will lose a little bit from the edges, but not anything really definite. That's as it stands now. That doesn't mean it can't change. But as it is now, I do not see the tremendous shift to where you will have your Gulf of Mexico up into Austin. That has been shifted much by your lightworkers. In Florida, the hurricanes that hit there were a foretelling of what is still to happen. Some of you have seen the different maps that are out. There will still be some problems. There will be some problems in New York City in some of the low-lying boroughs. There will be greater problems that you will see in California in many places and in the far northwest of Washington. The groups that have been trying to keep the Mississippi from changing course are going to lose that battle. It will change course. It is bigger than they are. It will change course and that means a whole system of economy as well as a few houses.

Now I would like to give each of you a blessing. The energies you call your guides are surrounding you. Know that these guides are actually aspects of yourself, and they are surrounding you. They send you love and light from their hearts. I come and place my hand upon your crown and send you energy. Dear ones, I bless you. Know that I am Amma, the divine mother of the divine mothers, and I am your mother. You grew from my womb, and I love you.

# 25

# Reincarnate Yourself

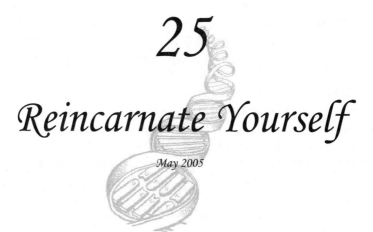

*May 2005*

$\mathcal{G}$ ood evening, everyone. I am Amma. I am the divine mother of the divine mothers, and I am your mother. There is not one of you who has not experienced my love, because I am with each of you. You grew in my womb. I loved you into being. I nurtured you as you decided what you would do in this lifetime and in your hundreds of other lifetimes, whether on this planet or another one, in this dimension or another. I am always here with you, loving you.

If I asked each of you what you would change about yourself, you would no doubt give me a list several pages long. I want you to know that I see you only in the perfection of the pure, unadulterated love that you are. If each of you could believe, totally and fully in this instant, that you are love and only love of the highest vibration, your entire life and being would change. Even your physical form would change. Some of you hold on to weight because you do not believe that you are lovable, and others hold on to illness because you do not believe you are lovable. You hold on to addictions or behaviors that do not serve you because you do not believe that you are the highest level of love and the manifestation of love. Can you even imagine what life would be like if you were to truly believe that—not in the head, but in the heart, in the depths of yourself?

There was one who walked this Earth, the one known as Jesus or Yeshua, who knew to the depths of himself who he was. If you are familiar with his words, you will recall he said that if you have the faith of a grain of sand or even of a mustard seed, you could move a mountain. If you believed that much that you were love incarnate, you could do anything. Love is not an emotion. It is a state of being, an energy that guides and transforms you. It is what you are made of. It is in your DNA and in all those little proteins that make up your DNA.

This is my first message to you today—know that you are love and that you are beloved. I love you; with all of my being, I love you. There is nothing imperfect about you in my eyes because I see who you truly are, and you are glorious. When was the last time you were told that you were glorious? You are in the depths of yourself and the depths of your soul. Work on taking this message from your head into your heart and having it change your very self.

I've been teaching about encodements and would now like to show you how to work with them in more depth. Even if you have never heard of encodements, you will be able to do this work. The next few times when I gather with people, whether it is in these regular monthly sessions or at other times, I will be giving instructions on how you can change your life plan by working with your encodements.

## YOU DIDN'T THINK YOU'D BE HERE IN 2005

Every one of you, before you incarnated, did not believe you would be here in the year 2005. You knew it was highly probable that the people of this planet would choose to self-destruct. Think of what your 1960s looked like. Did it not seem that you were on the path of self-destruction? Most of you came here for the big bang of ending, not the big bang of beginning. Then something happened.

In 1987 with the Harmonic Convergence, the energies of the planet changed. All of the buildup before Y2K was the buildup of what was, before 1987, very probably going to happen—the world as you knew it would self-destruct. This would have happened in a period of several months, with literally millions of people (although not all) leaving the planet. The fears of Y2K served to release the "what was to be" and allowed the new energy of "what will be" to enter. Then came the new year of 2000 and you celebrated what you called the turn of the century, though it was really the end of one century, not the beginning of a new one. But in your belief system, it was the turn of the century, and that belief overrode the arithmetic involved.

You each had encodements that mapped out how your life was going to run until the year 2000. To allow for the possibility that you would live past the year 2000, you had a few other encodements, but you did not have encodements to the degree that you had for your life before the year 2000. Many of you have felt rather rootless, like you're drifting, and suddenly you don't know what you're going to do with your lives. That is because everything was supposed to be over, and you didn't need to know what to do with a life after 2000. But you are still here.

Now you have an opportunity to reincarnate yourself. You could easily choose to leave your body, if, on a soul level, you would like to. There are many of you who have made decisions on a soul level to stay longer than you originally thought. You wanted to watch what is going to happen to this planet now that it is in the new energy as well as see the wondrous beings who are here. As you look at the planet right now, it doesn't look that great. Look at the wars and horrors going on. And yet you have probably heard it said that things are not as they seem.

## THE MEDIA GIVES FACTS, NOT TRUTH

I want to say something else to you that you have heard many times: Do not believe everything you read. There is very little truth in your newspapers and news magazines. There is almost no truth in your television or radio news. I'm talking about truth, not facts. They report incidents that do indeed happen, but not in the context of what is happening on the planet.

The truth is that change is occurring. Love is being known more and more. Whatever your stance is on the highly political issue called capital punishment, I want you to know that when your judges said no one should be put to death if they committed murder under the age of eighteen, that was a raising of the level of belief of what life is. [Channel's note: We're in Texas, a state that puts more people to death than most countries.]

There are no unredeemable lives. When you grow up in a home filled with animosity, hatred and abuse, you add artificial encodements of the belief that you are unworthy and unlovable. You begin to believe you deserve the abuse, that what people say about you is true. Dear ones, I ask you: Why do you choose to believe lies about yourself? Why do you choose to believe that you have no value, that you are worthless, that you cannot achieve, that you cannot have dreams for yourself? It is a choice of what to believe. Some of you grew up in such situations, and you chose not to believe those messages. If, however, you believe that you are worthless, stupid and without talents or gifts—well, dear ones, please choose something else to believe! It is that simple. A choice can be made in the deepness of yourself that will change any artificial encodements you have.

You must learn how to control your thoughts and feelings—what comes into your eyes through watching and reading, what you bring to your ears and listen to and, more importantly, what goes on in your brain. Those are your own thoughts. You say more negative things about yourselves than anyone else has ever said! It doesn't matter if you grew up in a home in which you were told ten times a day how worthless you were. You have reaffirmed that within yourself more times than you could ever imagine.

## HOW DO YOU FIGHT ARTIFICIAL ENCODEMENTS?

Let's talk about how to make it easy to change these debilitating beliefs. How does one go against artificial encodements? We will work to make these changes. This is where the life plan comes in. Let us say that you have been a writer and have decided that you no longer wish to pursue writing but would rather try something new in your life. Maybe you'd like to be a computer programmer, or we could reverse the process and go from computer programmer to writer. Let us say that you do not have the encodements to do that. You can ask for them. If you do not like your life, or if you just want something different, you can choose to make the change.

The first aspect of this change is perhaps the most difficult—you must determine how you want your life to look. You can discover that by asking some important questions, such as, "What would I like to learn?" Before you incarnated, the whole planning process concerned what you wanted to learn about and how you wanted to grow. Did you want to grow in the area of learning about relationships? The usual answer is yes. So how did you want to learn this?

Did you want to learn to love yourself more? You might think that if you're going to learn to love yourself more, then you need to be in a family that will give you lots of love. Yes, that is one choice. Ironically, you learn more about how to love yourself when you grow up in a family that does not know how to love. Then you have to make decisions and choices that are contrary to what you were taught. When you place yourself in a family of people who do not know how to love, then you have to be stronger in resisting that message. When you break out of that bond, there is nothing that can take the knowledge of love away from you, because you have learned it to the core of your being.

## WHAT DO YOU WISH TO LEARN?

So first begin with, "What would I like to learn?" Then ask, "How would I like to learn it? What would I need to do?" This seems rather simple. It is not, because you are here on a planet where wisdom is not the ruling factor. Consider asking the encodement technicians to activate and place within you encodements for tapping into divine wisdom. Do this process in consultation with others—your guides, angels or higher power. Seek out mentors or other high-level beings who walk upon this planet. You could do it yourself, but having more resources helps you to see various possibilities. You are limited by your belief system.

You did not plan this lifetime by yourself. The encodement technicians who worked with you were the final step. Your guides helped you look at different possibilities and ramifications. You then built a framework of what you wanted to learn. Various levels of choice were built in. Younger souls are given very little choice. Older souls, which most of you are, are simply given a foundation. You then built your house or structure however you wanted. Younger souls coming onto the planet now have many more choices than you were given—and then there is free will once you incarnate, which can change many plans.

So first, what is it you wish to learn? Think about that for a moment. What do you wish to learn most right now? Do you wish to learn about love? Let me tell you that there is nothing you can learn on this planet that is not about love. If you think it is about money, it is still about love. If you think it is about personal power, it is still about love. Everything is about love. The choice is how you wish to learn about love and in what way. This is your first task: What is it that you wish to learn?

## NO CHOICE IS INSIGNIFICANT

This sounds like goal setting, does it not? In a way it is, and it is on a very deep level. The choice you make about what you wish to learn is the pivotal point of your entire plan. It will decide the rest of your life. Let us say that you wish to learn how to be true to yourself no matter what anyone else thinks, does or says. The one known as Shakespeare said, "To thine own self be true." You can probably recall many times when you have not to your own self been true, perhaps in this very week.

This one [the channel] got in touch with a previous lifetime and asked what its purpose was. It was not a very happy life. Its purpose was for her to learn that no choice is insignificant. There are ramifications to every decision. For her in that lifetime, it was learning about the ramifications of her choice as a sixteen-year-old girl to have a temper tantrum when her father wanted to go to the country to visit cousins. She didn't want to go because she wanted to see her boyfriend. Her father chose to delay the trip until the next day. The Nazis came that night and killed most of her family. No decision is insignificant.

Each decision has repercussions, even the time when you go to bed or your choice to read a particular book. How many times have you read about the irony or the amazing coincidence of somebody missing a plane by five seconds and that plane went down? Or if a person had only waited for a brief hug, he or she wouldn't have been killed by a car that sped down the street. No choice is insignificant. When you decide what you would like to learn, it might be just a few words long, but it can focus tremendous energy on where you want to go. That is where you can start if you wish. It sounds a little overwhelming, but it is of great importance.

Let's say that you want more prosperity in your life—most people do. I'm not using "prosperity" to signify only the energy you call money. I'm talking about prosperity in many, many ways. So we will say you would like more prosperity and you have blocks against receiving it. Suppose you say that you would like total abundance in your life, coming to you from every direction and in every way—financially, emotionally, physically, spiritually. Sounds pretty wonderful, doesn't it? What could be the unintended consequences of that choice?

Think right now of what would happen if you had all the financial resources that you could possibly desire. How would your life change? You might think that would be wonderful, but I can tell you that if you had unlimited financial resources, an unintended consequence could be that you would not know what to do next in life. With that much money, you would not need to work anymore. You would begin to wonder if you had friends because of your money or because of who you are as a person. You would also have to take care of taxes and handle the things people said about you because you had money, like that you weren't spiritual because you have money. It might even be that, because you had money, you wouldn't meditate as much. Perhaps people would slander you when you gave money away, even if your heart was in the right place. Unintended consequences—how would you deal with them? [Channel's note: You could develop another set of encodements to work with each one of these unintended consequences.]

## CHANGING YOUR ENCODEMENTS WILL CHANGE YOUR LIFE PLAN

When you make a change in your encodements, the way your life is progressing will change. If you don't like the results of the encodement work, you can ask the encodement technicians to change them back. You cannot, however, change the events that occurred due to the changes. If you choose, for instance, to have a certain wondrous car—the biggest and best car you can choose—an unintended consequence might be that you become full of yourself, don't pay attention and kill someone when you run a stoplight. You can change the encodement about the car, but you cannot change the death of another. I'm using hit-you-in-the-gut examples, because I want you to realize that unintended consequences can be major.

Let's say you want to alter your encodements so that you feel more loved than you do now. It is possible to change the encodements to accept greater love. I recommend that you not have them changed all at once, because all the new energy coming into you might overwhelm you. Make the changes a little bit at a time. The best encodement plan for your new life will be similar to an architectural plan. Many just see the plan for the façade of the building. There is also a plan for the electrical, the plumbing, the foundation and all the other things that go into making a good structure. The plans demonstrate how all will interact and interrelate. In working with your encodements, the best plan takes into account as many interrelationships as possible.

## HOW WILL THE CHANGE MANIFEST?

Decide first what you wish to learn and ask yourself how that will manifest in the physical, emotional, mental and spiritual layers. Each of these has sublayers. In the spiritual, for example, does it mean you'll learn in a community, or will you be a hermit? If you intend to make encodement changes in your life plan, will the relationships with the people you now have in your life change? Your vibration will change. Others will not be attracted to you and some might actually be repelled. Your vibration and theirs will no longer be compatible. These are consequences to consider when you change things in your life.

People say they want certain things to change in their lives and then they don't like what happens. How many of you have heard the stories, or perhaps experienced it yourselves, about marriages that were stronger when they did not have physical or financial support? Much of this is about belief systems, which can be changed by working on your encodements. You can choose to have encodements for financial abundance while also having encodements to stay connected to people. At the same time, you can work with your encodements so that you are disciplined to stay spiritually connected. There is one who you have all heard of who does this, although not through conscious encodement work. Her name is Oprah. She has learned how to go from poverty to tremendous abundance and how to do things with her life and her money to serve others. She has not lost her center. She is an example of what can happen. She is a very public figure, but there are others who are not so public.

Hopefully, you are coming to a better understanding of the complexities of making certain decisions. I'm not saying don't make them. If you choose to use this path to change your life, you will learn more than when you were originally planning before incarnation. You will be making the choice without fully knowing that you are love. Until you came into this body, you had no doubt that you were love. In fact, that is why some of you chose such tough lives this time. You ask, "I chose this?" Yes, because when you knew you were love and were surrounded by love, you also knew you could handle it. It's just that you forgot that you are total love surrounded by love. You were supposed to forget. Now you can remember.

## CHOOSE SOMETHING TO WORK ON AND TRY IT OUT

Let us now do a little encodement work. This is what I want you to remember: There might be unintended consequences. Some you will like these consequences, some will feel uncomfortable and some of you won't like them at all. Just go back and do more encodement work. You do not necessarily have to change everything. Just ask if there can be some adjustments made.

Choose a small part of your life to work on. Let it be something you can measure so that you will know the result. Now think of what the unintended consequences might be. Since you haven't experienced this new role yet, you're somewhat limited in how much you can know, but give it a try. Now get in touch with your encodement technicians. Someone has called them engineers, and that is also fine. You can call them whatever you want. Getting in touch with them is very simple.

*Enter your heart center from the back of your heart. You will know you are in the center because it feels different, more expansive. Continue moving deeper into your heart center. You have now entered the space of no-space and the time of no-time.*

*You are entering into the most sacred part of yourself. When the great prophets like Moses and Abraham touched God, they did it through this space. When Mohammed and Buddha touched God, they did it in this space. Continue moving inward until you find your altar, no matter what it looks like—that sacred space within yourself.*

*Now ask your encodement technicians to come. They have all come now whether you've experienced them or not. Those who are clairvoyant or clairsentient will see or sense them. Know they are here. They have worked with you many times. They worked with you before this incarnation and have worked with you as you slept. They have especially worked on developing encodements after the year 2000. Now focus on what you want to change. Ask the encodement technicians if there are any artificial encodements that are preventing what you want from coming into your life. You will get a yes or a no. Just accept whatever it is; don't question it. Most of you received a yes. Now ask what would be the consequence of asking that those artificial encodements be removed.*

*You now have a choice. If you liked the answer, you can ask the technicians to remove those artificial encodements. If you didn't like what they said, you can choose to keep the encodements as they are. You can even ask, for instance, what would happen if you only had 10 percent of the artificial encodements removed, or if you had them removed more gradually. You now have information. This is where freedom of will comes in; you have a choice, so make it. Ask for those artificial encodements to be totally removed, to have a percentage removed or to leave them as they are.*

## NOW FOCUS ON YOUR NATURAL ENCODEMENTS

*The next step is to ask if there are any natural encodements that have been damaged or deactivated that prevent you from achieving what you would like. Again ask for the consequences. Keep asking questions until you get the information you need. Again, you have a choice. If you are comfortable with the consequences, ask the technicians to please repair the damaged encodements and activate any that are deactivated. The third step is to ask if there are any natural encodements that have not yet been activated that, if they were activated, would help you attain your desire. This means the encodements were already put in place, but for whatever reason, they are not yet activated. If the answer is yes, ask what the consequences of this would be. Again, dear ones, you are faced with a choice. You can ask the technicians to activate these encodements gradually if you think it would be overwhelming to have them activated all at once.*

*The final step is to ask if there are natural encodements that could be placed within you to facilitate your receiving what you wish to receive. If the answer is yes, be sure to ask about consequences. Some of you might receive information that it can be done but that it would be best not to do it all at once. Just ask what you need to do and how to do it. Ask if it must be done consciously or if it can be done in your sleep state. You can simply set it into motion now. And again, now is the time of choice. That is it. Now you know how to contact your encodement technicians.*

*Play with them, and I do mean play. Have fun. Try different things. Pay attention to the changes that occur.*

## THINGS YOU CAN DO WITH THIS TECHNIQUE

Let me give you a few examples of some other things you can do with this technique. You might be able to relieve pain. The one you loved who is no longer a part of your life due to death or leaving in some other way can still cause great pain. You can go to the encodement technicians and ask them to please deactivate the encodement that connects you to that person, or to turn those encodements down so that it doesn't hurt as much. You and another being might have made a choice to be partnered in this life. It could be a partner by marriage, a friendship, a business partner or a parent. Then something happened in this world of free choice and one partner left earlier than expected. The encodement for that person is still active. You can have that encodement changed to relieve the pain of separation.

You can do this same thing with places of business and locations. In the case of possibly moving to another country, it would be very helpful to ask if there are any natural encodements for that country or place that are not yet activated. If there are, ask to have them activated. If there are none, ask that they be put in so it will be easier to live there. You can play with the encodement technicians by asking to stimulate other encodements you might have for where you might live. That is a way to find out if there are any other encodements within you that, by your life choices, you decided not to pursue. These encodements did not get stimulated or activated. Play with this. Let your imagination run wild. If you can think of it, it can be done. Remember that the encodement technicians always say yes. They won't mention consequences unless you ask. Are there any questions on this? Does anyone wish to share anything?

## ON OTHER PEOPLE'S ENCODEMENTS AND RECEIVING UNCLEAR RESPONSES

*Can you work with other people's encodements?*

You can do this only for your child up to the age of five. You can also do this for a grandchild up to the age of five if there is a deep soul connection. After that age, you can only lead them through the process. There is no way to change other people, even for the better. They must do it themselves through their own free-will choices. You can work with the encodements of the planet. She's always willing to release artificial encodements that don't serve her.

*In going through the process, I got clear answers in the first two steps, but at the third step nothing was clear; it was just confusion.*

That would be a sign that the answers are more complex than we have time to go into here. You might need to sit down with pen and paper or at a computer and write out the questions and the answers to see how one leads to another. Here I have just been taking you through something very simple to get you started. It can become more complex as you work with the encode-ment technicians.

*What if the answers from the technicians are unclear?*

Then you ask them another question. Just continue asking. The lack of clar-ity isn't meant to put you off. It is meant to help you be clear. Their lack of clarity has more to do with your own lack of clarity. You might not even be con-scious that you are not being clear. They know how serious this work is.

## CONSEQUENCES, RITUALS AND ALTERING THE DIVINE PLAN

*One of the problems I have with this is that you don't know all the consequences of your choice. So even with the help of the technicians, it's like flying solo. Even with all the questions you could ask, you still don't know what is going to happen, yet you have to make a choice.*

Yes, it is challenging, and this is one reason why you wanted to come here! You can always go back and change things, but you can't change the conse-quences. You recently had a powerful experience involving a ritual. Rituals like bar mitzvahs, the Christian sacraments and Native American sweat lodges activate powerful encodements. They are not to be taken lightly. They bring you into a different level of belonging, whether you want to call it the morphogenic field or some other term. They open up avenues for other energies to come in—the energies not only of faith but of spirituality. These consequences are far-reaching.

*I keep coming back to the fact that we come here with a divine plan and that by doing this, we are somehow manipulating that divine plan. That seems scary. My own thought is that the choices we make are part of our divine plan. Do you have any comments on this?*

Remember that you had many encodements set until the year 2000. Since that time, you haven't had many encodements, because you didn't think you would be here. You cannot manipulate God or the divine, so you are not manipulating in the negative sense even though you are making choices to make change. If, for example, someone has decided to stay in addiction for a number of years and that was in his or her plan, he or she can decide to change the plan and become sober. We look at that as a good change. On the soul level, it might not be, but here on the planet, we look at it in this way. That isn't any different than what we are doing with the encodements.

Perhaps you do not want to change the definite path of your life, but you would like to change things to make the path easier to travel. The first thing to ask is if there are any artificial encodements that are interfering with your life path. Remember that artificial encodements were not put there by the encode-ment technicians. They were not originally in your plan. It's like a computer virus getting in. It's not your operating system. That's not any different than asking if there are any belief systems that are not serving you. You can look at it in that way. By removing artificial encodements, nothing integral has been changed in your life path. Even though you can choose to change something integral, if it isn't supposed to happen on your soul level, it won't change no matter what you decide.

## TIMING AND RESPONSIBILITY
*How often do you need to change your encodements?*

It would be very beneficial if, before you go to sleep at night, you ask if you have acquired any artificial encodements throughout the day. Then ask what would happen if they were removed. If you like the answer, then ask that they be removed. That's called encodement housecleaning. It is something you can do on a daily basis, and it will prevent your having to do major work later. In other words, what you are asking is if any other energies, thought forms or beliefs have come that are now affecting you. Then you ask that they be removed. You can go to the encodement technicians as often as you like, but be sure to ask them those important questions. Sometimes they will tell you, "That is enough for now." You have a physical body and it can go into a healing crisis if too much change takes place at once.

*How should I view my own responsibility for the choices and the questions I am asking? I call in the encodement technicians and they do something magical that causes certain consequences. It seems that we should be taking responsibility for the choices we make, which means we must be careful in how we view this process.*

Yes, you are exactly right—you must take responsibility for your choices. That is why I keep emphasizing the consequences. Let's talk a little about the responsibility you mentioned. The encodement technicians have a responsibility to answer the questions you ask and to do the work as you asked it to be done. This means that if you ask for a change without realizing the full dynamics of what will happen, you would have an unintended consequence.

The encodement technician's primary responsibility is to work with you on your deepest level. They will do nothing that is against your soul purpose, no matter what you want. There is very little that you are going to ask that will be contrary to your soul purpose—very little. Quite frankly, it would rarely come to mind if it were against your soul purpose. There are very few people whose soul purpose is to live in poverty, but they might want to learn what poverty is like and might do that for several reasons. There is a woman in this city who has lived in poverty and studied it. She now writes and lectures about poverty and has become quite wealthy doing that.

## YOUR SOUL PURPOSE IS TO LEARN HOW LOVE IS MANIFESTED
Your soul purpose is to learn how love is manifested. Each of you will do that in a different way. That's why your guides sit back and let you run amok. It's not their job to influence your choices. Their job is to give guidance when asked, on a conscious or subconscious level. And their job is to love you. You

have this group of beings surrounding you with total and absolute love at all times, no matter how many times you might go against their guidance. They still love you, even though they might find you amusing.

There really isn't much that you can ask that will be against your soul purpose. What I am presenting is a way to reincarnate yourself without your physical body dying, your coming again into somebody's womb, being born, growing and going through that process again. Some of you might have heard of the term "walk-in." This is where another being's energy comes into you. This process we are working on is like making you your own walk-in. The difference is that you're not changing the soul. By the way, reincarnating yourself can be done very simply by making a choice to be different and then acting upon that choice. Your encodements would then be changed by the encodement technicians. We can talk about this more at a later time.

*Can the consequences be harmful to other people?*

Yes, they can. Any choice we make can be harmful to other people. It's a heavy responsibility. I talked earlier of a situation where someone had a special new car that he was proud of and liked showing it off. He ran a red light and, as a result, someone was killed. That's a consequence that was harmful. The same would be true of the choice to drink and drive, which could also lead to a serious accident. You could make a choice when you are very young to experience stealing. When you steal, you deprive someone of something. That is another type of harmful consequence. Making choices is a serious responsibility.

I wish now to leave you with a blessing. I place my hands upon you. Feel one on your head and the other on the back of your heart center. Feel the love I have for you and the love that is you. Even as we have been talking, I have been loving you and working with you. Feel that love now. Experience it. Dear ones, allow yourselves to be the love that you are. I see, know and experience the love that you are. I am Amma, the divine mother of the divine mothers, and I am your mother.

# Predictions 2003

# Discover the Power of Living from Your Heart Center

*D*ear ones, you ask for information about your upcoming year 2003. I wish to tell you how beloved you are. More than that, I desire that you come to know who you are. If only you knew and believed who you are, you would not need me to tell you how beloved you are. You would be the beloved for yourself and others. I do know that as this world of yours is structured, you will not come to that realization until your mission is over, but that is what I yearn for you to know.

## MIRACLE CURES ARE NO MIRACLES

This next year, much more information will come to light that will reveal how wondrously you are made. Your scientists will soon discover how to "turn on" the latent DNA. There will be the physical proof they need to demonstrate that all parts of the DNA are important and have a role. There are no filler items in the DNA. Within the decade, great advances will be made in helping the paralyzed to regain sensation in parts of their bodies they thought were dead. The world will look in wonder.

These advances will come about as some scientists realize they need to release the paradigms of the third dimension to accomplish what they will call a miracle. You have some very spiritual scientists who are aware of interdimensionality. They have been to the space vehicles of those who are imparting to them the methods to bypass the belief that paralysis cannot be changed. They are learning how to move between dimensions and how they can enable molecules to move between dimensions. In addition, they are learning how the beliefs, emotions and spiritual energy one has can be focused interdimensionally to activate the "sleeping" or latent DNA.

Once this is done, you will soon find how to regenerate the pancreas, liver (its ability to regenerate now is the third-dimensional key to the beginning of this understanding), nerves, spleen and other cells. The way will open for the cure for diseases such as diabetes, MS, Parkinson's, Alzheimer's (which will be discovered to be several types of dysfunction, just as there are a number of types of cancer), AIDS and all autoimmune disorders.

These discoveries will come from Russia, and those in the Western world will not believe them for some years. The mistrust of anything from Russia as well as the mistrust of anything that cannot be studied in the prevailing method of Western science prevents the acceptance of these great discoveries.

Your scientists in Russia have learned how to subsist in their culture by depending upon their own inner strength and inner knowing. That is why they are able to make these advances. They have discovered the spiritual nature of the individual and that healing must occur with the activation of the spiritual. That activation begins with the activation of the heart center. They will break from the paradigm of looking at isolated causes and effects and will begin to see the holistic aspect of healing.

## WORKING FROM THE POWER CENTER

Your energy workers will be discovering more healing techniques. Already simple but previously unknown information about additional energy structures in the human energy field is being given. Several people are channeling this information at this time. It is important for each person not to be competitive when this information comes out. If all work together and realize that this is not "their" information or technique, tremendous advances can be made in changing the patterns of the way emotions are held in the body. An understanding will come as to why it is more difficult for some people to "let go" of the past than for others. Psychology will be advanced greatly by these new techniques that are coming and will soon become public.

I encourage those of you who are receiving this new information about the energy body and healing to be looking for each other. Bring the information together. Do not be like your scientists who withhold information because it is "theirs." This information is for everyone. All of you will benefit. Withholding this information from humanity will grievously delay advancement in healing the emotional and mental aspects of individuals.

As you are working for peace, you will discover more about the power of your thoughts and beliefs. You will become more aware of how to use the energy around you, within you and of which you are made. All will be used for the good. You will soon discover that the greatest advances will be made when you are working from the power center of your heart. Your heart center is the activation center of your entire self. From this area, you will be able to amplify the energy of the atoms to change the molecules. You will be able to "move mountains." None of these discoveries can be used for ill. The heart is the activation center for all these "powers" that will be manifested. These energies will respond only to the vibration of love.

## DIET FOR HEALTH

Most diseases on your planet can be eliminated by changing your diet and how you relate to one another. Your researchers have shown that countries whose people begin to eat in the Western way develop diseases they did not previously have. They have also noted that health decreased when family units were dissolved.

The role of diet will be coming to the forefront as a way of curbing disease. The focus on diet at this time has predominantly centered around weight gain and loss. By centering on weight loss rather than on the health benefits of diet, people have their intent on weight loss rather than on health. The result is that many people lose weight in an unhealthy manner. Weight loss should not be the goal; health should be the goal. Weight loss, when necessary, will result when healthy eating habits are developed.

Much research is available about the destructiveness of the current Western diet. Most of this research is not able to find its way into general publication due to the influences of the food industry. If healthy eating was the focus of everyone, much of your food industry would go out of business. They would need to change what they produce and serve to stay in business. This would be good; however, it would require a tremendous expenditure of money and, more importantly, a change in thinking. Notice how much of your economy is based upon the food industry. If every person quit drinking and eating anything containing refined sugars, flours and chemicals, what do you think would be left on your grocery shelves? Each missing item on the shelf represents a loss of money and a company in financial trouble. This would mean the loss of many jobs. Your economy would be greatly affected. Do you now see why there is resistance to change in the food industry?

However, let me speak directly to you who are reading this message. You have the deep desire to change your consciousness, do you not? Most of you reading this will answer yes. This is what you must do for the greatest facilitation of change; I will begin with the third-dimensional realm.

## LISTEN TO YOUR BODY

Change the way you eat and drink. This is the simplest of what I will suggest, and it will have a powerful impact. Each of you has different needs in regards to your body. Learn to listen to what your body is telling you. Make contact with and communicate with your elemental body. Before you put something in your mouth, ask if this will give your body support. If the answer is "yes" or "neutral," continue the path from hand to mouth. If the answer is "no" or "not entirely," then don't eat it. However, if you have to choose between foods and drink that your body elemental says "no" or "not entirely" to, choose the "not entirely" foods, since they will have some elements of support.

A healthy individual need only drink one thing—pure water. There is very little pure water; most of it is trapped in the glaciers. Those of you who drink bottled or purified water are under the illusion that it is pure because there is nothing in it. That is not true. The molecules are not in the "pure" construction.

There are two simple things to do to increase the benefit of water for your body. The first is simply to add a pinch of sea salt to each glass. The second is to bless it. You can bless in any way you wish, but for those of you who prefer particular words, I give you these: "Thank you, Blessed One, for the gift of this water. I ask you to fill it with light and love. I ask that the molecules of this water move in unity with the structure of purity and love." While saying this prayer and for a few moments afterward, focus on your heart and see the energy from your heart go through your hands into the water. A similar blessing upon food will help your body assimilate it.

## BLESS WHAT IS NOT NATURAL

Cover your body in clothing that gives you joy and feels good. Notice what does this. Notice what colors give you the most pleasure and when.

Avoid as many chemicals as possible. This means that as much as possible, wear and use items made from natural sources and live in an environment that is from such sources. Bless all things that are not natural. Even that which is manufactured from chemical elements is of the light; simply bless those substances.

What I have said is not a command for you to become obsessed in this area. Obsession is not good for the spirit. Simply choose from what is available that which will most benefit you. Your body will respond to the energy of the substances you eat, drink, wear, breathe and use. Bless them all.

Have you noticed my emphasis on blessing? The quickest way to consciousness is simply to be conscious—you might call it awareness, if you wish. When you bless anyone and anything, you are being conscious of their blessedness, and just as important, reminding them of their blessedness. When you remind the molecules of their blessedness, they will "remember" and realign themselves. You will assist them in their remembering by activating your heart center and sending them that energy.

## CONSCIOUSLY LISTEN AND WATCH

Since you wish to be conscious, be aware of what you put into your eyes and your ears. No, I am not speaking of contacts and hearing aids here; I am speaking of what you listen to, what you watch and what you read. There are a very few of you who are able to remain conscious no matter what you put into your ears and eyes. Most are unable to make decisions about what will remain within your mind and release the rest. If you think you are one of the few able to do this, answer this question: How often do you do or buy something because of advertising? I am also speaking of your workshops and spiritual endeavors. Do you go into the deepness of your heart and ask if this book, event, television show, movie, newspaper or retreat is what you need at this time in your life? If you do not, then you do succumb to advertising and need to be more selective about what you put into your eyes and ears. Simply go into your heart and ask what is best for you.

It would be better if you listened and watched only that which uplifts you. When you must watch other things, then pay attention to what they do to your moods and thoughts. Release all that lowers your vibration. Send light to that which is of lower vibration. Activate your heart when watching the news or listening to the radio. Elevate your love vibration so that the lower vibrations coming toward you do not affect you. When you see or hear horrors or misfortune, immediately activate your heart and send the love energy from your heart to those involved. When it is fiction, send the energy to the producers and writers of such things.

## THE KEY TO RIGHT RELATIONSHIP

Now I wish to speak briefly of right relationship. I have already given you the key to right relationship. Activate your heart, send love energy and ask, "Is this the relationship I need to be in at this time?" Dear ones, every relationship, be it with a person, place, thing or activity, can be for your highest good. Every relationship will teach you about love, about loving yourself and loving others. Every relationship will teach you about nonjudgment. Will you open yourself to learning the lessons contained in the relationship? Do you leave a relationship before learning the lesson simply to have to repeat the same lesson in a new package? If your new relationship is the same lesson in a new package, then the lesson is about you, not the other. Stay and learn the lesson. Then you can move on to a new lesson in a new package.

Right relationship begins with your relationship with yourself. You have been told this for many years. You will not be able to be in right relationship with any person, place or thing, including All That Is, unless you are in right relationship with yourself. How does one get in right relationship with the self? Simply stay in your heart. Have compassion for your life and your struggles. Accept responsibility for everything—yes, I do mean everything—that rises up from you. You are not responsible for what others do to you. But you are, dear ones, responsible for how you respond to what others do. If someone assaults you through thought, word or deed, that is that person's responsibility; how you respond to that person is your responsibility.

## THE MOST POWERFUL FORM OF DEFENSE

Your planet is moving out of the vibration of using physical weapons to respond to assaults, and humans tend to hold tightly to that which is most ready to be released. This is one of your more destructive characteristics. It is time to release the physical weapons. That is why your governments are so anxious to use them again; they are not able to release them. As long as they hold on to those weapons, they will not be able to find another way of bringing peace. You must show them the way. You bring peace by activating the most powerful force of defense. Unlock the tremendous energy that is contained within your heart. Continually send blessings to others; even those you disagree with. Love is the force that will bring lasting change.

You find that difficult to believe, do you not? It is love from which you and all around you were made. It is love that will overpower that which is not love. If each individual reading these words would activate the power contained in the heart center, which is the entryway to the power source of All That Is, then the destruction on your planet can be overcome. The low-vibration thought forms will be overpowered by the high vibration of love.

You are willing to do this but are not sure how. Let me tell you; it is very simple. Do the following exercise now.

## EXERCISE: ALL BEGINS IN YOUR HEART CENTER

*Bring your attention to your heart center, just to the right of your physical heart. Focus on that area. Breathe in and out of that area. Yes, you have heard this many times.*

*Now, keeping focus on the heart center, also focus on the pineal gland. See the heart-shaped form contained within the pineal gland. Now expand that heart-shaped form to center around the pineal gland. Expand it to around the pituitary, all the while continuing to breathe in and out of the heart center.*

*Now connect the two hearts, the one from the heart center and the one around the pineal and pituitary glands, with a beam of energy. Breathe into the entire structure. Allow it to expand to encompass you.*

Whenever you need protection, do this. It would be best to have this structure surrounding you at all times. When you feel attacked, expand the structure and send energy from your heart center, from the center of the structure, to the person attacking you.

The exercise I have just given you will also increase your health. You understand the effect of chemicals and food upon your body, even if you do not use the information, but you do not fully understand the effect of right relationship, of coming from the heart center. Right relationship begins in your heart center. The power to change your life, to change the world, lies within your heart center. The body needs the vibration from your heart center to function at its best. For your body to be in the best of health, natural law requires that you live from your heart center. This is where your power is located. Discover it. Use it. Accept responsibility for the power that is you.

Dear ones, all that I have said can be summed up very simply. The power to change yourself, to change the world, to manifest miracles, will come from your learning how to live from the heart center and harnessing the energy contained therein. Advances in science, in consciousness, in peace will be made as you learn to live from the heart center. Activation of the DNA and the healing and regeneration of the body will come from living from the heart center. This i⸱ what the scientists in Russia have discovered; they have discovered how to ha⸱ ness this energy. Watch for this information. Pay attention when it comes. You will discover that what you call miracles are not miracles at all. The advances you will see are the result of natural law, which requires the emanation of the love vibration.

I encourage you, dear ones, to practice living from your heart. I encourage you to learn about the power of the love vibration. I encourage you to believe you are love. When you do, you will move mountains. I am Amma, the divine mother of the divine mothers.

# Predictions 2004

# Your Consciousness and the Planetary Being

*D*ear ones, I wish to speak to you about several things. My purpose is to prepare you for the possibilities of what is coming to you in your year of 2004 as well as the coming decade. You have heard many things through teachings in religious, scientific and spiritual groups. I wish to open the possibilities further so that you can prepare yourselves to accept what is happening. This will make the transition easier for you as individuals and for your planetary collective.

Let us begin with your planet. Many of you who read this are aware of your planet being. This is a play on words. Your planet is a being, and your planet is being. Beings by their very nature "be." Your planet is a being, dear ones. Although you can refer to the planet as "she" or "he," your planet is neither. Your planet is a fully-realized, androgynous entity. Your planet is a fully-realized, multidimensional being who continues to grow and develop. This one you call Earth has both consciousness and will. Earth has agreed to host you and allow the use of the many resources within the planetary body. This was a conscious decision made in response to a question presented by the oversoul, or group of souls, who wished to experience a life of duality on the surface and, yes, subsurface of the physical body you call Earth.

Your planet has a physical life cycle just as you do. If you wish to gauge that life in years, you will not be able to do so. You gauge your year as to the Earth's revolution around your Sun, but the embodied Earth being has no measure of time. The planetary consciousness did not enter into the plan of duality as you did. Earth agreed to host you for your own experiences and because it knew that tremendous spiritual growth would result by being such a host. The embodied being had full awareness of what challenges lay ahead by being such a host. There was an agreement that your oversoul and the Earth's being would do what each needed for spiritual growth. The experiment and experience began.

When the souls upon the Earth were in contact with their own oversoul and thus with the Source, they were also in contact with the being embodied by the planet. What you would now call a magical and wondrous relationship occurred. When the souls lost connection, they also lost connection to the being of the planet. Disaster occurred. This cycle has been repeated three times, with this being the third cycle.

You have before you the possibility of two events. You may continue in the cycle in such a way that most of you will be eliminated from the planet's surface. (This, by the way, will also result in the leaving of some of the souls who live beneath the surface.) This option will be difficult for those left. There will be much physical—as in the Earth's physical—violence. Some has already occurred with volcanoes, hurricanes and such. There is, however, a second possibility. The souls upon the planet will get back in touch with their own oversoul and the being embodied by the planet.

Dear ones, as much as you might think otherwise, it is this second possibility that is nearing. You see so much violence and focus on that violence. You believe that the violence is a sign that the disasters you have heard through your ancient scriptures and new channeling are coming true: "Those upon the Earth will be destroyed." Not so! Every day more people are connecting with the oversoul. As they do this, they become aware of the oneness of all, including the planet who has so graciously housed you.

As awareness of the oneness increases, more will connect with the being within the planet. People will become aware of the tremendous androgynous being whose body they are living upon. There will be more reverence, honor and respect for the body of the being you call Earth. You will witness in the next fifty years tremendous changes in how people live upon this planet. Even your corporations will change. All of this will occur as the consciousness of everyone upon the planet elevates.

Many will still be leaving this planet in order to experience the newness of the rise in consciousness. Many people mired in the old consciousness of duality and limits to abundance will choose to leave their present bodies. They will have finished their work in bringing about the change and will then want to participate in the change in a new body. It will be easier for them in this way, especially public, political, corporate and religious figures.

You might wonder how these of the old consciousness helped to bring about the new consciousness. How do you walk if you do not have something for your feet to push against? For the new consciousness to be revealed, you had to decide against something to move toward something (remember, you are on a planet of duality). Those of the old consciousness gave the gift of providing you with something to leave or to change. Honor them. Bless them. Do not curse them or hold them to be less than you. You lessen yourself when you do so.

## THE DEVELOPMENT OF CONSCIOUSNESS

First, know that consciousness simply is. There is no need to develop consciousness; you simply need to be conscious of it. Once conscious of consciousness, you then learn to use what would be seen as the dramatic power of consciousness in your day-to-day life. That which you call magic (not the illusions of magicians, although that also incorporates consciousness) is simply the skill of combining the consciousness of the individual with the consciousness of the elements. The limit you have placed upon yourselves is that you believe this skill requires certain personal attributes such as deep spiritual connectedness or initiation into some esoteric mystery school.

Dear ones, there is no need for "spiritual connectedness" or an initiation. You are already spiritual. You cannot be anything other than spiritual. This means that you are already connected; you simply are not aware of this connectedness. An initiation is a process that was developed centuries ago to have the populace believe there was something hierarchically special about certain individuals. An initiation is simply a ceremony of demarcation of something you have learned. And what is it you have learned? You have learned to access the power that you already are.

What you will see happening on your planet is the growing awareness that you have tremendous talents and powers. Yes, some of you are more aware than others of both your connectedness and your talents. An example might help here. You enter a room with which you are unfamiliar. You wish to listen to music. You find what you think is the box to play the music, but you are unable to find any buttons or dials to turn it on. After much time, you look at the box and you think to yourself, "I wish I could just look at the box and say 'On,' and it would turn on." Just for fun, you then look at the box, focusing all your attention upon it. Then you say "On." Oh, how surprised you are when the box does indeed turn on. This is a wondrous experience, and you begin to experiment with what else you can do with this box and your focused intention.

The box was there. It was simply waiting for you to discover how to make it play. You had all the powers you needed; you simply needed to learn to use them. Consciousness is a part of you. You simply need to learn how to use it. Have you ever seen a stone mason make intricate designs in stone using nothing but a hammer and a set of chisels? The tools are very simple, but learning to use those tools takes dedication and commitment.

Many of you know that spirituality is in a resurgence. It will continue to be so. Those of you raised in a particular religious tradition who have left that tradition might be looking to other traditions to strengthen your spirituality. Because you were so wounded in the religious tradition of your youth, you believe that all that tradition is invalid. After you feel your spiritual connection is strong, go back to the teachings, especially the traditional scriptures of your past religious tradition. Read them through your now more open and more aware heart. You will find truths and secrets of spiritual growth within those scriptures. In many cases, they are secrets because they have been spoken of rarely or not at all.

In the next decade, many people will be going back to the religions of their youths and discovering the truths and joys contained therein. This will lead to a greater expansion of a global spirituality. As an aside, spirituality is from within the deepest aspect of yourself and religion is from outside of yourself. Take whatever you hear from the outside into your heart and decide whether it should stay there as is or be altered or released. Even that which you do not deem truth can teach you truth.

In your present world, there are certain belief systems that shape your awareness of consciousness. These beliefs limit you. The development of your awareness of consciousness rests upon how quickly you will be able to release the limits. It is possible to release the limits within the blink of an eye; you simply need to let them go. The sooner you release the hot poker, the sooner you will quit being burned.

## LOSE THE HOLD OF LIMITING BELIEFS

Many things will be happening in the next ten years that will begin to loosen the hold of limiting beliefs upon you. The use of thought to move things has been experimented with in your laboratories. Toy trains have moved upon tracks simply with the power of the mind. There is even the development of a wheelchair that will move with the thought of the one sitting in it. As amazing as that sounds—a quadriplegic able to move in a wheelchair by thought—do you see the limiting belief? Some of you do. Some do not. If the quadriplegic is able to use the power of the mind to move a wheelchair, which most people consider inanimate, why can't the same person speak to the cells to move in the direction of regeneration and walk? "What if the person has no legs?" you ask. Yes, that would be a problem in your world. Why not think the growth of legs? Why not think health? "Impossible," you say? Ah, those are the limits, dear ones; those are the limits.

Your society will begin to break out of those limits. It is already discovering the power of thought and belief. There is much study occurring and many miracles being seen. You do not hear about it in the United States and Western Europe, because these advances would have a tremendous effect upon the profitability of companies. Those whose focus is profit will do all they can to sabotage the efforts of using the power of the mind. In fact, they use their knowledge of the power of the mind to keep you in the box of your limiting beliefs. This occurs through advertising and what you call disinformation.

Become aware of advertising. Notice it. Much drug advertising does not mention what the drug is used for. The message simply is to check with your doctor and ask if the medicine is for you. The subliminal message is that you need something outside your very self to bring you to health. Notice how the advertisers word the side effects. They do it in such a manner—using a soft tone of voice and music—to imprint upon you that the side effects are minor and will have little negative effect upon your body. Notice how they use the power of the mind to form beliefs and fear in those who listen. If you do not notice, if you do not become aware, you are not using your own inner power.

## ALTERNATIVE VERSUS ALLOPATHIC HEALTH CARE

This method of advertising will ultimately backfire on the advertisers and help bring about the quickening of use of what you now call alternative methods of healing. Since more people will be drawn to using the drugs advertised, more people will have side effects, some devastating. There will be lawsuits. People will then go into fear. Their fear will propel them to look at other ways they can be made well. A large minority of these will begin to find alternative means of health care.

What will also speed the advance of alternative health care and ultimately the awareness of consciousness is the price of health care. Those who can no longer afford traditional Western health care will look for alternatives. They will find these alternatives to be less expensive, less invasive and more empowering than the system they are now familiar with. As people move to other forms of health care, there will be a continuation of false information coming from those who are worried about loss of income. There will be continued attempts by government agencies to stop alternative health care. Much of the new health care will be based upon consciousness, the ability of the mind to form material reality. Nothing will be able to stop this except for individual fear. This is known by those in power. You will see much more information released to keep this fear at high levels.

But as people go into despair and anger because either they or their loved ones are not being helped by allopathic health care, they will look to other modalities. In order to do this, they will need to break the structure of the energy that allopathic health care has formed. Within this structure are beliefs that allopathic is the only form of health care that cures; that alternative or complementary health care is substandard and a waste of time, money and energy; that people who use a modality other than allopathic health care are weak and demented. Understand that there are good people in allopathic care who truly believe that how they are treating patients is the only healthy and sane choice. There are others, however, who are aware that there are other treatments that not only cost much less but are less invasive, but they do not wish to give up their profits.

For those of you who are in what you call alternative, holistic or complementary health care, be aware that the competitive and profit structure of allopathic care is an energy that permeates all health care. Just as those in allopathy would be served by other modalities, so also will you be served by learning and being aware of other modalities, including the allopathic. Humans tend to believe that what they do or believe is the only right way. There are many different ways, just as there are many different people. Be aware of other modalities, and be true to your inner voice telling you to refer someone to a provider of another modality. Be connected to the energy of healing. It is a specific energy, activated by connecting your heart and brow chakras with an actual structure containing all the information of healing. After connecting your heart and brow chakras, simply ask to connect to that energy. You will be connected.

## YOU CAN CHANGE ANYTHING: SOME SPECIFIC PREDICTIONS

Regarding health care: There will be much anguish seen in the news media and among those you love about the pain and suffering caused by the profit motive of the allopathic system. By the middle of the next decade, in about ten years hence, there will be definite changes in not only the structure of health care, but in the beliefs of responsibility regarding health care. The general populace will begin to see that the individual is responsible for personal health care. This will result in greater numbers of people learning to access the powers of their consciousness to change the structure of their bodies to the cellular level. This can already be done. More research from other countries will be revealed that will support this. Nonrefutable evidence will be seen in changes in the physical abilities of certain public figures.

Regarding the political system: There will continue to be much rancor. More people are feeling helpless and hopeless about their political system. If things continue the way they are presently, there will be a rising up of the general population against issues being political rather than for the people. They will begin to look for leaders willing to look at the general well-being of all people. Although you will see some of this in this next presidential election, the separatist political energetic structure is very strong. Beliefs will need to change. This will begin to occur in elections by the end of the present decade.

Regarding the moral climate: There will be continuing revelations of the deceit and shadow side of corporations and political and religious figures. Although this will continue to increase the sense of helplessness and cynicism of the general population, it will also increase the anger. The result will be new people taking a leadership role and beginning to change things. There will be a strengthening of the belief of personal responsibility. The lack of personal responsibility is a result of fear and despair. Both of those emotions are immobilizing. As anger comes into prominence, there will be more activity to change things. The anger will result in violence as is already seen in terrorism on your planet. As the energy of spirituality and awareness of consciousness increases, the anger will be transformed through heart energy. New ways will be discovered to produce changes that do not alienate, but heal.

Regarding the prison system: Injustices will continue to come to light. There will be philosophical discussions between those who believe in retribution and those who believe in reformation. As awareness of consciousness increases, people will learn the power of moving to their heart center. This will lead to a focus on reformation rather than punishment. Although this is beginning, it will not occur in force for at least ten years.

In the nonpublic arena—which is that arena not noted in newspapers, radio or television—there are two opposing forces occurring simultaneously: the increase of despair and the increase of optimism. The despair comes from those who have not yet connected spiritually to the Source from which they came. The optimism comes from those who have connected.

## CHANGE YOUR WORLD!

Those of you who are connected to your Source, which is most of you reading this information, are in awe and wonder of the changes within you. For the most part, you enjoy this as a personal experience. You have not, as yet, learned to use your newfound connections within the concept of oneness. Yes, you intellectually believe and have some experience of the oneness, but you have not yet learned to use the power of the oneness to change your world. If you want your world to be different, gather together and change it.

Connect each of your major chakras, the seven within your physical and the one above your head (those of you aware of the others can incorporate those also). Feel the power of the connection. Ask for support from the spiritual beings who are ready to help. Ask for an increase in the vibration of that connection. Now, from the heart of yourself, simply make that intention—connect to the "one heart." Again, simply form the intention.

The community inherent in your religions is a powerful force. Learn how to use the connection I have outlined in communion with each other. Learn to live every minute in this manner. The sooner you do that, the sooner things will change, even in the blink of an eye.

You are blessed, my children. I bless you every minute of every day. I am Amma, the divine mother of the divine mothers. I am your mother.

# Predictions 2005

# Stay in Your Heart, Live from Your Heart, Be in Your Heart

*D*ear ones, people want predictions to help prepare them for whatever is coming in the next year. I want you to know that what is coming is . . . life. You will need to manage the events in your life, whether you are told about them months before or not. Most people, even if they do know what is coming, make little preparation. For instance, your financial advisor will tell you to save money for retirement or you will not have enough money to live on. You all have heard this. You, dear one reading this message, have you followed the advice of your advisor? Only a few of you have, and I smile as I say this.

What I would like to do is share with you some general possibilities and ways to manage possibilities. First I want you to know that what everyone is sharing with you in this wonderful journal are possibilities. It is up to you to either manifest the possibility given or form a new possibility.

## DIPLOMACY IS MANDATORY

There is a great possibility of social unrest in the United States and the world at large. You now know who is the president of the United States. This individual must act quickly to mend fences with other countries. The United States is virtually alone in its political stand in the Middle East. The people of Great Britain will not support for long their country's involvement as it now is in the Middle East. There is a strong possibility that by the time you read this, there will be a new prime minister in Great Britain.

As the people of the world express their displeasure with the policies of the United States in thought, word and deed, the people of the United States will be confused as to why they are being maligned. Citizens, including your-self, do not understand the difference between the government of a country and its people. The low-vibration energy projected through thought and deed onto the United States will add to a sense of unrest in this country. The unrest has the possibility of expressing itself in violence but not to the degree you witnessed in the 1960s.

Several things can be done to change this possibility. One is on the govern-mental level. Diplomacy is mandatory. Part of diplomacy needs to be the atti-tude that the United States government does not have all the answers. Diplomats will need to turn to social scientists to learn about the peoples of var-ious countries. This will lead to a greater understanding and acceptance of the ways and cultures of others.

## TRY ON OTHERS' FEELINGS—BUT STAY IN YOUR HEART

You as individuals can do much to change what is happening. First imagine what it must be like to live and experience what those in other countries are experiencing. This is best done by releasing all your experiences of your pres-ent culture and beliefs. Of course you cannot do this completely, but do the best you can. Research what newspapers and citizens of other countries are saying. Attempt to feel as they do. By "trying on" their feelings, you can come to some understanding. This will change the energy you send out to others.

You might have the fear that if you do the research suggested, you will be filled with low-vibration energy. There is a simple way to avoid that event. As individuals, stay in your heart. Stay firmly planted in your heart. You will read these words many times in this message, as they are the key to living your life in peace and joy.

If you experience fear, go back to your heart. If you experience anger, go back to your heart. If you experience jealousy, go back to your heart. If you experi-ence anything not related to the energy of love, go back to your heart. By stay-ing in your heart, further energy that could lead to unrest will be avoided. If you send love to those who express hate, you cannot only lessen but eliminate the impact of their energy upon you. The more of you there are who send love, the less unrest on the planet there will be.

You have heard how important it is to be in your heart. You have heard it so often that you might give only intellectual assent to its importance. Where is your energy now, dear ones? Are you now in your heart? If you could set a timer for every seven and a half minutes and check it, would you be in your heart? If you take seriously the notion that you can alter your reality, then spend concen-trated time exercising being in your heart.

When you are in your heart, low-vibration energy cannot become attached to you. When you are in your heart, you will be able to listen to and hear what others are saying beyond their words. When you are in your heart, you will be able to make decisions about how you live your life without making judgments about how others live their lives.

## DO NOT GET INVOLVED IN LOW-VIBRATION EMOTIONS

Know also that another way to change what is happening in the world is for you to simply not get involved with the emotions of what is happening. You do not need to research and read what is happening—you will certainly hear from others what is occurring in this world of yours. For those who say, "But Amma, how can I help heal the planet if I do not know what is happening?" It is very simple, dear ones. Stay in your heart. When you stay in your heart, only love energy will be emanating from your personal vibration. When you are not in your heart, your personal vibration of that which is "not love" contributes to the low-vibration energy on the planet.

If you wish to be more actively involved in the healing of the planet, you still do not need to know the particulars of what is happening. Simply—note that I am saying "simply" often—consciously intend that love energy go directly from you to a place of low vibration. You can choose the particular place, or you can direct the love vibration to a particular place.

## PEOPLE WILL TAKE CONTROL OF THEIR HEALTH CARE

There is a wondrous event occurring in the United States of which most people are unaware. It has been occurring over the past few years and will increase dramatically in the next ten years. People are going to be taking control of their own health care! Most people miss what is happening because they read only about those without insurance and without the ability to buy the medications prescribed.

Dear ones, the continued increase in the number of people without insurance and the problems with the drug companies are what will propel people to take control of their own health. The pharmaceutical industry, in its marketing efforts for every dollar, will greatly assist this happening in two ways. First, they will continue to raise drug prices, to the extent that many people cannot afford them. Second, by pushing drugs through every available resource, many people will be having reactions, even leading to death. This will result in lawsuits bringing about the demise of many drug companies.

People will become afraid of taking the pharmaceuticals and will explore other means of achieving health. What many see as a grave injustice—not having health insurance and not having affordable medication—will actually lead to greater numbers of people turning to complementary and alternative forms of health care. This will be occurring especially in the population of parents looking to care for their children.

What can you do for yourself? The answers have already been given to you many times. Eat a healthy diet. Put as many live foods as possible in your body. By live foods I mean those whose enzymes are living. Drink water that is as pure as possible. And . . . stay in your heart!

If you are a person whose body needs some animal protein, eat only animals who have been fed and killed as humanely as possible. The energy of fear, which is in a precious animal when it is killed, will affect the taste and energy of the meat. You can remove this low-vibration energy by blessing the food.

Those of you who are vegetarian will say, "There is no reason to eat animal products." Dear ones, if you are not presently living in a body that needs animal protein to function to its fullest, then you cannot understand the need. For those of you who do need animal protein, a few ounces (three to four) every two to three days is sufficient for the working of your body.

Whether you eat foods of animal or of plant origin, have the food be as clear as possible of pesticides, antibiotics, hormones and other manufactured substances. This includes avoiding those genetically modified foods that produce their own insecticides.

## BLESS WHAT YOU PUT IN YOUR MOUTH

Bless everything you place into your mouth. Give thanks to the animal or plant who gave its life that you may live. Ask the energy of the food and the energy of your body to come together in the way that is healthiest for your body. Instruct your body to release all substances that are not necessary for the health of your body. Devise a simple prayer or blessing that includes these elements and say it aloud before you eat or drink.

Use your own words, but for those who need an example, try the following while sending energy from your heart to your food and drink; say this aloud if possible: "Thank you for giving the gift of your life so that I may live. May the love from my heart transmute any vibration of anger or fear contained in this food or drink. I ask that the energy in every molecule of this food rise to its highest level. Dear physical body, accept the gift of these nutrients. Take in all that you need. For any substances contained within this food or drink that are not compatible with your healthy functioning, eliminate them quickly and easily. I give thanks and ask blessings upon all those who brought this food and drink to my use. So be it."

Instead of pharmaceuticals, learn about herbs that will support your body. Use only organic herbs whenever possible. Almost all that is needed to heal the body is found in that which grows naturally. When you find it necessary to take pharmaceuticals, bless the drug and inform your body that it is coming. Ask your body to eliminate whatever part of the drug will have a negative impact.

## THE TECHNOLOGY TO ACHIEVE MIRACLES IS IN YOU

Be open to various healing modalities. Do not reject all avenues in allopathic medicine. Go into the altar within your heart and communicate with your body before using any form of health care. I tell you, my dear ones, that there is little that cannot be healed within the body by simply changing what you put into your body. I am not speaking simply of food and drink; I am also speaking of what you read, watch and listen to. What thoughts and beliefs do you keep in your mind? If you do not like how your life is going, change your thoughts and beliefs. There are many precious beings who have brought in information about how to do this. If you wish to take control of your life as much as you are able to control it, incorporate beliefs and thoughts that will manifest what you want from your life.

There are many wonderful healing modalities available to you. They will not have long-lasting effects unless you place only that which is healthy into your body and mind. Your Western society, especially your U.S. society, looks for the quickest way to achieve the goal. You have accomplished much in this search. You have forgotten, however, that the greatest power for fast accomplishment is within you. There are technologies to help you achieve whatever goal you wish; however, dear ones, the most powerful technology is found in your own mind and heart.

When you stay within your heart center, you will unleash the power within your mind. When the heart and mind work in synergy, you will have what others will call miracles. You have within you the ability to change things within an instant. The difficulty is that you do not know that. Ah, but the children do.

## THE NEW CHILDREN NEED YOU AS YOU NEED THEM

Oh, dear ones, yes, it is true that wondrous children are coming onto the planet. You have heard of the Indigo children. These individuals began their appearance about forty-five years ago. There were just a few. Now there are many. These children are here to teach you of the possibilities of life when you remember who it is that you are. These children remember.

You have heard much of the Indigo children. Parents, read and follow the information about how to assist these wonderful children. Those of you who are Indigos and are reading this, follow what has been found to assist you. There are children of several other rays now coming onto the planet. You have the children of the crystal and the rainbow rays and now, for the past few years, those of the platinum ray. All of these children come with special gifts, just as you yourself came in with special gifts.

These children are not better than you or more special than you. They do have memories, gifts and talents that you might not have. Understand their gifts and talents using this example: Some of you are accomplished musicians and some of you play music, whereas others delight in music but are not able to produce it. Just as you enjoy and respect those who exhibit great musical talent, enjoy and respect these children.

Parents wonder how to treat these children. Aren't they so special that they need different ways of eating, different ways of discipline, different methods of education? Actually, they do not need anything different than what you need. What do I mean by that? You flourish when treated with honesty and dignity—so will these children. You learn best and with joy when taught by methods that fit your style of learning—so do these children. Your body is healthiest when it receives the highest quality of food and drink—so are these childrens' bodies. When you read various books and articles on the best ways to relate to these precious children, you will find that all the information will apply to you. If you had been raised as you are being told to raise these children, you would not have the difficulties you now struggle with. Their energies, however, are more sensitive than yours to imbalances in your food, air and water.

What is the difference between you and the children of the newer rays? The difference is that they know to the depth of their being who they are and also that you are awakening. Learn from them and realize at the same time that these children need you. You have wisdom and information to give to them. They have wisdom and information to give to you. Neither of you is better than the other. These children simply have different gifts and talents. In fact, many of these children had bodies who you might have known just a few years ago, perhaps even months ago.

Souls incarnate in the ray that is needed at the time when they incarnate. Many who are now incarnating as the children of the new rays have incarnated many times in other rays. These souls have now taken on the energy of the newer rays. They remember more of what they knew while on the other side and are ready to teach and to move the population to be who and what they truly are—love.

## BROADEN YOUR DEFINITION OF SLAVERY AND AVOID IT

Relationships among peoples are gradually changing on your planet. Although there are those who still do so, most of the population no longer believe it is right to keep one bound in service to another. You have called this slavery. More people are recognizing that each person is to be treated with respect and dignity, no matter what his or her physical abilities, spiritual development, sexual orientation, age, gender, social status, religion and more. The key to changing relationships is to broaden your view of what slavery is. When you use another person for your own purposes without his or her full and uncoerced agreement, then you are participating in slavery. A rather broad definition, is it not?

The way to avoid being in slavery or being a slave master is to view each person from your heart. If you look at each person from your heart center and relate to each person from that same heart center, you will relate with freedom and joy. Great wonders can occur when you see others through your heart. When they also see you through their hearts and you then join together heart to heart, you will be amazed at the miracles that can occur. All will cooperate with one another for the highest good. You will find the teachings of the great masters being manifested.

## DECIDE HOW YOU WILL LIVE

Dear ones, it is time for you to decide how you will live. Will it be from your heart or from your own self-will? This is a critical time for you as an individual.

If you choose to live from your heart, you must be vigilant in discovering those times when you are not in your heart. Practice being in your heart. Practice as many times as you can, for as long as you can. When you are able to go to sleep in your heart and awaken in your heart, you will know that you are becoming more embedded in your heart. You will come to know who it is you truly are. There is no wondering who you are if you are in your heart.

Dear ones, there are many wonderful words in this journal you are reading. Read it from your heart. Only then will you be able to hear the fullness of the messages. Not all the messages are for you in particular. When you read from your heart, you will know which ones are for you. Blessings to you, my dear ones. I am Amma. I am the divine mother of the divine mothers. I am your mother.

# Epilogue: Learning to Be Love Incarnate

### By Cathy Chapman

*T*he question I am most often asked is: How did a woman who lived for twenty years in a convent end up channeling Amma, the divine Mother? How, indeed! Life takes interesting twists and turns. If you had told me twenty years ago that I would be channeling, I would have laughed as I wondered which psychiatrist could best to work with your delusions. I would have also protected myself very carefully with the blood of Jesus from the evil that you had just spoken. Ah, spiritual journeys are amazing adventures!

## MY BEGINNING AS A CATHOLIC

Yes, I was very much a Catholic. I wouldn't really call myself a fundamentalist, since I believed in birth control and a women's right to ordination, which are both big no-no's in the Roman Catholic Church. What is amazing is that my current spirituality and the teachings of the Catholic Church in the spiritual domain are very similar. The Catholic Church has a very strong mystical side. The problem is that it prefers its mystics either quietly praying in a convent or monastery—with an emphasis on quietly—or resting peacefully in the grave. Live, public mystics are often silenced.

When I was in my late teens, I joined a mystical movement in the Catholic Church known as the Charismatic Renewal. This very mystical group practiced the gifts of the Spirit: healing, tongues and the interpretation of tongues, prophecy and teaching. Tongues, or speaking in tongues, is when an energy—the Holy Spirit—comes through you and you pray in other languages. Interpretation of tongues is when you interpret these prayers in the language of those present. Prophecy is when the energy of God comes through you and you have words of knowledge that can be given to the people. I was very familiar with the power of the Holy Spirit coming through me and words coming through my mouth. The gift of prophecy is what channeling is.

Toward my later years in the convent, at about year eighteen of my twenty years there, I participated in a program called Healing Touch. That is where I learned more about the energy that I felt in my hands when I prayed over people. I always called it "the power of the Holy Spirit coming through." That is why my hands got hot as I felt this power coming through them. I learned about chakras, auras and meridians. I learned how to focus my intent more precisely.

## CHANNELING PASSES THE FRUIT TEST

There was only one problem. This stuff was New Age—occult—and that meant that it was of the devil! "Oh, God," I prayed, "what am I going to do? God, if this is wrong, if this is going to pull me away from you, I trust that you will stop this." So I waited to be stopped. I waited for God to save me from what I had been told was an evil, an abomination. Instead of being saved, God pushed me off the cliff and into the deep water. "Oh my God, save me! How can this be right? God, are you sure? I trust you. I know you want nothing less than for me to be with you forever. Are you sure?"

In the Gospels of the Christian scriptures, Jesus says, "By their fruits you will know them." Well, okay, God. This sure seems to pass the fruit test. I'm happier and more at peace. My clients are becoming happier, healthier and more at peace. They are coming in contact with the deep spiritual essence within them. Some call it God, some Spirit, some universal energy.

As I learned more healing techniques, I found myself growing spiritually. I became a Certified Healing Touch Practitioner and, for a while, an instructor; I studied Reiki, pranic healing, the Melchizedek Method and the BodyTalk System. I found myself more in touch with God, Spirit, All That Is, than I had been while in the convent.

I had been in the convent for twenty years when I left to further explore this new spiritual life. The spirituality I was now delightfully—and yes, at times, fearfully—exploring could not be held within the confines of the convent or Roman Catholicism.

My mom had introduced me to reincarnation through the book Many Lives, Many Masters by Brian Weiss. I had read the book and become furious. It made so much sense. This was a big problem. I was looking forward to getting out of this lifetime because it was so hard. I didn't want to do this, learn these same lessons, again.

## A NEW-LIFE EXPERIENCE

Five years ago, I was in an automobile accident that changed my life. No, it wasn't a near-death experience. It was a new-life experience. In the long instant that the accident took, I thought I was going to miss her [the woman in the other car]. I ended up sideswiping her. Neither of us was hurt much. I was really shaken. I'd had accidents before, but I'd never had this reaction. I took a long bath about an hour later. While soaking in the tub, I had images of the fire department coming and using the jaws of life to pull a dead body out of each car. I had almost slammed into the rear of her car at more than sixty miles an hour. I had images of two funerals, the driver of the other car and my own. There was grief swirling around me. This went on for about forty-eight hours. I knew, very clearly, that that was the time I had "planned" to leave this life. On a soul level, I had made a choice to stay here. I was now in a whole new life!

Not long after the accident, energies began to come through such as I had felt when in the Charismatic Renewal. I let them out. The energies described themselves as Melchizedek, Quan Yin and Djwahl Kuhl. One day another energy came through. "Who are you?" I asked. "I am Amma, the divine mother of the divine mothers. I am your mother." "Uh, say again?" I asked. "I am Amma, the divine mother of the divine mothers. I am the mother of Quan Yin, White Buffalo Calf Woman, Athena and the one you call the blessed Mother. They are my children. You are my child."

Later she brought a memory to my mind: I had just professed first vows, my first formal pronouncement of my commitment to poverty, chastity and obedience. We were all on a retreat in which we prayed over scriptures from the Bible. Suddenly I had this image in my mind's eye. The feminine aspect of God, with the deepest brown eyes imaginable, was dancing around the Earth. I could have fallen into her love and lived there for an eternity. She was touching everyone with joy and delight—the starving, the depressed, the holy, the unholy, everyone. I was in awe and speechless—an unusual occurrence! Within that memory I heard: "That was me introducing myself to you twenty years ago." Oh, wow! The feminine aspect of God. In the Kabbalah, she is in the place of Binah: Amma, the divine mother of the divine mothers.

At first, Amma came through my crown. I was wiped out at the end of each session. One day I asked if she could come in in a way that did not leave me so tired. She then introduced me to the altar in the sacred space that is entered by going through the back of the heart center. "I will come in through the back of your heart center." What a difference that made!

## DISCOVERING YOUR INNER AUTHORITY AND LEARNING TO KNOW YOURSELF

Amma's purpose with me is to give information and tools to help us become the love that we are. I certainly find that it is happening with me. (By the way, people tell me that Amma has a bigger smile that I do.) I have learned, and I teach, that there is no outside authority that knows better than our inner authority. The key is discovering how to get past that little ego, the little i am, and find the big ego, the I Am presence. (For those who don't know, "ego" is "I am" in Latin.) The I Am presence has the wisdom and the knowledge—all that I need to know.

Amma tells everyone to read and listen to wisdom figures, including herself. Make decisions based upon your own inner knowing. Become responsible. Only by accepting responsibility can you leave victim consciousness. You cannot blindly follow the teachings of a religion or a channel, even Amma, and be true to yourself. Learn that you are love incarnate. Live the reality of being love incarnate. Know that everyone is love incarnate.

I laugh about where I am now. I believe—no, that's not correct; I now know—that things I once believed in, like hell, are not true and limit my ability to access my personal power. There is no hell. God really, truly does love everyone, so much that there is no way that God will confine anyone to someplace separate from God. How can God deny something that is a very part of God's self? Life is growth, and God loves us through it, whether in this lifetime or another, this dimension or another, whether you are playing a saint or a sinner, whether you call God "God" or "All That Is" or "universal energy" or "Source" or your own personal nickname.

I still struggle with my personality. I still get flashes of anger, although I am not nearly as defensive as I used to be. I handle events, even my brother's recent passing, with acceptance and some tears. I have few doubts about myself. I still have some resistance about where I think I'm going—but not much. I still make judgments about myself and others, but I let them go quickly.

I have often considered myself lazy because I like free time. I recently went on vacation expecting to do some work with Amma regarding a class I was teaching, and Amma wouldn't come in! That had never happened, not since I had begun channeling her. At the end of vacation, she said, "You needed a vacation. You needed to rest." I still eat that wonderful Texas ice cream called Blue Bell to excess whenever I buy it. But peace and joy pervade my life. I no longer look for other people to complete me, although I wouldn't mind a life partner. I'm discovering that healing can come easily by simply asking. I work with clients on an increasingly higher level each day. I'm accepting myself more and more as Amma takes me to realms I'd previously only read about.

## NOW AS YOU TRAVEL YOUR PATH, KNOW THAT YOU ARE LOVE

There are many paths to peace and joy, to becoming the love you are. Amma's path works for some people, other paths work better for others. The information I have does not belong to me. It is yours, and mine, but not to own. Amma has been very clear about that.

What I am doing is exactly why I joined a wonderful group of women known as the Houston Dominicans in December of 1975. I am of service. I am a healer. I want to share the wondrous power of God. Now I am learning about this statement in the Christian Gospels where Jesus says, "You can do this (all of Jesus's works) and more." That's my goal in life. To learn how to do and be what Jesus said (my paraphrase): "Be all that your potential holds for you. I have given you tools that will move you further than you could ever dream. Forgive seventy times seven times, release all anger, judge no one (including yourself), be of service, be true to yourself and do all this from your heart—from love." And that sounds just like Amma!

I am no longer Roman Catholic. I am, however, truly catholic: universal. Everyone can be in communion. The only thing that keeps it from happening is each individual's fear of oneness. And Amma is my mother. She is your mother. And guess what? It doesn't bother her, diminish her or insult her if people don't believe that. She doesn't care if you don't like her, don't love her or think her words are unimportant. She has only one response. She loves. That is what she teaches me. That is what Jesus, that good Jewish guy, taught more than two thousand years ago. Hmm, maybe I haven't gotten too far away from what Roman Catholicism could be if it went back to the foundation of the message of Jesus.

My day is filled with studying; reading deep books and novels; working as a psychotherapist using Body Talk, soul healing, encodements and hypnotherapy; playing with my dogs; and sharing Amma. I write. I visit with friends. I go to the movies. I travel. I watch this beautiful world of ours in wonder. I feel the vibrations as they rise in the planet. My goal is to be the love that I am and to teach others to do the same. I am love incarnate—and so are you! Claim that now, out loud. Say it: "I am love incarnate!" As we each recognize that reality, this world will change. You and I can change now. The rest of the world will eventually join us!

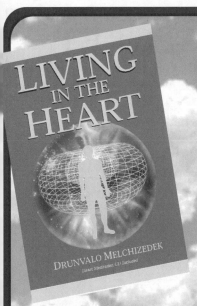

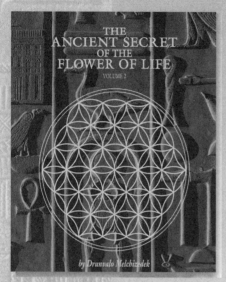

## SHAMANIC SECRETS for PHYSICAL MASTERY

The purpose of this book is to allow you to understand the sacred nature of your own physical body and some of the magnificent gifts it offers you. When you work with your physical body in these new ways, you will discover not only its sacredness, but how it is compatible with Mother Earth, the animals, the plants, even the nearby planets, all of which you now recognize as being sacred in nature.

It is important to feel the value of yourself physically before you can have any lasting physical impact on the world. The less you think of yourself physically, the less likely your physical impact on the world will be sustained by Mother Earth. If a physical energy does not feel good about itself, it will usually be resolved; other physical or spiritual energies will dissolve it because it is unnatural. The better you feel about your physical self when you do the work in the previous book as well as in this one and the one to follow, the greater and more lasting will be the benevolent effect on your life, on the lives of those around you and ultimately on your planet and universe.

$25^{00}$ SOFTCOVER 544 P.
ISBN 1-891824-29-5

## Chapter Titles:

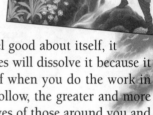

- Cellular Clearing of Traumas and Unresolved Events
- Feeling is Our Body's First and Primary Language
- The Resolution of Fear, Trauma and Hate
- Dealing with Fear, Pain and Addiction
- Shame, Arrogance, Safety and the Inability to Trust
- The Role of Trauma in Human Life
- Letting Go of Old Attitudes and Inviting New Energy
- The Waning of Individuality
- Clearing the Physical Body
- Using the Gestures to Protect, Clear and Charge
- The Flow of Energy
- Connecting with the Earth
- Communication of the Heart
- More Supportive Gestures
- Sleeping and Dreamtime
- Responsibility and Living prayer
- Communicating with the Natural World
- Life Lessons and the Vital Life Force
- The Sacrament of Food
- Working with the Elements
- Communication with Those Who Would Follow
- Elemental Connections
- Taking Responsibility
- Creating Personal Relationships

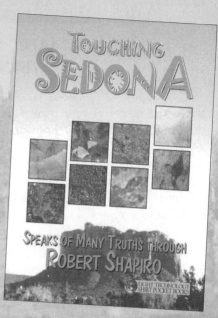
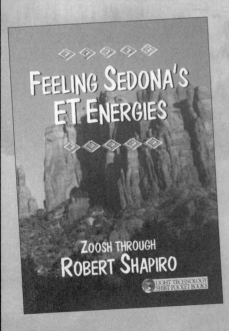

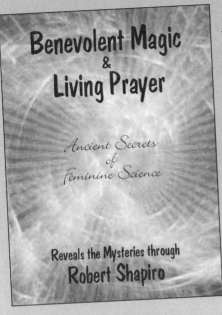
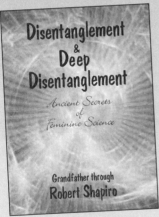
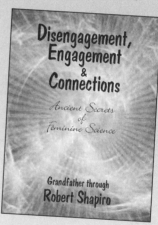

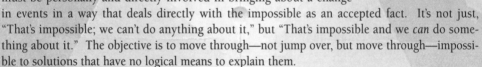

PRETTY FLOWER
THROUGH
MIRIANDRA ROTA

# Pathways & Parables for a Changing World

Here we are! We know this is a powerful time; we have successfully birthed ourselves to be present during the grand awakening. We can feel it—the call to powerful living! What makes some solutions for powerful living easy to grasp whereas others seem slippery and elusive? Maybe the slippery and elusive solutions are so different that they feel like a foreign language, one we haven't yet learned to speak. Maybe the elusive solutions are poking at the conclusions we've spent our entire lives developing. This book is about practical solutions called pathways. Have you ever asked Pretty Flower a question only to have her answer begin with, "Once upon a time . . ."? At the end of her parable, did you ever find yourself saying, "Huh?" and then, "Oh!" Yes—it's easy, simple. That's what the parables are all about: a shift in consciousness, spiritual awakenings galore. But don't let me keep you a moment longer from these easy pathways, delightful parables and simple solutions for your powerful living!

—Miriandra Rota

Interwoven within your story, dear beloved ones, is the truth of who you are. Interwoven within the fabric of your being are the encodings that contain all knowing and the capability to venture forth in the fulfillment of your heart's yearning. And within your heart's yearning resides your beloved innocence, which holds the wisdom you seek while creating your story. Blessed are you.

—Pretty Flower

## Chapter Titles:

- We Are All Journeyers
- The Fulfillment of Your Own Knowing
- Truth Does Burst Forth!
- Ripples in the Timeline
- Friendship and Truth
- The Light Within
- The Energy of Completion
- The Spring of All Springs

LIGHT TECHNOLOGY PUBLISHING
PO Box 3540 • Flagstaff, AZ 86003
928-526-1345 • 800-450-0985 • FAX 928-714-1132
Or use our online bookstore: www.lighttechnology.com

$16$^{95}$
SOFTCOVER
ISBN 1-891824-53-8

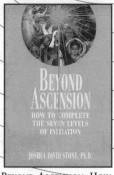

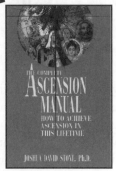

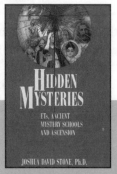
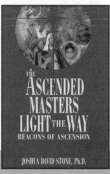
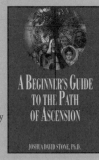

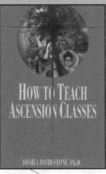
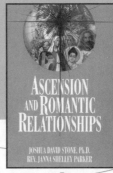